All Worth Their Salt: The People of NWI

Jeff Manes

DEAR DOROTHY,
HOPE YOU ENJOY THE BOOK!
Jeff Manes

Copyright (etc)

Publisher; Jeff Manes and Mike Echterling

Printed in the United States of America

Manes, Jeffrey, 1957-.
All worth their salt: The people of Northwest Indiana / Jeff Manes.
p. cm.
ISBN 978-0-9970047-0-0

1. Northwest Indiana – Interviews – 21st Century. 2. Indiana – Calumet Region – Interviews – 21st Century. 3. I. Title.
977.29 –dc22

Cover designed by Conservation Mike Echterling

First Edition

"The Post-Tribune is very fortunate to have such a great columnist as Jeff Manes. He gets the stories firsthand from people all across the region – the young 80-year plus crossing guard, the stories of the Kankakee River's rich history, the steelworkers' tough jobs in the mills. They seem to jump off the page."

– Thomas Best, Eau Claire, Wis. (letter to the editor, Post-Tribune)

"What I find refreshing about Jeff Manes' Salt column is it isn't about the sorority queen or company president or the sports hero. Instead, it is about 'Joe Average.' Yet, it turns out 'Joe Average' always has a deeper side and achieves great things or makes the world a better place. Thanks for this uplifting and entertaining column in a world of crime, disaster and dire headlines."

– Faithful reader (appeared in the Post-Tribune's anonymous "Quickly" column)

"Jeff Manes does with words what the best musicians do with music, the best directors do with movies, the best artists do with paint. He makes you feel it. This book is the real deal."

– Ted Kosmatka (Nebula and Theodore Sturgeon Award nominee)

"I had tears running down my cheeks while reading Jeff Manes' column about Anita Heath. What a beautiful human being she is, and what a wonderful world this would be if more people were like her."

– Faithful reader (appeared in the Post-Tribune's anonymous "Quickly" column)

"Our region stretches from the shore of the Michigan to the banks of the Kankakee. It extends from the heaviness of industry on which our community is built to the lightness of the nature we treasure. Jeff Manes is uniquely experienced to understand our story, uniquely talented to tell it."

– Andrew Steele, former "Neighbors" editor, Post-Tribune

"From streetwise Marty Jakubowski to sweetheart Eleanor Bartz, Jeff Manes' columns are incredible. He should make a book of them."

– Faithful reader (appeared in the Post-Tribune's anonymous "Quickly" column)

Contents

A Note to the Reader

It was January of 2005 when the first of these human interest columns was published. Approximately 1,000 have been written since. Some of the folks featured in this collection are now deceased. Some have changed occupations since being interviewed. Their stories and photographs will appear as they did when first published – without updates.

It was a daunting task, selecting but 100 of 1,000 interviews. The ones chosen appeared in print from 2005 to 2012.

– JM

All Worth Their Salt:
The People of NWI

Introduction

Salt. The human body contains about four ounces of it. Without enough salt we perish. It was for salt that Mahatma Gandhi marched.

Around 1900, certain social leaders in New York claimed there were only 400 people worth knowing. In disagreement, author O. Henry wrote a volume he called "The Four Million." He thought everybody was worth knowing.

In more recent times, Raymond Carver, dubbed the American Chekov, spoke of the laborers and service workers who formed his submerged population: "They're my people, I could never write down to them." Ray Carver grew up on a small river town of 700 souls.

I have had the advantage of growing up along the bayous of the Kankakee River and atop the carcinogenic coke batteries abutting Lake Michigan. I'd like you to get to know your neighbor, those living, sometimes eking out a living, just across the alley or down the road. Their names don't usually appear in the newspaper. The obits, maybe. But they are all worth their salt.

Everyone has a story to tell.

– Jeff Manes

Salt of the Earth

George Wesselhoft *(Apr. 2005)*

"Shall not one line lament our forest race..."
– Simon Pokagon, son of Leopold Pokagon

George Wesselhoft lives in Lowell's Indian Heights subdivision on Cherokee Drive with his wife Cathy. They have raised three children.

Wesselhoft, 82, is a Korean War veteran and a past commander of American Legion Post 101 in Lowell. He was involved with either the Cub Scouts or Boy Scouts for more than 25 years and retired from Lever Brothers in 1987 with 39 years service.

Like the late, great Chief Leopold Pokagon, Wesselhoft is a devout Catholic; he's a member of St. Edward's Church in Lowell. George also happens to be 1/8th Potawatomi.

* * *

How did you lose the finger, George?

"In the service," he said. "I worked in the mail room out in the hangar. We rode in a moving van, with benches all around the inside. My ring caught on something. It bent the ring and squeezed it tight, cutting off the circulation. Because the ring was squeezed tight for an hour before they removed it, my finger never healed properly. It got hard as a rock and just dried up. They ended up sawing it off four months later."

Lever Brothers?

"Yeah, we always got blamed for American Maize's smell. Before

Lever Brothers, I worked at Youngstown Steel in East Chicago. One day we had a job working on the hot rails up above on the cranes by the ore docks where they empty out the ships that come in.

"After lunch break, we were about half-way up to the job site, when I decided to climb back down and check the lockout. Somebody had removed the lock from the hot rail switch. The switch was on. Those live rails would of fried the lot of us. We were lucky.

"Well, I didn't stay in the steel mill long. Soon after, through a fella at the Holy Name Society, I got the job at Lever Brothers in Hammond. That was 1948; I moved to Lowell in 1967."

What did you do at Lever Brothers?

"I did everything. It was a bid-and-bump situation. I worked about every job in the plant. We used to make everything. There were over 1,300 employees back then."

You were born in Oklahoma City.

"Yes, but I was raised near Fort Bliss in El Paso (Texas). My mother died when I was 11. She was bed-ridden the whole time – asthma, TB, heart problems. She had divorced my father after a year. He was an alcoholic. He wouldn't provide milk or nothin'. The booze came first.

"My mother, grandmother and I lived with my mother's step-brother. Grandma had a stroke in '35 – paralyzed her left side. This half-uncle of mine graduated high school in '36 and had a scholarship, but didn't go to college. It was hard times; he had to take care of us. But he couldn't get a job except with the National Relief Administration or the WPA. He tried to get hired in town for 10 cents per hour."

Talk about growing up in that environment.

"We lived in a shack – no paint on the outside. You know, a lot of guys wouldn't do what my uncle did, take care of my mother, his mother, and me.

"In 1940, my mother died. She had a brother who lived in Hammond. He sent money for Greyhound bus fare for us. We stayed with him for a couple weeks, then the three of us got a place in the Harbor. Grandma died in '45. I went to school at St. Mary's in East Chicago and then Bishop Noll (Institute.)"

What happened to your dad?

"I didn't meet him until I was about 14. My uncle sent me back to Texas to meet his aunt and uncle in 1943, I stayed with them for a little while, then they put me on a bus to Shepherd Field Air Force Base in Wichita Falls, Texas, so I could meet my dad. He picked me up with his second wife at the air force base. I rode in the rumble seat of a '35 Chevy.

"It was during the war and, with the rations going on, we'd go down a hill and he'd shut the key off to save gas, then turn it back on–Pop! Pop!

"I returned to Indiana and got married. I'd make trips almost every year back to Oklahoma to see him and my grandmother; she lived with my father by then. It was her, my paternal grandmother, who was half Potawatomi.

"My dad had spent some time in prison. While in prison, they beat him with barbed wire. My old man didn't take any shit from anyone, but the scars that man had on his back... . Eventually, he had to have his legs amputated. Never quit drinking, though; he'd sit there with no legs and get drunk."

You and Cathy raised three children.

"Yes, but I also had two children, Robert and Dennis, by my first wife. She died in 1969 out on 141st Avenue. In 1974, my oldest boy, Dennis, also got hit by a train – right before Christmas."

Can you tell me more about your American Indian ancestry?

"Let me show you this laminated card I carry in my billfold: Citizen Potawatomi Nation, George H. Wesselhoft, one-eighth Potawatomi."

"The settlers would barter with the Potawatomi, promise them this and that. The grain traded or sold to the Native Americans was rotten and moldy. The store keepers who sold them goods were in cahoots with the government. The government would get them in debt, then mortgage off their land. A lot of treaties were signed before The Trail of Death in 1838 – 3 cents per acre.

"My great-great-grandfather, Nan-wesh-mah, was born in 1812 between Warsaw and Rochester, four years before Indiana became a state. When he was 7, he was taken by his grandfather, Chief Chebass, to Fort Wayne where he attended a mission school and learned English. He was adopted and named Abraham Burnett.

"By the time he was 24, he was an official interpreter. In 1837, he went to Washington, D.C. with the delegation of chiefs trying to persuade the government not to force the Potawatomi to go to Kansas. When he was in Logansport, he was painted by George Winter, a famous pioneer artist. Abraham Burnett was 6-feet, 1-inch and known for his extreme strength. They say he would beat all challengers at lifting contests."

George, I have a photograph of my great-great grandmother on my mother's side that I cherish. Her married name was Georganna Sypult. She was full-blooded Cherokee.

"Abram, as he was sometimes called, dressed well in public; usually in a coat, trousers, tie, dress hat and cane. He died at his farm in Kansas in 1870 at the age of 59. They buried him near Burnett's Mound in southwest Topeka."

* * *

As I drove away from his well-kept, but modest home, I thought about this man who worked two jobs for nearly 30 years and had two loved ones killed by trains. A man who told me, with sincerity, how lucky he has been several times during our conversation.

George Wesselhoft. Proud Potawatomi. Livin' on Cherokee. Indian Heights.

Leona Bowman *(Nov. 2006)*

"Parents learn a lot from their children about coping with life."
– Muriel Spark

Thanksgiving – a time of gratitude. Heading south over the Kankakee River bridge, I exited Shelby and Lake County and entered Newton County and the town of Thayer.

It had been more than 30 years since I'd driven down the mile-long gravel road that dead ends at the Bowman residence.

When I pulled up, Leona Bowman, 70, was standing at the mailbox in front of the same house where I spent so many nights.

She lives alone, now.

* * *

"Come on in, Jeff, " Bowman began in a voice sounding as comforting and homespun as it did three decades ago.

Been a while, Leona.

"I remember those days so well. You and Dale Allen. Coffee?"

No thanks.

"Now tell me, Jeff. How did you get into writing? When I first read your column, I said to myself, 'Why, this can't be the same little hooligan...'"

Ahem. So, Mrs. Bowman, you were raised in Shelby?

"Yes; there were 10 of us Strickhorn children. I had six older brothers. Raymond was killed in a car wreck down at Fort Benning; Eugene was killed by a train in Shelby; and Charles was killed by a horse.

"Jeff, do you remember my kids at all?"

All of them. Greg, Lisa, Jeff, and Dale, of course. I know you called him Dale Allen because your husband went by Dale.

"They were great kids. You learn from your children. I did. Maybe because my kids had what they had – except for Dale Allen.

"They were never hospitalized at the same time. It was difficult. A child with cystic fibrosis spends a lot of time in the hospital."

I remember when I'd sleep over. The little ones slept in those noisy tents.

"They finally done away those tents. The technology has advanced a lot with CF, since my children have died. My kids taught me how to appreciate life. They knew their's was going to be short-lived. They knew that."

Even Greg? The youngest.

"Greg didn't, you're right. But he was only 6 when he passed away."

Leona, I know Dale didn't have CF; he was your oldest. The disease seemed to strengthen with the birth of each child.

"Yes, they died in the opposite direction that I gave birth to them. Greg in 1975, Lisa in 1983, and Jeff in 1989."

You and your husband weren't afflicted with cystic fibrosis.

"No. It is a genetic disease, though. Both parents have to be carriers. When Greg died, that was the hardest for all of us. I think it impacted Dale Allen the most. They didn't have the counselors in the schools like they have now. My husband and I had each other. Maybe we didn't consider what Dale Allen was going through at the time. He was 17 when Greg died. I don't think he ever dealt with it."

Leona...

"Lisa sat me down and told me how she wanted her funeral and everything. She lived to be 18. Her life's goal was to graduate high school, and she did. She graduated in May; she died in November.

"She knew how upset I was when Greg died. It took a while to get over it – you never get over it. Lisa said, 'Mom, I don't want you crying like you did with Greg.'

"I said: 'I know, Lisa, but this is not easy for a mother to listen to. You just keep talkin.'I'll listen.' That was the hardest talk I've ever had. And I've had some tough ones.

"When Jeffery's time came, he said, 'Mom, I want you to give my guns and fishin' stuff to Dale Allen. You and Dad can have my car.'

"Jeff lived to be 26. The doctor predicted he'd live to be 40. But when he had his appendix taken out – it's those secondary things that get you.

"Jeff told us he never wanted to be put on a ventilator. They took him away by ambulance. But Dale Allen said, 'No, I can't let him go yet.'

"So, we put Jeff on the ventilator and it brought him right out of it; he was still in intensive care though."

What did you tell Jeff?

"We explained to Jeff the reason we put him on the ventilator. He couldn't talk because of the ventilator, but wrote a message to Dale Allen, 'This is not living.' He came home and lived another three weeks."

Dale Sr.?

"He died of lung cancer the day before Thanksgiving, eight years ago. Now, when you write this, don't make me seem like I'm needy or anything like that."

You break my heart, Leona.

"You take care, Jeff Manes."

* * *

Today, the mother who buried three of her own, finds solace driving to Rensselaer five days a week.

Leona Bowman baby-sits 1 year-old triplets.

Joshua and Carmelletta Bradley *(May 2010)*

"I'm a consecrated boy...
I'm a singer in a Sunday choir
Oh, my mama loves me, she loves me
She get down on her knees and hug me
She loves me like a rock
She rocks me like the rock of ages
And loves me
She love me, love me, love me..."
– Paul Simon

I first met Joshua Bradley a couple years ago while covering a Neighbors story for the Post-Tribune. He was part of Highly Flavored, Inc.'s Social Justice Leadership summer program.

Today, Joshua is a senior at Thea Bowman Leadership Academy in Gary and a member of the National Honor Society. Joshua lives with his mother, Carmelletta, and his brother, Marc-Anthony Bradley, 7, about a block from what was Horace Mann High School in Gary.

Carmelletta Bradley works full time and is currently attending Governor's State in University Park, Ill., where she on the dean's list. Her major is interdisciplinary studies.

As a 14-year old eighth-grader in Harvey, Ill., Carmelletta had a book bag slung around her shoulders while waiting for the school bus.

She also held Joshua in her arms.

* * *

Talk to me, Carmelletta.

"We'd ride the baby bus to school; it was for mother and child," she said. "They had a daycare at school. I remained in school the entire time and graduated from Thornton (Township) High School."

What was next?

"It took 10 years, but I earned an associate's degree in occupational therapy in 2006 from South Suburban College (in Illinois). I'm working four jobs to make sure my family stays afloat."

Josh?

"Yes, sir?"

You really don't have to call me sir.

"My mother proved a lot of people wrong," Joshua said. "She made something of herself and made sure I had a roof over my head."

Plans after you graduate from Bowman?

"I was nominated to be part of the Indiana University Bloomington Groups Program, but I'll defer my acceptance so I can study abroad in Germany for one year."

Explain.

"I also was accepted into the Congress-Bundestag Youth Exchange Program, which was sponsored by the Nacel Open Door Program," Joshua said. "I'll attend IU Bloomington my sophomore year."

Well, congratulations.

"Because of the Social Justice Leadership Program, I was able to display my character. There were like 10 students in the SJLP; I was the one chosen to go to Germany. It was an excellent group of students.

"My mentor, Ian Herron, is a former SJLP student who also did the Congress-Bundestag Youth Exchange Program; he's been walking me through the entire process."

Added Carmelletta: "Joshua will stay with a host family in Germany. It's fully paid except for personal expenses which comes to about $4,000."

Joshua said, "I once was nominated by the People to People Program to go to France for a whole summer, but I wasn't able to go because of financial issues."

Sprechen sie Deutsch?

"Some," said Joshua. "Through the SAILS program, I took German in 2008. The first two months overseas will be spent learning the German language. I took four years of Spanish at Bowman."

Your impressions of Bowman?

"It's a great high school, a beautiful school," Joshua said.

Favorite subject?

"I'm really into English. It wasn't always that way, but now, I understand the importance of it. If you know how to write, you can learn anything else. Math comes natural to me, but English is my favorite."

You look like a linebacker, do you play sports for Bowman?

"Not since my sophomore year; at 6 feet 1 inch and 210 pounds and attending Thea Bowman, a lot of people assume I got an athletic scholarship."

Added Carmelletta: "There was a time when Joshua wanted to be a rapper and a basketball star. He won a lot of trophies for sports, but I told him the one thing people can't take away from you is your knowledge. That's why he turns the pages."

OK, enough academia. For the first 10 years of Josh's life, before Marc-Anthony came along, it was just you two. Care to talk about those years?

"I had to teach some things to myself because I didn't have a male figure to learn from," Joshua said. "But my mother, she was there for me; she taught me how to stand on my own two feet and to strive for something greater – for my ethnicity, my community, and my people."

Any rough patches in the mother-son relationship?

"Not really," Carmelletta said. "We have a relationship where he talks to me about everything and vice versa."

Josh?

"Go ahead, son," Carmelletta said. "Tell him whatever you want. Say it."

"The worst childhood memory for me in this household was when she had to find her way, too," Joshua said. "She ... lived with somebody else for a while when I was about 10 years old. I stayed with my grandmother. It was like grind time. I felt almost like an orphan."

Your mother is a good person, Josh. You know that.

"It only lasted about six months," Carmelletta said.

Added Joshua: "I also remember when she asked me if I wanted to meet my father, and I told her, 'No.' It came to a point where I felt like not seeing him made me stronger. My mother didn't have to stay, but she did. He didn't."

Added Carmelletta: "Wow, you've never told me that one. I wish you'd have expressed that thought instead of just saying, 'No.' But I appreciate that you just said it."

Josh said: "Mr. Manes, if you don't put anything else in the newspaper about me, please let the people of Gary know that I'm trying to bring something back to the community. I hear things said about our generation; they say we don't want to do anything, that everybody just wants to rap or stay in the ghetto. I hear people say that we don't have any motivation. I want to prove that you can make something out of nothing."

Added Carmelletta: "I come up with different slogans for my sons to live by like, 'Be positive and productive and you will gain respect and power.' Every morning before Joshua leaves for school, I tell him, 'PPRP.'"

Carmelletta, any final thoughts on parenthood?

"Children don't ask to be here; as parents we have to make sure they get all the life skills they need. You have to be open-minded and not too set in your ways. Never try to have a friendship, but definitely a partnership.

"Joshua is a wonderful son. He has a good head on his shoulders. I'm proud of him. He has taken everything I taught him and utilized it. When he goes to Germany, he will be well-equipped."

* * *

Carmelletta is a strong woman who does the very best she can to raise and provide for her sons.

Joshua will become the first male Bradley to enter a college classroom.

And the walls come tumblin' down.

Kenny Hirata *(Dec. 2005)*

"Shikata ga nai." (It cannot be helped.)

Kenny Hirata is a proud American. He was born the son of a truck farmer back in 1928 in Stockton, Calif. He fought for this country during the Korean War.

He has been a very successful and well-respected businessman in Lowell for 50 years.

When Hirata was 14, he and his family were forced to move from their home. They were placed on an Indian reservation in Arizona.

The Hiratas' crime? They were of Japanese descent.

* * *

"My parents came from Japan," Hirata began."My wife's parents came from Japan. After the attack on Pearl Harbor, the U.S. Government incarcerated all people of Japanese ancestry. I think there were about 10 of these so-called camps in the United States. My wife and her family were sent to Wyoming. My family was sent to Arizona.

"They told our family to report to the county fairgrounds by a certain day. They said to bring only what you could carry. My father was a truck farmer; one of his major crops was tomatoes. He grew a lot of tomatoes for Del Monte and Heinz. He had to abandon everything.

"One morning, our neighbor, who was a Caucasian – a good neighbor – drove us to the fairgrounds. From there, we were put on a train to what they called the 'assembly center;' it was like a homemade barracks. We stayed there for a few months, then we were sent to the relocation camps.

"My parents took it pretty good. They figured, 'We're aliens, the government is doing what they feel is right; it cannot be helped.' They accepted it. There was no fighting, no rioting."

What were the conditions of the camps like, Mr. Hirata?

"The perimeters were fenced. Armed guards were posted. All of the sites were located in desolate areas, far from the general population. We raised most of our own food while in the camps. The government liked that. They didn't have to feed us. The doctors and nurses among us took care of the sick."

How long was your family kept there?

"About two years. Then, they allowed us to move out. The government gave everybody $50 each and a train ticket to go wherever we wanted to go. A lot of people chose the Midwest because of all the industry. It was 1944 by then. The war was still going on.

"While still in the camps, my future brothers-in-law were drafted as soon as they turned 18. Like me, they were born in the United States. At 18, they were considered red-blooded American citizens, you see.

"When Uncle Sam started drafting all these Japanese-Americans, the (Japanese American Citizens League) went to Washington, D.C., and asked if they could form their own infantry battalion with all Japanese-American and Hawaiian people; they wanted to prove a point."

The birth of the 442nd Regimental Combat Team.

"They are still the most decorated infantry division in the history of the U.S. Army.

"While we were held at the camp, our farm had been ransacked, our personal belongings taken.

"My family ended up resettling in Cleveland. I graduated from an all-boys Catholic high school. My parents were devout Buddhists. The Korean War broke out around 1950, and I was drafted by the army. I spent two years in the infantry. It was OK."

How did you end up in Lowell?

"When I was in the army, one of my best friends was from Lowell – Bob Kuiper. We got mustered out in '52. I came to Lowell and visited him and his wife a few years later. In 1955, the Kuipers came to Cleveland to visit us.

"Bob said, 'Why don't you move to Lowell?'

“Bob talked me into moving. I started up a body shop; it was a struggle. With two kids at the time, I thought we were going to starve that first year, but it worked out.

“My wife of 55 years, Chiyo, was a bit apprehensive when we first decided to move to Lowell. She said: ‘My God, people around here have never seen an Oriental face before. What’s it going to be like?’ I was confident it was going to be OK. I had made sergeant by the time I got out of the service. I felt I could deal with people.

“I had a few confrontations when I first moved to Lowell; most of them were in a bar. Bob told me, ‘Kenny, I think at this point in time, you should join the VFW and the American Legion.’ So I did.”

“I eventually started a little three-car garage where the doughnut shop was; now it’s Curves. I stayed there five years, then I put an addition on. After five more years, I moved to this location. That was back in 1966. Since then, I have added on eight times.”

You’re pretty much retired now.

“Yes, my son, David, has taken over the business.”

When did you really get into drag racing?

“I tinkered around with it after I got out of the army. Once I moved to Lowell, I built a dragster. We won the U.S. national championship in ‘63 and ‘65. I got out of it from about ‘73 to ‘96, and then, in 1997, David got into it.

“He participated at the Joliet National where he set a track record for his class. From a dead stand still, David traveled the quarter-mile in 5.16 seconds. Since then he has won four national events”

Exactly how fast was David going?

“At the 1/8th-mile mark, he was traveling 231 mph. At the quarter, 276 mph. We’re not professional, by the way. We have few sponsors. It’s out of pocket, mostly.”

You’ve led quite a life, Kenny. Were your parents ever compensated?

“Back in the ‘80s – 40 years later – my mother received $20,000. My father was already dead.

“Imagine if you can, your family today, being told that in a month or so, you would have to leave your home, and that you were only allowed to take a suitcase worth of your life with you. What stays? What goes? Valuables were sold for pennies on the dollar – some got rich off our misfortune, our relocation."

* * *

As a 14-year-old boy, he was told he could only take what he could carry.

Stand proud, Kenny Hirata.

You've carried more than most could take.

Jack Callahan *(Oct. 2006)*

"You never got me down, Ray"
-Robert De Niro as Jake La Motta in "Raging Bull"

With a name like Jack Callahan, he was destined to be a fireman or a pugilist. Callahan has put corned beef and cabbage on his family's plate doing both. For the past 18 years, Jack has fought fires for Hammond. As Kid Callahan, he fought men in another ring of fire. Jack Callahan is one of the nicest guys I've ever met.

The Kid is 52 years old now. He graduated from Hammond Tech in 1973. Today, he and his wife, Fran, reside in Thayer. Their son, Jack Jr., will attend college this fall. Young Jack is the first student in the history of North Newton High School to be accepted to Notre Dame.

Jack has worked his 24-hour shift. He also has worked out at the gym. At 5 feet, 9 inches and 165 pounds, we stand eye-to-eye. I wouldn't want to stand toe-to-toe with him, not again. Like Rocky Balboa and Apollo Creed, we don't want a rematch. The first one was brutal. We went the distance in a Cal City 13.1-mile race.

* * *

Was Hammond Tech pretty rough?

"I had quite a few fights back in high school," he said. "You had to stick up for yourself. It was an era with a lot of racial tensions. Some of the black kids would say, 'Gimme a dollar, man.'

"A lot of the white kids were intimidated. They'd give up the dollar. I'd say, 'You know what, you ain't gettin' my money.' I'd end up fightin' two or three of them, sometimes I got my butt kicked. But you know what, they quit messin' with me.

"My best friend is a black man. His name is Octavius James. He's got me into fight promoting now. One in a Million and Jack 'Kid' Callahan Promotions.

"Octavius takes care of me like I'm his brother. I've never been a prejudiced person. When you lay your life on the line with guys on the fire department, you realize there's good and bad with every race."

How did you get into boxing?

"Through Dennis Hardesty. We opened up the Whiting Boxing Club. I started boxing amateur, went something like 19-7.

"I really liked the one-on-one competitiveness of boxing. I was about 25 years old back then. I didn't turn pro until I was 27. I fought Golden Gloves and Park District. Always the runner-up. I fought some good fighters out of Chicago. Collins, for example, won about five Golden Glove titles.

"I turn pro. I tell myself, I'll get five fights and I'll get out; I go 5-0. I say, I'll get 10 fights; I go 10-0. Well, I figure I'll fight for the state title one day.

"On May 17, 1986, at the Holiday Star, I fight Mike Pollack in a 12-rounder for the state title. It was a tough fight, but I won by unanimous decision."

Then what?

"I find a note on my door from Hardesty, 'Call me right away.' Dennis says, 'We're flying out to New York in the morning, you got a world title fight.' I'm like, 'Yeah right.'

"He tells me to go to Sportmart and get a nice sweatsuit and new suit and tie. He tells me I'm going to be on an undercard with Tyson and Biggs.

"I asked him, 'Who am I fightin?' 'Matthew Hilton,' he says."

Matthew Hilton. Egads.

"Hilton was 26-0 with 23 KO's at the time. He had just knocked out Wilfredo Benitez. I didn't blink an eye. I didn't ask how much the purse was or anything. The next day we flew out to New York City.

"There I am, sittin' at a press conference with Sugar Ray Leonard, Mike Tyson, Don King, Merchant, Biggs. I'm like, do I belong here? I stood up and said, 'I want to thank you for the opportunity... .' It was awesome."

How did you fare versus Hilton?

"I wasn't prepared. I went from club-fighter status to topnotch world-class status. But the opportunity was there and I took it. I ended up getting cut and they wouldn't let me come out for the third round – but I got my picture in Sports Illustrated. And I wasn't on my butt either. In the photo, I'm takin' a shot to the body, and I'm throwin' a shot, you know."

Fighting southpaws?

"Big difference. I remember this lefty, Bobby Sands, down in Alabama. He was ranked in the Top 20 in the world. I was on the undercard of the Randall 'Tex' Cobb fight. What a character Cobb was.

"Sands was beating me through six rounds of an eight-rounder. I started landing body shots. I dropped him with a body shot in the seventh.

"In the eighth round, I dropped him again. I ended up winning by TKO."

Jack, tell me about the latter stages of your career as a prizefighter, then we'll move on to other aspects of your life.

"I fought in Melbourne, Australia. It took 24 hours to get there. Really a beautiful country. It was for the British Commonwealth Title against Troy Waters. He was ranked No. 2 in the world. I couldn't come out for the fourth round. I got cut. I didn't realize how bad it was.

"We stood toe-to-toe for three rounds but he caught me with an uppercut and a hook. I went down to one knee. I took a standing eight. The bell rang. I went back to my corner. I said, 'Pete, I can't see, wipe the blood out of my eye.' He said, 'No shit, your entire eyelid's hangin' off.' I said, 'What can you do?' He said, 'You can't see, the fight's over.'

"I had to move up to middleweight to fight Lonnie Horn. He came in at about 166. He was 19-2. I was 27-2. I went 12 rounds with him. It was a good fight. I was 40 years old."

What was your record as a pro when you finally hung up the gloves?

"I ended up 30 wins, 3 losses."

When did you become a fireman?

"I was 33. The age limit is 35. It took a couple years to get on at the fire department. They start you in fire service for a year, on the engine, fightin' fires. There was an opening for the fire department's ambulance service. Everybody on the department has to be an EMT. I was on the ambulance for 10 years.

"I've answered calls for gunshot wounds and I've delivered babies.

I could write a book. I got off the ambulance. I couldn't take it anymore. You see kids who have been hit by cars... I'd had enough."

You're an acting captain now.

"Yeah, for the past six years. We average about five or six calls per day. It's a pretty good job."

You got completely out of boxing for a while.

"Yes. I had the tragedies of losing my sons."

Jack, I can't imagine burying one of my kids. Let alone two.

"If you have children, you understand. If you don't have children, you don't know. We lost little Patrick when he was 7; he died in an automobile accident on May 7th of 2000. I was at the fire station when I got the call. My buddies had to drive me home. It changed my life completely. Nothin' was the same.

"Two years and three days later, I lost my oldest boy, Shannon. Brain aneurysm. He was 25. Again, I was at work when I got the call.

"I'd go into rages; it would just tear me up. I had to stay busy. That's when I met Octavius; he hired me as a trainer – I was refereeing. I started training guys like Johnny Novak and Jimmy Holmes."

Future plans?

"I work with a lot of amateur fighters right now at One in a Million in Merrillville. A good number of them are from DeMotte, Lowell, etc. There's no boxing club between here and Lafayette. I'm looking for an empty building that I can put a gym in. I'd like to start an amateur program. Maybe turn a couple of them into pros."

* * *

He has survived the mean streets of his youth, the fight game and battled countless blazes.

Remarkable likenesses of Shannon and Patrick are tattooed on the insides of his powerful arms.

He says Jack Jr. keeps him going.

Joyce Carol Oates claimed that boxing had become America's tragic theater.

Maybe so.

One thing for certain, life has thrown him some hard punches. And he's been down to one knee.

Each time, Jack Callahan has risen from the fire and ashes.

Sister Peg Spindler *(Jan. 2009)*

"Speak up and judge fairly; defend the rights of the poor and needy."
-Proverbs 31: 9

It was almost New Year's Eve; I had a date with a nun.

Sister Peg Spindler was born in Gary. She is the director of Sojourner Truth House, also in Gary.

Spindler, 61, and three other nuns reside in the convent located on the STH grounds near 13th Avenue and Madison Street.

* * *

Sister Peg, do you have any ties to Lowell?

"Yes, I was in raised in Cedar Lake, but went to grade school and church at St. Edward's in Lowell."

Well, the reason I ask is, there's a large marker in one of Lowell's cemeteries where four people were laid to rest. They and 600 others perished on Dec. 30, 1903, when Chicago's Iroquois Theater caught fire. As of 2008, it is still the deadliest single building fire in U.S. history.

"I believe they were relatives. My dad's parents also are buried somewhere in Lowell; I was never taken to the grave site."

High school?

"Andrean, class of '66. My dad, who was not Catholic, insisted that we go to Andrean High School. I must say that I received an excellent education at St. Edward's and at Andrean."

I must say you have an excellent vocabulary.

"I must say I remember doing that book, 'Thirty Days to a More Powerful Vocabulary;' it was part of the summer reading program at Andrean – and you were tested on it, too."

Let me guess, with that flaming red hair of yours, mom was of Irish ancestry and Roman Catholic.

"Yes; her maiden name was Morrison, my grandfather founded Morrison Construction."

When did you get the calling?

"Probably as far back as grade school. I went back and forth with it through high school. Finally, by the time I finished my senior year, I said, 'Well, I'm going to try it, and see whether I like it or not.' So, I went off to the convent and here I am 40-some years later."

This site has been known as Sojourner Truth House for 11 years; you resided here many years before that.

"Yes, I joined the sisters of St. Cyril and Methodius, which was founded for Slovak immigrants. I taught here at Holy Trinity Slovak Church for 15 years."

Children of Eastern-European descent?

"When I came here, my students were all black; the church was half and half. By the time I left, the congregation was completely African-American. I loved teaching here. But the diocese closed it all down; we won't go into that.

"About 10 years ago, I transferred my vows to the congregation of St. Agnes out of Fond du Lac, Wis. I went on a sabbatical from '94 to '97 in Hyde Park (Chicago); I received a degree in theology. That's where I met the Sisters of St Agnes. I'm making a very long and circuitous story, short."

Sojourner Truth House is a ministry of the Poor Handmaids of Jesus Christ.

"Yes, after a two-year study, the Poor Handmaids saw the need for a woman's center here in Gary. They bought these empty buildings for next to nothing. This particular building was the parish and school hall; the actual school is that abandoned, dark-red brick building next door – you can still read the Slovak words for Holy Trinity etched into the facade.

"All these buildings were a mess; the Poor Handmaids took a big risk by sinking a lot of money into renovating all this."

You have two major fundraisers here at STH.

"We hope to make close to $50,000 at our annual Walk-a-thon in June. We're just finishing up our Thanksgiving Non-Event."

Non-Event?

"We send out fancy invitations, telling people how much money they can save by not showing up, renting a tux or limo and not having to get their hair fixed. All they have to do is buy a non-ticket."

Pure genius.

"We have people like Bill and Ila Langen, from Lowell, who donate every month; that's their way of helping us. Other people make large donations once or twice a year; we had a person who gave a dollar towards the Thanksgiving fundraiser."

But there came a poor widow who gave only two mites... .

"We treasured that $1 donation as much as if somebody had given us $10,000 – which nobody did.

"We also get food and clothing donations from all kinds of outlying churches; the Gary churches are really generous, too."

The women and children who come here during the day are from area shelters.

"Yes; we do case management with them. Here at STH, we've grown by leaps and bounds; I don't know if that's good or bad. I'd just as soon work us all out of a job, but that would take major economic systemic change. The nuns are only part of the staff. We also have a volunteer nurse, volunteer assistant in the food pantry and case managers.

"It's a very creative staff; we're always tweaking our groups because we don't have these women very long. What we want to do is help them glimpse the potential inside themselves and inside their children. We can't change them from point A all the way over here to B. But maybe we can help them see that there is a B. We give them a good meal at lunch. They must go to groups; if they're not going to do that, then there's no point in coming here. We're all about growth and stability; that includes staff – we all learn in this process."

How's "business"?

"In 2008, we've seen 30-some women per month from the shelters and 20-some children.

"Community-based clients, who are no longer or never were in the shelters, can come in every 30 days for food and every 90 days for clothes. That's where our huge numbers come from. In fact, November was our fifth consecutive month of more than a total of 1,000 clients served. We've never had that. Never."

While waiting to interview you, I couldn't help but overhear your phone conversation. You'd make a good union griever.

"That was the Gary Housing Authority; they're in trouble with the feds and everybody else because of mismanagement in the past. There's a 75-year old lady who walks with a cane."

Yes?

"In September, she paid her security deposit to the Al Thomas senior citizen building near 11th (Avenue) and Broadway. They said it would be ready very shortly. Well, very shortly still hasn't happened. I'm putting pressure on them downstate. How long does it take to fix up an apartment?

"The system does not work for these little people. It perpetually holds them in poverty. Gone are the days when there was job training. Remember all that job training and childcare money during the Clinton years? Where is it now?"

Well, I've... .

"I've got single women who get $170 per month in food stamps. They can't buy toilet paper, soap or deodorant; hence the stereotype, 'Poor people smell.' Well, duh, make a sensible program!"

Talk to me, Sister!

"And Gary's transportation system – terrible. But they're supposed to go get a job. Well, there aren't any jobs in Gary, so they have to walk to Merrillville. Compound that with the fact that some of them have children.

"Jeff, the rich are getting richer and the poor are getting poorer. If you want to grow terrorism, that's a perfect mix. I'm serious."

I believe you.

"I don't care if you live in Briar Ridge."

Who, me?

"Those people aren't any better than the people who come through here. Maybe they made a few good choices; maybe they had the money to cover up the bad choices they did make.

"We're all in this together. How we care for our most vulnerable citizens tells you what kind of society we are. And right now, we ain't doin' so good with that."

* * *

A couple of decades ago, while on the board of Lake Interfaith Families Together, Spindler sat in on a training seminar in East Chicago. She remembers a young man from Illinois who led one of the breakout sessions. She said he stood at the blackboard with his sleeves rolled up and spoke with passion.

His hair is “salt-and-pepper” now.

And as president-elect of the United States, that man has vowed to cure some of this country’s ills.

Godspeed.

And Barack Obama can rest assured, a red-haired nun from Cedar Lake will continue slugging it out in the trenches at 13th and Madison in Gary.

It’s a habit that becomes her.

Bernice Pittman *(Dec. 2010)*

"Jesus loves me! This I know,
For the Bible tells me so
Little ones to Him belong
They are weak but He is strong."
– Anna B. Warner

Jesus has His helpers here on planet Earth. One of them is Bernice Pittman of Crown Point; she is a crossing guard.

Twice a day, Monday through Friday for more than 20 years, Pittman, 80, has escorted Solon Robinson Elementary School students across the street. She had just finished her morning shift when I interviewed her; the thermometer read 9 degrees Fahrenheit.

Bernice enjoys baking, painting ceramic angels and has a great collection of old movies. She also works the fish fries at the Moose Lodge, walks two miles per day for exercise and has a delightfully raspy voice.

* * *

"I'm going to have to buy a new icebox," Pittman began.

Why's that?

"There's no more room left to display all the photographs of my grandchildren and great-grandchildren."

Where were you born?

"Right here in town."

Maiden name?

"I was Charlie Campbell's daughter. He worked at Letz's a long time ago when I was first born. I believe it was a machine shop here in Crown Point. He taught himself how to read blueprints. To me, he was the greatest man of all. After he retired from Helix, he worked as a handyman at The Boston Store."

The Boston Store?

"It was like a department store, right next to Twelve Islands Restaurant."

I know where that's at.

"My sister Ida and I eat at Twelve Islands every Tuesday. She works in the kitchen at the school. My other sister and her husband were bus drivers; they just retired."

Your neighbor, Dawn Kirk, told me you're known as Mrs. B around these parts.

"You know how that got started? My great-nieces couldn't pronounce Aunt Bernice so they called me Aunt BB. My great-grandchildren call me Grandma P. My cousin's wife across the street goes by Mrs. C."

Mrs. B, please tell me neighbor Dawn goes by Mrs. D. I mean, the residents of Oak Street are starting to sound like something out of a Dr. Seuss book: One fish, two fish, red fish, blue fish. This one has a little star, this one has a little car. See how many fish there are?

"I don't think she does."

You grew up during the Great Depression.

"We never went hungry, but we ate a lot of oatmeal and chicken. To this day, I'm not fond of chicken.

"Right after high school, I worked for Indiana Bell and then Illinois Bell and eventually Ameritech. I started out as an operator and then became a supervisor. I worked for the phone companies for 33 years."

*Tell me about being a telephone operator in the late 1940*s.

"I had to wear a headset with a mouthpiece."

Inebriated callers?

"There were a lot of those."

Could operators listen in on conversations?

"Yes, but we were not supposed to do that. If you got caught, that was trouble."

Mrs. B, did you eavesdrop a time or two?

"Oh, yeah."

Remember party lines?

"Sure."

When I was about 10 or 12, I used to listen to Mrs. Filipek across the street. I'd swear I was being as quiet as a mouse, but every time, she would say, "Wait a second, Juanita, one of the Manes boys is listening again."

"What would you do then?"

I'd shout out at my little brother, "Jace, get off that phone," and then hang up.

"Children can be as ornery as the Dickens, but they eventually grow out of it. I have a son and daughter from my first husband. I waited 16 years before I got remarried to Virgil Pittman. I have 23 great-grandkids and they're all different and I love everyone of them."

I think you love all kids, whether they're blood kin or not.

"I really do. I have memories and scrapbooks."

Tell me about being a crossing guard.

"I arrive at the job site at 7:45 in the morning; school starts at 8:30. In the afternoon, I get there about 2:45; the kids get out of school at 3:30. I get them across the street and make sure I can see them walking to their houses."

What intersection do you work?

"Greenwood (Avenue) and Main (Street)."

Tools of the trade?

"My stop sign and my reflective vest."

You probably get to know those children well as they ascend from kindergarten through the fifth grade.

"Yes, I have kids from way back when I first started come by and say hi to me. When I came back from hernia surgery a car drove by with a sign on it that said, 'Happy to see you; we're glad your back.'"

How many crossing guards are there within the Crown Point Community School Corp.?

"There are 15 of us and five substitutes."

Any close calls?

"Once, when I was out in the middle of the street and the kids were already starting to cross, a car came flying toward me; I shouted to the children not to move until the car got by us. The driver never attempted to stop"

What happened then?

"We're supposed to take license-plate numbers of cars that don't do things the way they're supposed to. But when you're trying to watch out for all those kids, you don't have time to write down numbers. Keeping the kids safe comes first.

"I'm very cautious about my kids. There have been so many scary things going on; I don't like that. I remember one little boy whose father was a cop. He came to pick him up. It was during a time when people who were not really police officers were impersonating police officers. One day, a squad car stopped on Main Street and that little boy started to get in the police car."

And?

"I put my arm around the child, looked at the man, and asked the little boy, 'Is that your father?' He said, 'Yes, Mrs B., that's my dad.' I explained, 'I'm sorry, but I wasn't going to let him that car until I knew everything was OK.'"

Do you get paid?

"Yeah, we get paid, but I'd work for nothin'. I love the job."

* * *

I have to agree with Dawn Kirk when she said that crossing guards are underrated. Mrs. B is an earth angel.

Char Seramur *(Apr. 2010)*

"Time is an important factor to most people, and time is my business – in fact, my only business. I am a commercial-type clock, that has hung on the wall, in the same place, a Lowell business place, since 1922... ."

– Fremond McCarty, from the beginning of his ode to a Regulator wall clock that hung in The Corner Barber Shop for 55 years

Char Seramur, 77, has resided in Lowell her entire life. She raised three children, is a member of Three Creeks Historical Association, and lives with a rat terrier named Daisy.

I've known Seramur for quite a while; she's a daisy, too.

* * *

"I don't tweet, twitter or text," Seramur began. "How boring is this interview going to be?"

Charlotte, just continue talking and let the readers decide.

"I grew up in an old two-story house here in town. We rented half of it out for extra income.

"My dad planted a redbud tree when I was about 10. That redbud still stands; every spring, it blooms beautifully."

Tell me more about your father.

His name was Fremond McCarty.

Great name.

"He barbered in the same location, Commercial Avenue and Clark Street, for 58 years. It was called The Corner Barber Shop."

School days.

"I walked to school; it was only a block from our house."

You speak of the Romanesque-style schoolhouse destined for the wrecking ball.

"What a beautiful building it was. It had beautiful wood floors. There was a huge golden oak staircase with turned newel posts.

"To see it in the condition it's in today saddens me; something should have been done many years ago to preserve that historic building."

Radio days.

"We had a floor model Philco. My mom liked to listen to 'My Gal Sal.' I liked 'Jack Armstrong, the All-American Boy.'

"We also did a lot of ice skating at the old mill pond off of Main Street. We'd stay out there for hours.

"My dear friend, Marcia Carlson, and I, have talked about that. We truly believe we grew up in the very best of times. None of us had much, but we knew how to make our own fun.

"The electronic things kids have today, sometimes I wonder what they have to look forward to. We didn't get everything we wanted."

Are you a dyed-in-the-wool-Democrat like Marcia?

"No, I'm more conservative. But in the past year-and-a-half, I've become more of an independent; I'm not a Tea Party patriot or anything like that. I watch a lot of C-SPAN."

The homefront during World War II.

"I remember hunting for milkweed pods."

Why?

"The silk was used to make parachutes. People also bought war bonds. I think they were $18.65; if you kept them for a period of years, you'd get $25.

"We turned in aluminum, even gum wrappers, although there wasn't much gum to be had. My mother melted paraffin and added a drop of peppermint extract to it; that was our gum. We saved everything; each member of the family had a ration book. Here's mine."

Obviously, you've continued to save everything.

"When the siren went off, my dad was in charge of Fremont Street. It was like an air raid drill. He'd put on a helmet and he had this huge flashlight. We'd turn out the lights and pull the shades. We expected to hear bombers come over.

"When the war was over, they closed down Commercial Avenue. Bill Weaver had an appliance store where the tae kwon do place is now. He mounted a big speaker onto his storefront and played music; the townsfolk did a gigantic snake dance down the middle of the street. We were so happy the war was over."

Happy Days.

"When I was a freshman, maybe, I remember the farm boys coming into to town on a Saturday night. They'd been in the fields all day, and after they got cleaned up, they'd cruise up and down Commercial Avenue with their polished cars. They were all tan, shiny and smooth."

The cars?

"The farm boys. We looked forward to that."

You did say you knew how to make your own fun.

"A few years later, I learned to drive a '36 Ford."

What kind of Ford?

"A blue one."

Let's fast forward to the 21st century. Hobbies?

"I like flower gardening and baking for the firemen and EMT's; they're my boys. In fact, I made them chocolate chip cookies today; I saved some for you."

It is unethical for me to take gifts of any kind.

"You can dunk."

Well, maybe.... Your mother taught you how to make wool braided rugs.

"Yes, now I'm passing it on to Sharon Speichert, Janice Hamm and Joyce Bradley every Tuesday. They're doing so good, I'm going to take them for a field trip when they're done with their rugs."

Minnesota Fabrics?

"Mi Ranchito restaurant for margaritas."

Tell me more about these rugs.

"They're made from old wool skirts and coats. It's just like braiding hair.
They last forever because wool repels soil. Both sides are useable. I'm working on the wrong side right now."

Wrong side right now?

"It's like fabric, there's a wrong side and right side. Your shirt is worn with the right side out."

Right side out?

* * *

Lowell is a small town, and word travels fast. Seramur is dealing with some serious health issues. When I questioned her about it, she told me she was grateful she didn't have Parkinson's disease, arthritis or dementia. She can still braid rugs.

"Jeff, I've had a pretty darn good life," she said.

The daughter of Fremond McCarty believes she grew up in the best of times.

I believe Char Seramur has made the most of her time for 77 years.

Rosa Maria Rodriguez *(Dec. 2010)*

"Among poor people, there's not any question about women being strong – even stronger than men. They work in the fields right along with the men. When your survival is at stake, you don't have these questions about yourself like middle-class women do."
Dolores Huerta, co-founder, United Farm Workers

I interviewed Rosa Maria Rodriguez at the union hall of United Steel Workers Local 1010 in East Chicago; she is the financial secretary there.

Rodriguez, 56, has been married to Pedro Rodriguez for 18 years; they live in Portage.

* * *

"I was born in Texas," Rodriguez began. "Then, we moved to the Brunswick neighborhood of Gary in the early '50s. When I was about 12, we moved to downtown Gary. Where we moved to was nothing but doctors and lawyers. It seems like as soon as we moved in, everybody else moved out."

High school?

"I didn't go to high school; I was locked up from the ages of 14 to almost18. I learned at the age of 3 to shut up and put up."

What do you mean by that?

"I was molested from the ages of 3 to 12 and I kept my mouth shut. By the time I was 12, I realized if I fought, they couldn't touch me. I learned to protect myself and I took it out to the streets; I became a bully. I would beat up people just for the heck of it – boys, girls, teachers... . I couldn't tell my parents my secret."

Was it a family member who was molesting you?

"A family member and friends of the family. I was 36 before my parents found out. In the meantime, I was this uncontrollable child they didn't know what to do with."

Rosa, it was fight or flight; you were angry.

"I wanted negative attention; I robbed a gas station. I only got $257, but I got the attention – and I also got arrested. Finally, just before I was 15, they sent me away. I was supposed have my quinceanera that April, but instead of wearing a beautiful gown, my father watched them drag me away wearing shackles. He cried like a baby."

Your mother?

"She is the strongest individual I've ever known. She was one of the first women to operate a forklift back when the women only picked the fruits and vegetables. She's one of those quiet individuals who does what she has to do. She's doesn't look for recognition or glory.

"My mother was hospitalized because of tuberculosis when I was a little girl. I had to stay with relatives. That's when bad things started happening to me."

To which correctional facility were you sent?

"Indiana Girls School, located at 2596 Girls School Road, Speedway, Ind."

A year or so after you were released, you had a baby.

"Yes, she drowned when she was 5. I was unmarried at the time and making a dollar an hour. Less than two weeks later, thanks to affirmative action, I got a call from Inland Steel Co.; they wanted me to start that Monday. I told them that I had just buried my daughter."

And?

"My dad grabbed the phone and said, 'She'll be there Monday morning.' I was sent to the 12-inch Bar Mill; it was 1978. I was 24. Just before my first day on the job, my dad told me two things: 'No. 1, you don't let nobody do your work, and No. 2, you don't shit where you eat.' That has proved to be some of the best advice I've ever received."

Explain the latter, please.

"Leave your personal life at the mill gate. You are there to do a job. I never dated any of my workmates; very rarely would I stop after work with them.

"Some of the women who were hired in the '70s were looking for husbands. Some of them got bad reputations. I had my dad, brothers and cousins all out there protecting me."

You eventually married.

"Yes, I have two sons, Moises and Erick, from my first husband. The marriage lasted about five years."

The mill?

"I learned there wasn't anything I couldn't do in the mill; all I had to do was try. I was the first woman to become a bandsaw operator at the 12-inch Bar Mill. I also was the first woman to make it to the mill floor at the 12-inch; I was a guide setter. Currently, I'm the only woman in the world who is a vacuum degasser."

Those are production jobs; you also worked maintenance.

"Yes, I was a mechanic when I had my accident."

Rosa, you took one hell of a fall at the blast furnace.

"We were having trouble aligning a coupling. The guy I was working with left the job site to get a crow bar so we could pry the flanges into place.

"I picked up the gasket and started to place it on the flange; when I did that, I perfectly teeter-tottered the grating I was standing on. It had never been welded down."

How far did you fall?

"Almost 30 feet. Luckily, I landed on a pile of graphite. If I had fallen six inches in either direction, I would have hit some steel piping or landed on railroad tracks."

You didn't come out of it unscathed.

"I broke my back; they gave me a 50-50 chance of ever walking again. That was in 1987; to this day, right now, I'm in pain. But I deal with it."

How did you deal with it during the '80s?

"Morphine and Vicodin; I became a full-blown addict by '89. In 1990, I gave my life to God. I've been clean for 20 years. But I still have nightmares of falling."

The union?

"I come from a long line of unionists and steel workers. My great-uncle was an organizer for the mine workers. My grandfather worked in the copper mines of Mexico and the coal mines of Pennsylvania."

You've done your part to support the miners in Mexico.

"All those copper miners in Mexico want is to be able to come out the same way they went in."

You mean safer working conditions.

"Los Mineros have been on strike for more than three years. Some of the strikers have been kidnaped and jailed unlawfully. Their wives have been attacked and their children have been segregated from their peers."

I'm sure the Mexican miners are grateful for the support they get from American Steelworkers.

"Yes, but it's still bad down there. We watched the Federales dressed in full riot gear protecting the mines while bringing in scabs. It was sad to see the desperation on the faces of the striking miners."

Some people you really look up to?

"The president of this local, Tom Hargrove; the president of the United States, Barack Obama; and my mother."

One of your goals?

"To become a mentor at 2596 Girls School Road."

* * *

Rodriguez has been a community activist in East Chicago for many years. She also sits on the board of the United Way and is a member of Women of Steel. She's a strong woman who has worked right along with the men.

As little Rosa Maria Salas, she was strong, too. She had to be; her survival was at stake.

Ron Styck *(Jan. 2011)*

"You cook good rabbit, pilgrim."
– Will Geer, from the film "Jeremiah Johnson"

To me, Ron Styck's dad always seemed to be easy-going – a gentle giant and a methodical man. He was a farmer.

My dad, was, let's say, more fiery – an Italian-American who didn't spare the rod. He was a steel worker.

Maybe that's why I've never forgotten the following prelude to this interview – a classic tale of crime and punishment.

When Ron was about 6 and his sister 4, they followed their father around as he did chores one sunny day. While Percy – not a lot of Newton County farmers named Percival – was preoccupied repairing something with baling wire, baling wire being a panacea to the farmer much like duct tape is to the suburbanite, Ron said to his diminutive sibling, "Lana, touch that."

"That" happened to be an electric fence. Lana was jolted immediately to the ground.

Percy had overheard Ron's command, but couldn't react in time to protect his darling daughter.

Above Lana's wailing, "Big Perce" looked Ron in the eye, and calmly said, "Son, you know what you have to do."

With bottom lip quivering and a solitary teardrop rolling down his chubby cheek, the boy looked up to his father and nodded. And that's when little Ronnie grabbed the electric livestock fence with both hands.

The smoldering chip off the old block took it like a man.

* * *

Ron Styck, 51, lives south of Lake Village and west of U.S. 41 in McClellan Township near the state line. He has been married to Judy for 27 years; they have raised four adult children: Chad, Tara, Stefanie and Cody.

I hadn't seen Ron in 35 years, but he waited for me in his pickup at the end of his long, snow-covered driveway the evening I came to interview him. He wanted to make sure I didn't get stuck.

He's that kind of guy.

* * *

Ron, remember when we used to hunt rabbits near Ira Porter's place?

"Yeah, that area still has lots of rabbits," he said.

How much land do you farm?

"About 6,500 acres."

Didn't you also purchase some of the land surrounding the ghost town of Conrad?

"I bought 800 tillable acres from Jennie Conrad's heirs; the Nature Conservancy bought the wooded portion."

During the off season, you operate an excavating business.

"Yeah, we have an excavator, a dozer and a scraper."

Do you do a lot of work for TNC?

"Yes, we help TNC create wetlands. We've also dug some ponds or depressions for them over by Bogus."

You refer to what remains of Bogus Island. Ron, you live in a very historic area; right where this house sits was once part of the largest natural lake in Indiana.

"My yard is part of Beaver Lake's beach; you can really tell during the daytime. When I dug our pond out back, I found all kinds of arrowheads."

Ron, do you know much about the Black Marsh? The legendary wolf hunter, "Kankakee Ned" Barker, considered it one of the most treacherous bogs on the face of the earth. That's where the trumpeter swans nested by the thousands.

"I farmed that muck ground; it's right next to Cherry Island. I used to flood that area so I could duck hunt it. I'd have a few swans show up every year. TNC owns that now. When I drove my combine through that muck, I could kinda feel the ground wavering."

Ron, do you care to talk about when you got shot in 1997?

"I was turkey hunting with a friend. I went on one end of the property and he went on the other. Right at daylight, I heard a shot. I thought, 'Well, he got his.'

"I wasn't seeing anything and by 7 a.m., I had to get out of there – planting season. As I walked back to my truck I heard a gobble; I figured I'd have just enough time to try for that one. I snuck up toward some big bluestem (tall prairie grass) and stood up against a wild cherry tree. I started calling and it called back. The turkey was just on the other side of some pines."

And?

"POOM! It was like a cold sting and a shockwave hit me. It knocked me against the tree. I thought I'd shot myself. I fell over and couldn't get back up. My lungs started gurgling. I thought, 'This ain't good; I'm gonna die here.' I figured my friend had gone home after bagging a turkey."

Did your friend shoot you?

"Yeah, remember Babe Stojanic?"

Sure, he was like a father to both of us.

"He had just given me some really good 3-D camouflage; it blended in like you wouldn't believe. I was holding my shotgun in front of my chest. My bottom hand was gripping the stock. It was cold out and my hand had turned kind of pinkish-red."

Your buddy thought your right hand was the head of a wild turkey.

"Yep. I blacked out and I guess I laid out there for quite a while. It's real sandy and they had trouble getting to me. Judy and the kids were there when they carried me to the ambulance. They had cut off most of my clothing."

I'd imagine more than your right hand was red by then.

"My youngest daughter fainted when she saw me. Butch Cain, the Lake Village fire chief, blew oxygen into my face in the ambulance. I remember everything from then on."

From what range were you shot?

"About 25 yards."

Lord. What kind of ammunition hit you?

"A duplex load of No. 4s and 6s. The No. 4s are bigger shot; they did the most damage. There was a perfect outline of my shotgun on my chest. The gun protected my heart and one lung."

Ronnie, you shouldn't be here; it's a miracle.

"My kids counted 176 BB holes from my waist to the top of my chest. I was lucky; it didn't pierce my intestines. But the blast did collapse one of my lungs and broke three or four bones in my right hand."

How long were you in the hospital?

"Four or five days; Judy says I came home too soon. I got an infection from leakage in my rib cage. They stuck a huge needle in my back and drained the infection. That was nasty.

"But really, I haven't had a whole lot of trouble. I still have BBs in my chest; it does more damage taking them out. I had a goose-down coat on that day. When I came home, my kids pulled feathers out of my chest and stomach.

"Jeff, you know where I was when I got shot?"

No.

"TNC's Unit H."

I'm not familiar... .

"Yeah, you are; it's where we used to rabbit hunt near Ira Porter's place."

* * *

Ronnie said when you go through something like he did it really makes you want to come home and kiss your wife and take good care of your kids.

He also told me he'd much rather be the person who got shot than be the person who accidently shot somebody.

Ron Styck is that kind of guy.

Jeff Manes (left) and Ronnie Styck after rabbit hunting during the blizzard of '67.

WORK

Shane Peck *(Sept. 2006)*

"Football is a game designed to keep coal miners off the streets."
-Jimmy Breslin

Shane and Sandy Peck are the proud parents of Steffan Peck, starting tailback of the Lowell Red Devils.

The Pecks have lived in Lowell since February 1999. That is the longest period of time Shane Peck has ever hung his hat in one spot during the entire 38 years he has spent on or under this earth.

Shane Peck is a hard rock miner.

* * *

Tell me about your line of work.

"The Pecks have been underground construction or coal mining since day one. That's basically what we do, you know what I'm sayin'? Our business is dangerous as hell.

"I've been doing it for 12 years. My brother has had well over 100 stitches and never missed a day's work because of it. He cut the end of his finger off; we taped it back together so he could finish the shift.

"We've been on A&E, The History Channel. All the Chicago news stations have covered us. We build anything underground. We're 300 feet down. We build tunnels and structures, mainly for flood control for the Metropolitan Water Reclamation District of Greater Chicago. We also punch into existing sewers and give them an overflow.

"There's about 160 miles of deep tunnel underneath Chicago. Some of the prettiest sewers I've ever seen are in the city of Chicago – completely bricked. Beautiful masonry work done long ago. They used mules that never saw daylight. They had stables underground from them.

"We didn't leave Eastern Kentucky to find work. They called us – men like my dad, men who do that kind of work. They didn't have experienced miners around here. These deep tunnels started in Milwaukee and Chicago back in 1977. We're from the mountains that border West Virginia and Virginia.

"Hard rock miners don't mine coal. We build the mines so the miners can get to the coal. The Pecks before me were the coal miners. They say my grandfather was heading into the mine to begin an afternoon shift while his father, Watt Peck, was being hauled out – he'd been killed. Father and son passed right by each other. They worked for Peabody Coal. It *will* stop here. Steffan will *not* be a miner – I'll kill him first. You know what I'm sayin'?

"There's different kinds of miners, too. Coal miners, gold miners, copper miners, salt miners. ... Dad worked for Morton Salt down in Louisiana – 2,200 feet straight down. He said it was the most beautiful thing he'd ever seen. Salt is blue. We penetrate the rock. We drill and blast. That's the fun part. I've probably set off the more than 300 charges."

Fire in the hole!

"We still shout that warning. She hits hard, Jack. I've used as much as 2,500 pounds of TNT. When you hit rock, you drill anywhere from 4- to 10-foot holes, then you load it with dynamite. You have to shore up the walls as you go, so rock don't fall and kill you.

"When you get down so far in, you don't come out to shoot – you just hide behind somethin'. It's like standing in the barrel of a loaded shotgun. It knocks your hard hat off. Your cheeks pound. My dad cain't even hear no more."

How long have you and Sandy been wed?

"I've been married to the same woman for 20 years. I'm only 37. We got married right out of high school – didn't have to or anything. I was goin' into the Air Force and I just knew someone else was going to nab her up, so I married her. The way we move around, you've got to have one hellaciously strong woman.

"Sandy's awesome. She's also from the Appalachian Mountains. The only thing going on down there is coal mining; it's a poverty stricken area. But for some reason nobody wants to leave. Except for the hard rock miner. He tramps out."

That's got to be tough on the kids.

"It is. Steffan was born in Florida. He's lived on Grissom Air Force Base in Indiana. He's lived in Kentucky twice. He started school in Beaver Dam, Wis. – that little hillbilly could play some ice hockey, too. Now he's back in Indiana.

"We're nomads. I went to three different schools during my fifth grade year. You know what I'm sayin'?"

You dip?

"I been chewin' since I was 7. My brother started when he was 5. We'd chew tobacco while we watched cartoons on Saturday morning. My mom would buy it for us by the roll. That's when we lived in West Virginia, before they found out it was bad for you."

How do you get to the job site?

"A man cage lowers us down. We carry meters for gases and explosion. We still wear cap lamps. The work is brutal. There is a couple of days every year where I have to literally crawl around on the floor. Sandy rubs my back until I can stand up; I go to work."

What union are you out of?

"Local 2. That's the sewer, tunnel, and miner part of the Laborers' Union.

My dad is still a member of the UMW. In West Virginia the United Mine Workers is a very strong union.

"In Kentucky, a lot of guys are nonunion. They'll go under the ground for $10 per hour. That's ridiculous. I remember one Christmas Eve, a friend of mine named Gary Emmett had his face removed in an accident. I was just coming in for the graveyard shift.

"I hear, 'Man down!' My brother Marty wrapped what was left of Gary's head in a towel. When I got down there, he was making a gurgling sound. It was his death rattle.

"It was wet on that particular job, another good friend of Gary's was a guy named Randy who saw the whole thing. Randy's yellow rain suit was bright red. I'll never forget what Randy said to me as he stood next to Gary, he looked at me and asked what I was getting Steffan for Christmas."

He was in shock.

"We also had a guy cut in half. Usually when a man dies underground, whether it's West Virginia or Chicago, it's major news.

People like to read about it, I guess.

"I've only had one serious injury while working foreman. That was a 25 year-old boy. A bundle of re-bar fell and shattered vertebrae in his back. The local paramedics came to the job. They refused to go underground.

"Here I've got this man, who I'm afraid to move, and he's laying in icy water. About five of us took off most of our clothing and stuffed him with it. We had a stretcher down there. I'm thinking, 'I'm responsible for this man.'

"We picked him up in unison and rolled him onto the stretcher. We wrapped him up like a mummy with duct tape. The paramedics told him we did exactly what needed to be done. He thanked all of us. Today, the company and union are paying for him to go to culinary school.

"My dad had all the toes on one of his feet severed while underground. They reattached all five of them – stitches and pins. But there's no feelin' left. He walks with a limp. Tell you what, for a man approaching 60, he can still kick the ass of most 25- year olds."

Shane, there's easier, safer ways to make a buck.

"We're just people tryin' to make a livin'. You got to find somethin' you're passionate about – and give 110 percent. We take pride in our work. What we do is not a job, it's a lifestyle. Being a hard rock miner is like bein' on Star Trek. We go where no man has ever gone before. We have a geologist that goes along with us checking out the rock. We were drilling in a new spot and I noticed a hole in a wall of rock. It was a perfect circle about two feet long that looked like it had been drilled with a auger. I asked the geologist about it. He tells me that was where some kind of extinct sea creature had been. The rock we're going through is 40 million years old."

I hope your family is able to reside in Lowell for years to come.

"Jeff, Lowell is the best place I've ever lived. The people are friendly. It reminds me of the town my wife is from – only flat. This has been a good place for Steffan to grow up in. That boy would give you the shirt off his back – but don't cross him. He don't like bullies. And don't mess with his mama. He's also a mama's boy. As far as football, I tell Steffan, 'Son, you give a 110 percent or don't play at all.' I tell him that – ever' day."

* * *

And when the city folk carp and complain about their office jobs from atop those ivory towers, let it be known there is a hardcore, hard rock miner more than a football field's length below them. He's watching out for his men, his brother, or his daddy. And he's about to set off another charge... .

"Fahr in the hole!!"

And he doesn't hear a mumblin' word coming from those skyscrapers. Shane Peck is too busy giving 110.

You know what I'm sayin'?

Kathi Wellington *(Apr.* 2007)

"I am a union woman,
just as brave as I can be.
I do not like the bosses,
and the bosses don't like me."
-Aunt Molly Jackson

I arrived at the Paragon Restaurant in Hobart just ahead of my friend Kathi Wellington. Kathi was raised in Hobart. She has resided in Portage for many years. I asked for a booth in the nonsmoking section. Angioplasty has convinced her to go from 55 cigarettes a day to seven. She ordered a Coke.

It was 10 a.m. and Wellington had been on the go for more than six hours. At age 50-plus, Kat Wellington is still a pistol.

* * *

"I'll give the waitress a good tip – used to work here," Wellington began. "Every time Bethlehem Steel would lay me off, Jimmy would give me a job waitin' tables. I was laid off three times. Once, for three-and-a-half years. I made good money in this place. I was a good waitress. Good legs. Run, run, run. This place fed my kids."

Kids?

"I have one birth child; Clay's 33. He has his Master's Degree. I made sure he worked summer help in the mills while he was going to school to ensure he'd stay in school – and to see what his mother did for a living. A lot of other kids came and stayed with us for a lot of years."

Foster children?

"Strays. Some stayed the night. Some stayed for years. Abused kids seeking shelter, mostly. I was like the little woman who lived in a cracker box house and had so many kids she didn't know what to do."

What are you doing for a living now?

"I teach Labor History at the carpenters apprenticeship school right around the corner. Let me tell you, I give them boys a *lesson!* 'What did we fight and die for? The eight hour day, benefits, safety... .' People come into a union and they don't even know where these benefits came from. I also teach an Interpersonal Communications class to the ironworkers. It used to be you took an apprenticeship – you got a journeyman's card. Nowadays, you also get credits toward an associate's degree. I also teach OSHA classes at Ivy Tech to people who are pre-apprenticeship, but are taking classes in hopes they will be picked for an apprenticeship."

The Wellingtons have a rich labor history themselves.

"My great-grandfather was from Wales – potatoes. When the blight hit, he migrated to Pennsylvania – coal. His boys came to Gary – steel. My dad went railroad – EJ & E."

You?

"After my divorce – steel. I applied for a clerical job and passed the typing test in 1978. I said, 'Okay, when do you think I'll start?' She said, 'I don't know. We're not hiring. We're just taking applications.' I had a baby to feed. I needed a real job that would pay me a man's wage. I said, 'Listen, what jobs are available?' She said, "Labor. 160" Plate Mill." I said, 'Sweetheart, I'll shovel shit and I will never look back.' My dad asked me if I passed the clerical test. I said, 'Sure did. I'll be shoveling animal fat in the underbelly of Bethlehem Steel's rolling mills.' The only reason I got my foot in the door was because of affirmative action; they *had* to hire blacks and women."

"Dad said, 'I've raised four daughters. You got more balls than most men I've known.' That's when he handed me this.. .."

Let me read that: "Llewellyn Wellington. Fifty-one years service. United Steelworkers of America. Signed, I.W. Abel."

"That's my grandfather's honorary union card. I never leave home without it."

How many years did you end up putting in?

"Twenty-five. Bethlehem went bankrupt on paper – for about five seconds. When I'm 62, I'll probably get about $600 a month from the government. Not enough to live on. I'll work until the day I die, especially now that I got this stent in my heart – $42,000 and rising. Good times."

You remained in the labor gang for most of your career in the mill.

"Yeah. I was also union rep for 17 years. I press for workers to go back to school and get that higher education. I got my own degree from the ages of 40 to 50, you know."

Memorable grievances?

"When I became a union rep they told me that when we are in the grievance procedure we are all on the same exact level. This one superintendent decided he was going to show me who was boss. I walk into his office; he's sitting halfway across the room behind this big huge desk with his arms crossed. Without speaking, he points to a chair. Like, sit. I dragged that chair all the way across the room while looking him straight in the eye. I swung that chair around to his side of the desk and sat next to him. 'Now, let's read this grievance together.'

His reaction?

"He turns bright red. Old school. Never dealt with a woman griever in his life. He just stared at the grievance without reading it. I said, 'Well, since you don't seem to be very talkative. Are you going to sign this and pay those three guys?' He signed it, then pushed the grievance toward me and said, 'Get away from my desk.' I smiled, 'Really gonna like doin' business with you,' and walked out. I took him to my level – real quick."

Have you had to deal with any fatalities?

"Randy Moehl was our Christmas star at Bethlehem Steel. He and his wife did Steelworkers for Kids. They'd help purchase and wrap about 2,500 presents and then take them to the battered women's shelters and workshops for handicapped children. April Moehl is one of my best friends. It's undignified the way Randy's death was handled. When Bethlehem went belly up, they did April dirty. Ma Beth? She didn't miss a half hour of production. Do you think Randy said to April, 'Give us a big special kiss this morning, darling. I'll be dead this afternoon.' Jeff, nobody should have to go to work and die today."

* * *

No doubt her young apprentices receive an earful. Hopefully, they'll heed her words on safety.

Kat Wellington: A card-carryin', smokin' gun. Fightin' the good fight, while on the run.

Dave Cooper *(July 2010)*

"I complained because I had no shoes,
until I met a man who had no feet."
– Karen LeDelle Manes to her eldest son, circa 1965

Dave Cooper was born at George Ade Hospital in Brook, but has lived in Lake Village all his life. He and his wife, Brenda, have four children.

Cooper, 38, likes to ride his Harley-Davidson, hunt, fish and is a member of the Southern Lake County Conservation Club.

Like his grandfather, Sam Cooper, and his father, Ray Cooper, before him, Dave is a pile driver for Thatcher Foundations out of Gary. He's been with the company for 19 years.

* * *

You were part of the first class of apprentice pile drivers in this area.

"Yes, in '91," Cooper said. "I did all my schooling, a week every quarter, for three years, in Elk Grove Village, Ill.; it's like 85 miles from Lake Village.

"Although I had moved up from being a laborer, apprentices got all the crappy jobs the journeymen didn't want. In '95, I became the first pile driver to graduate from a Chicago local."

To which local do Thatcher employees belong?

"Local 578, which is the sea level (578 feet) of Lake Michigan in Chicago. The lake level fluctuates, of course. If you get a stiff north wind, it'll come up a foot or so in a day.

"Once I turned journeyman, the business agent approached me about being a union steward; he told me I knew the rules as good as anybody."

Did you take the position?

"Yes; by '97, I was running jobs for Thatcher."

Fill me in about the trade itself.

"We're usually the first guys on a job site who are union. The sites are real rough; there are no mud slabs poured for walls. We do everything from the ground down by beating beams in the ground or putting in sheet piling to keep everything from caving in.

"When it comes to earth retention, the No. 1 thing is safety. We're protecting the guys with our bracing systems. We don't want anybody getting buried alive because something collapsed.

"In January of '02, I became Thatcher's safety director. I have a good boss. When it comes to safety, he'll say, 'If your idea works, we'll expand on it.'"

How's business in these shaky economic times?

"I'd say work is steady. We currently have a job going for the Corp of Engineers."

What job is that?

"Stage 7 of the Little Calumet River between Munster and Hammond. We also have a job at Washington Park in Michigan City; we'll be doing the dock wall. And, we also have a dock wall we're putting in at the Port of Indiana – 1,700 linear feet of sheet piling."

Your accident.

"I got hurt Dec. 27, 1999. Before that, I had a perfect safety record. Nobody is exempt when it comes to getting hurt."

What happened?

"I was on the Aux Sable project in Channahon, Ill. The crane failed. A pipe pile about 40 feet long and a half-inch thick fell on me. Anything pile drivers work with is heavy, even when you're shoveling Chicago blue gumbo (soil). The operator was fully competent. Good guy; I didn't point fingers."

Where did the pipe strike you?

"It blew my foot out like a bad tire. I yelled one time, but I kept my wits about me."

You probably went into shock.

"They said I did, but I don't believe it. I remember asking my lead man, 'Hey, is my leg broke off?' He said, 'No, but your foot's messed up.' I told him to make sure I didn't bleed to death.

“The paramedics cut all my clothes off. Once they looked at my foot, they figured I couldn’t make the trip to Joliet in an ambulance, so they called in the helicopter. They gave me morphine; that didn’t work. Then, they gave me Demerol and started playing ‘Slow Ride.’”

Injuries to extremities can be the most painful.

“During surgery, they had to cut half my foot off, then replaced it with a muscle from my back. They sort of flapped or folded it around so I could eventually walk on it. I have pictures of it.”

No thanks. What next?

“It never did heal properly. It was driving me up a wall. I wasn’t mobile at all. After two years of being off work and walking on crutches, I told an orthopedic surgeon, ‘I’m tired of dealing with this shit and I wanna go back to work – cut it off.’ He looked at me like I was nuts. Hey, it was half a foot with a muscle on it.”

And?

“He had me see another doctor in Joliet. This new doctor sits down and asks me: ‘What’s wrong with your fingers?’ I told him I was working on my tractor just before my appointment – there was some grease underneath my fingernails. We continued our strange conversation and then it dawned on me – he’s a psychiatrist. I asked him why in the fuck I was sent to him. He says, ‘Well, we have people who want stuff amputated.’”

Did you pile drive him?

“No, but I did say, ‘So, you’re making sure I’m not gonna buy a parrot and dress up like Long John Silver?’”

The shrink’s reply?

“‘Dave, that’s basically it. You’re more sane than I am. Get out of here.’

“Jeff, I’m very lucky. There are people who have laid out in battlefields for hours before care could get to them. I had immediate care.”

* * *

Dave Cooper’s left leg was amputated about four inches below the knee in 2001.

He says he still has his days. Sores can be a problem. But, he can work out of his house on his laptop if he has to.

And, thanks to a titanium prosthesis, he still can ride a Harley and hunt wild turkeys with his Uncle Joe.

Wessie Anderson *(June 2010)*

"In '61, war begun
In '62, bullets flew
In '63, slaves are free
In '64, war is o'er
In '65, Lincoln died."
–Old school lesson, author unknown

Throughout the 20th Century, European and Mexican immigrants found jobs in the blast furnaces and open hearths of East Chicago and Gary. But they weren't the only folks who migrated to Northwest Indiana in search of work.

In 1971, two weeks after completing a three-year stint in Vietnam, native Mississippian Wessie Anderson hired in at Inland Steel Co.'s No. 2 Coke Plant. He's lived in E.C. ever since and has been retired for seven years.

Anderson, 62, is married to Geraldine; they have raised four children.

* * *

Wessie, you were 13 or 14 years old in 1961, 100 years after the beginning of the Civil War. Tell this Yankee about growing up in the Deep South.

"Parts of Mississippi seem to be catching up with the rest of the world," he said. "I was raised about 40 miles east of Jackson. We used mules to help plow the cotton and corn. We also raised chickens and hogs to eat."

Sounds like your father was a farmer.

"My dad was a sharecropper. When not doing the white man's burden, on Sundays, maybe, we'd work in our small field. But the crops of the landowner, who also was a store owner in town, always came first.

"Some years, you had bad years with the cotton. Say, you only made five bales of cotton. The man would tell my dad, 'John, you bring your kids on down to the store.' And, we'd get new shoes and maybe a pair of pants and a couple of shirts for school.

"The store owner would put it all on a ticket. Every year, he'd say to my father, 'John, you almost made it out of the hole.' The next year might have been a real good year – 10 bales of cotton. And you just knew things were gonna be better because Dad was going to get some money. But every year, it was, 'John, you almost made it out of the hole.'"

How many siblings did you have?

"There were 12 of us kids – two sets of twins. I'm 6-feet, 3-inches tall; my twin sister is only 5-feet, 2-inches tall. She also is about five or six times lighter skinned than I am."

Education?

"I'm not an educated person. We missed a lot of school during the spring and fall because it was planting or harvest time."

Wessie, you're one of the sharpest mechanics I've ever met.

"I loved being a mechanic. My father also would haul what they called pulp wood in those days; now, they call it paper wood. When the transmission of his truck would go out he'd rebuild it at night. Me and my brother would stick the transmission back in before school.

"When I was drafted, I wanted to be a mechanic, but they told me I couldn't be one unless I agreed to do an extra year. So, that's what I did."

How long were you in the Army?

"From '68 to '71; my job in Vietnam was to rebuild differentials for Jeeps."

Let's switch gears. You've lived in East Chicago for almost 40 years. It didn't take you long to enjoy high school basketball in Indiana.

"Yeah, there was a bunch of us that went to all of East Chicago Washington's basketball games. We'd travel to all the away games. I remember in the mid-'70s, when Washington played at Lebanon. I believe Lebanon was rated No. 1 (in the state). Their gym was packed. Jeff, from the cheap seats, I got to looking around at that crowd and it reminded of a big white dog with one black ear – E.C. was the ear."

How did the Senators fare?

"We beat 'em. Jeff, I'd like to talk a little more about race."

My friend, talk to me.

"There were wounds from growing up in Mississippi. I been called 'nigger,' and I been called 'boy' and I've been spit on. Those wounds healed, but as soon as (Barack) Obama became president, they seemed to resurface."

Go on.

"I consider myself the 'in-between' generation. I believe race relationships took a step back since we elected a black president. This country is more divided than ever. It's hard for some people, say 55 and older, to accept Obama.

"That night when he became president, I didn't think of him as a black president; I thought of him as a Democratic president. I didn't care who ran; I felt anybody was better than what we had."

Wessie, is there anything I didn't ask you, that you wish I would've? Any words of wisdom?

"Jeff, there ain't but one race what God made, and that's the human race. We done come a long way, but we got a long way to go. All of us need to get downstairs together."

Downstairs together?

"Kneel and pray."

* * *

Wessie and I often worked on jobs together where our faces were caked with coke dust. From the neck up, only our eyeballs and teeth were white.

It's been almost 10 years since we were involved in an explosion in the mill. The lights fried immediately. Little did I know, two colleagues from my hometown, Lake Village, had perished on our fourth-floor job site.

Three of us ran down an incline in the dark, but couldn't seem to get away from the oxygen line that had exploded above. We couldn't see the pipeline, but could hear it rumbling near our heads.

I feared it was going to blow up again at any second. Disoriented, I didn't realize we had made it to within about 25 feet of ground level and a way out. I screamed above the deafening roar that I was going back the way we'd come.

That's when "Big Wes"snatched me up in a vise-like bear hug and carried me toward daylight and safety.

He didn't care about my color.

Bill Sheets *(Oct. 2010)*

"I was standing by my window
On a cold and cloudy day
When I saw the hearse come rollin'
For to take my mother away...
I told the undertaker:
'Undertaker, please drive slow,
For this body you are haulin'
Lord, I hate to see her go"
– Traditional
("Will the Circle Be Unbroken")

My Grandma Manes' wake was at Sheets Funeral Home in Lowell. Growing up, I don't recall seeing my dad cry. But it was with a tear in his eye that he shook Mr. Sheets' hand, and said, "Bill, you did a beautiful job on my mother. They are fifth-generation morticians. Bill Sheets is retired; his sons, Ken and Blake, run the business.

Sheets, 80, has lived in Lowell all his life; he's been married to Paula for 53 years.

Our conversation took place at the funeral parlor.

* * *

"This photograph is of Andrew Henderson, my great-grandfather," Sheets began. "He was an undertaker in Carroll County back in the late 1800s. He was instrumental in my paternal grandfather, his son-in-law, buying out this funeral home and undertaking in 1905.

"Martin Schurr was the previous owner. The books go back to 1876; if Schurr did business before that, I don't have any record of it."

What was your grandfather's name?

"William M. Sheets."

Was Sheets Funeral Home always at this location?

"No, it was downtown at 410 E. Commercial Ave. It was called Furniture and Undertaking."

Your grandpa sold furniture, too?

"Years ago, that was a common combination."

Is this photograph of your father?

"Yes, Kenneth A. Sheets."

So, you named your eldest son after your father and your father named you after his father.

"Yes, but we all have different middle initials."

Lowell High School?

"Class of '48; I went to school with your Aunt Shirley. Her maiden name is Imes. We're on the class reunion committee."

How has the mortuary business changed over the years?

"It's changing right now. But with that said, the more it changes, the more it remains the same. We still have traditional funerals, but there are other things that are available now."

Example, please?

"There are more cremations for one thing. When I was a kid, we usually went to the home. My dad did embalming at the family's house. We still have the equipment they used.

"We came to this establishment in 1941. The 1940s were kind of a transformation period for us."

Did they embalm people when your great-grandfather plied the trade?

"I think so; embalming was developed during the Civil War when they shipped (President Abraham) Lincoln back here."

Did your great-grandfather or grandfather go to school to become an undertaker?

"For about six weeks. But they had to be licensed by the state. I've been licensed for almost 60 years now."

How long is mortuary school now?

"A couple of years. I went to Indiana College of Mortuary Science in Indianapolis."

Have you had soldiers killed in action shipped from overseas to Sheets Funeral Home?

"Yes, one World War II vet in particular comes to mind. The government said we couldn't open the casket. They sent two guards. The father said, 'I won't believe it's my son until I open the casket.' The guards told the man, 'Well, the government said you can't do that.'"

That's heartbreaking.

"Unbeknownst to the guards, my father brought in some tools necessary to open the casket and placed them in the chapel."

And?

"He took the two guards downtown for coffee for about 45 minutes. The casket was closed tight when my dad and the guards returned. Legally, the casket wasn't supposed to be opened; Sheets Funeral Home didn't open it. Later, the man told my dad he was satisfied that it was, indeed, his son in the casket."

Closure. In my opinion your father did the right thing.

"Another thing that has changed is that funeral homes were the only providers of ambulance service until 1972. There were two funeral homes in town back then; we both had ambulances. We charged $15 to take someone to the hospital in Gary. We lost money. Gary had the nearest hospitals; later, Dyer opened up and then Saint Anthony's.

"I have a driver's license from when I was 14 years old; during World War II, if you could show the need for a driver for your business, you could get a license at 14."

Bill, it must take a special mind-set to do your job. It seems that being a mortician in a small town would be even tougher, when you start getting a little older and classmates and close friends become customers.

"Oh, yeah. Sometimes close friends pass away expectedly and sometimes unexpectedly."

Your parents?

"No, not on family. That would be like a doctor operating on his wife or son. We always have somebody available who isn't family."

Toughest part of the job?

"Accidents were hard to deal with when we had the ambulance service. The worst one was when we had six people killed in a head-on collision at Indiana 2 and Indiana 55. Five of them were high school students."

For some families or ethnic groups, a funeral is more a celebration than a grievous occasion.

"I had a person of Bohemian descent from Sumava Resorts who passed away; the burial was in Chicago. The family told me they had a car that would lead the procession. They told me they would be pulling into a tavern and they would be in there about 15 minutes. We went into three different taverns on the way to the cemetery."

* * *

A month or so ago, I approached Ken Sheets about being interviewed for this column. He declined, but said, "You really should interview my dad."

I believe Kenny was right. It's been said the good Lord gives us three score and 10, if we're lucky.

I'm glad I talked with Mr. Sheets, the elder.

Brian Mathias *(Dec. 2005)*

"... Up on the housetop, click, click, click
Down through the chimney with good St. Nick... ."
– B.R. Hanby, circa 1860

W. Brian Mathias grew up in East Chicago and graduated from the former Roosevelt High School where he wrestled for the Rough Riders.

After a six-year hitch with the Marine Corps, he became an ironworker. Mathias is a 73-year-old bull with a pair of guns on him like Popeye. He's been married to Judie 46 years; they live in Lake Dale.

His long, snow-white hair is often kept in a pony tail. He is bearded. When I mention his conservatism, he corrects me, "Oh, no, Jeff; make no mistake, I'm not conservative, I'm to the right of Genghis Kahn."

Mathias also is Kris Kringle and, at his request, to protect believers, the more common nomenclature (S.C.) will not appear in this column. Besides, I wouldn't want to get on the wrong side of this particular jolly old soul.

* * *

"I grew up right across the street from (St. Stanislaus Catholic Church) above the barbershop," Mathias began. "My father was from Wales. He wrestled, boxed, and played a lot of rugby. He called American football 'sissy ball.' My mother was from Narrows, Ky – family of 13."

Brian, you're the president of the Friends of the Library in Lowell, and you're a member of the Northwest Indiana Symphony Chorus.

"Yes, I was NWI Symphony Chorus manager for 10 years and a charter member – second bass."

Welshmen are known warblers.

"You have a unique voice, Jeff. Second bass?"

No, I was a center fielder. That's quite a gravy catcher you have there.

"Being an ironworker, and working outside, I always grew a beard every winter; I'd quit shaving on my birthday – August 20.

Leo the lion; with that mane, I should have guessed.

"I'd shave it off on April Fools' Day. I can remember working on top, welding on a boiler one winter. My beard was drenched from the heat and my hair was hanging in my eyes while icicles hung from my backside."

Been there, done that.

"Before I retired, we were on a job at Standard Oil. It was a blizzard; the wind was blowing about 60 mph, I told the guys, 'I think I'll do something that has never been done before.' They asked, 'What's next, Brian?' I climbed to the highest place they had – on top of a cat cracker. It was snowin' like the Dickens."

What did you do?

"I belted out 'The Hallelujah Chorus.' You know, Jeff, my daughters used to fight to take off my boots when I'd get home. I'd tell them, 'No need to fight girls; there's one for each of you.' They'd say, 'Gee, Dad, did you wade in water?' I'd say, 'No darlings; that's sweat.'

"We worked hard and played hard in those days, but it's dangerous out on that iron. After a while, you have to grow up. There's old ironworkers and there's bold ironworkers; there are no old, bold ironworkers."

Was your father an ironworker, too?

"No, my dad was a steel worker in the open hearth at Youngstown (Sheet & Tube Co.). He told me about the time when these whippersnapper bosses came out on the floor with shiny new helmets, and said to my dad, 'When are you going to be tapping that heat?' They tried to use the lingo."

"'When it's ready,'" my dad said.

"'How will you know? Do you realize that you have gauges that aren't working?'"

"Dad said, 'Yeah, they haven't worked for six months.'"

"'Well, how do you... .'"

"'You look at it. When it's ready, that's when we tap it.'"

"'Well, what about all these gauges?' My father told them what they could do with their thermocouples. Those old-timers could tell within 15 degrees, the temperature of molten steel just by looking at it; it was an art."

Your dad spoke his mind. The apple didn't fall far from the tree.

"Jeff, I was questioned about not standing when a judge in federal court entered the room. The bailiff said, 'Weren't you told to stand?'

" I told him: 'You know what? I took orders in the Marine Corps for six years, pal. I know my Constitution. I stand for no man, especially not one wearing a long gown."

Let's talk about the "Man in Red."

"I try to be the best 'Man in Red' there is because when I was a kid in East Chicago, I can remember some adults having to walk a 'Man in Red' up to his chair because he was so drunk. And that's probably how he got paid – by the bottle."

To me, you're the best. You're an Edmund Gwenn lookalike. Thomas Nast drew you! Brian, I remember my mother taking my brother and me to see St. Nick; the guy was wearing these gigantic black, horn-rimmed glasses. And he had this fake, glued-on cotton beard. I know this is naughty, but, well, it kinda made me doubt.

"How old were you when that happened, little Jeffy?"

Seventeen.

"I don't work the malls; it's gotten too commercial. Before you know it, they'll be wanting us out there by Labor Day. I work the nursing homes, hospitals, libraries... ."

Probably had a few beard yankers in your day, huh?

"Yeah, I can read 'em before they ever make a move. I'll say, 'Just don't pull too hard.' Their eyes will get real big and they'll say, 'Why, I wasn't going to pull your beard, S@^+@."

Get any kids who are, forgive me, "claustrophobic?"

"Oh, yeah. Usually after a little coaxing or watching their siblings sit on my lap, they'll warm up to the idea. My suit is velvet, with real rabbit fur; it's tailor-made. They start touching that soft, smooth velvet and they don't want to leave."

I'm sure you've heard more classics from the mouths of babes than Art Linkletter.

"I had one boy who would ask me for a vacuum cleaner every year. I finally asked his parents, 'Does he use them?'

"'Does he ever,' said his mom. 'He wears them out. Johnny just loves to clean.'"

Yikes.

"I had a kid ask me for a pillow case – nothin' else. There also was a family of 13 children; most of them just wanted coats. I try to make sure they get them.

"I had a girl ask me if I had a little house. I said, 'Like a doll house?' She said, 'No, for my family; ours burned down.'"

* * *

Since becoming a resident of south Lake County, Mathias has volunteered for Meals on Wheels, has been a volunteer fireman and was a regular blood donor until being diagnosed with prostate cancer.

Mathias said he grew up a minority – a Baptist among Catholics. He admits being a bit of a hell-raiser in his younger days, and he can still be feisty. He told me: "If everybody likes you, you're a hypocrite. I'm proud of the people who don't like me. I'm not wishy-washy like a politician. I fear no man. I do fear God."

After the interview, we paid a visit to my neighbor, the widow Mueller. Her health is failing. She calls Brian her Marine. Soon after, there was a knock at her door. It was Peter Muha, with holy water in hand. She calls Father Pete her priest.

Again, Mathias was the minority.

But then, W. Brian Mathias is one of a kind.

Helen Pollard *(Apr. 2010)*

"...Daddy loved and raised eight kids on a miner's pay
Mama scrubbed our clothes on a washboard ever' day..."
– Loretta Lynn

Helen Pollard was born a coal miner's daughter in Hopkins County, Ky. Today, she lives in Lake Village.

Pollard, 90, also is a retired steel worker.

* * *

"I'm sorry that I didn't keep the Sizemore in the middle when I married Tex because a lot of people know me as Helen Sizemore from when I was married to Skinny," Pollard began.

Both your husbands, Skinny Sizemore and Tex Pollard, are deceased.

"Yes."

Helen, let's start from the beginning – Kentucky.

"We were about 40 miles south of Evansville; it was tobacco and coal country. There was seven of us girls and one boy. During the Depression, my father made moonshine. We all had a chore to do."

What was your job?

"At 8 years old, I milked the cow. By the time I was 12, I was able to strain the milk and churn the butter. We were never on relief and never went hungry. My father didn't own the land, but he'd get a permit from the company to work the ground."

What did he grow?

"Corn, onions, potatoes, turnip greens – all the things you needed to survive. We had a root cellar, but there was usually extra that we couldn't store."

What happened to the surplus?

"We'd set it out beside the dirt road with a sign that said 'Free.' I had a sister who got diphtheria; we were quarantined for 21 days. They put a sticker on the house."

Then what?

"We lived in company houses. You've heard the song that goes, 'I owe my soul to the company store'? ('Sixteen Tons,' by 'Tennessee' Ernie Ford.) That's how it was for us. You got no real money."

Scrip.

"We called them 'flickers.' They were coins to pay bills with, to be used at the company store only. They had you tied down, but it got a little better when they finally made a union; the men had to go on strike to get it."

Your father?

"We'd have a tub of warm water waiting for him when he came home from the mines. We had no bathrooms. The first thing he always done was cradle that jug and take a drink of corn liquor. We were told never to touch it. None us seven girls ever drank."

Never, even later in life?

"We were told not to."

Did your dad smoke?

"Rolled his own; mother dipped snuff."

Education?

"I went to a one-room schoolhouse until the eighth grade; I took seventh and eighth grade at the same time."

High school?

"I walked five miles twice a day to get 2 1/2 years of it. Then, I married Skinny when I was 16; he was 15 years older than me.

"Skinny and I lived in a company house, too. He was working up on the tipple when the mine exploded and killed 15 men. He had two brothers in there. We moved to East Chicago in the spring of '42. Our son was 5 at the time."

Where at in East Chicago?

"Magoun Avenue; people in East Chicago would ask me if I was a hillbilly. I'd say I was, then walk away like I had one leg shorter than the other from all those hills and hollers."

The mill?

"I hired in at Inland Steel in January of 1945; I was never off sick in 30 years."

What department?

"The Tin Mill; there was 100 of us women in that unit flipping tin. I did that for five years; then, I became a shipping clerk. Inland quit making tin around 1970."

Sumava Resorts.

"We moved to Sumava in 1955, once our son graduated from East Chicago Roosevelt (High School). Skinny and I built a house right on the Kankakee River.

"There was an old trapper who lived by himself in a little shanty next to us. He lived there before there ever was a Sumava. I remember him warning us to never trust the ice on the river. I'd take food to him when I had something left over."

How long did you live in Sumava?

"For 37 years. But Skinny was a real bad diabetic and died in '77."

My dad said you were a very good poker player in your day.

"Used to be; I currently belong to four bunco clubs and a euchre club. And I've attended at least 40 Kentucky Derbies.

"I'm also a red hatter and a diehard Democrat. And I do biscuits and gravy every Tuesday morning at the Lake Village Grange."

Tex?

"We got married in Vegas and had a few good years before he got colon cancer. He lived eight more years; they put two bags on him. I took care of him.

"We lived in my house in Sumava for a while. Tex never said anything, but he wasn't happy. You see, Tex had a father who drowned in the Kankakee River while duck hunting. Jack Sirois found him about three months later; he was hung up in a logjam under the river bridge."

Never trust the ice on the river.

"We moved here in '91. I've had a strange life: I married a man who was 15 years older than me when I was a young woman; I married a man who was 15 years younger than me when I was an old woman."

Do you ever miss living on the Kankakee?

"I've been to Sumava a few times to eat at Lukes Restaurant, but haven't gone back to the house. Out of sight, Jeff, out of mind."

* * *

Charles Sizemore is a brilliant artist who taught chemistry at

Hammond High School for 44 years. The odds of him becoming a success were favorable from the start.

You see, he was born the son of a coal miner's daughter who showed up for work at the Tin Mill ever' day for 30 years.

Albert Bailitz *(Nov. 2011)*

"Chim chiminey
Chim chiminey
Chim chim cher-ee!
A sweep is as lucky
As lucky can be"
– Richard M. Sherman and Robert B. Sherman

Albert Bailitz was raised in Cedar Lake and graduated from Crown Point High School. He lives in Valparaiso with his wife Bobbie; they've been married 17 years. He has four adult children from a previous marriage.

Bailitz, 53, is a chimney sweep who has been in the business for 30 years.

* * *

"I used to work in East Chicago at Combustion Engineering on Railroad Avenue and 151st Street," Bailitz began. "They closed down in the '80s. I was kind of doing the part-time handyman thing. Then I read about becoming a chimney sweep and decided to give it a try. I've been full time now for 23 years.

"I'm getting to the point where, at my age, I'll be weaning myself from the field for the next five years. Someone has to be the figurehead."

It's probably going to be tough for you to let go.

"Yeah, it is. I like the field work. I can still get around and do all the work, but sometimes the recuperation time takes longer. It's all physical, brushing a chimney. The old body is saying, 'Hey, slow down a little.'

"But we've evolved from the old way of just brushes and rods to where it's more mechanical sweeping, with a drill and spinning things out. As new tooling becomes available, we try to stay on the cutting edge. Most of our work is spent educating our customers."

Explain, please.

"Like how to use their fireplaces the best way, how to minimize the creosote buildup and still use it with less risk of a chimney fire. The more the client knows about how a system works the better it is for us. The customer will realize the value of having the maintenance done."

I remember when you were based out of Cedar Lake.

"Yes, after I got divorced, I moved to Griffith for 10 years; we had a shop in Highland. Then, we moved to Valparaiso because a lot of customers were moving from Lake to Porter and LaPorte counties."

How long have you been in Valparaiso?

"For seven years. We get a lot of calls from farther east, even southern Michigan. We try to do about a 40-mile radius from Valpo. Lake County is still a big part of it. Our main source of business is word of mouth."

Codes probably have changed through the years.

"You have to know the ins and outs of different fireplace construction and systems. Construction methods vary, on say, a house that was built in 1910 compared to a house built in 2010."

Explain tuckpointing.

"Sure, we do all types of masonry repair, but everything is focused around a chimney. Tuckpointing is basically grinding out mortar in between brick or stone or block and replacing it with new mortar. The process on that could be grind it, powerwash it, and then put in new mortar.

"We have different colors that we can blend in with our mortars to give it an aged look if we're only doing a partial chimney repair. Plus, we have water repellants that we use now that have 10-year durability. Water is the enemy of chimneys."

Albert, for years I worked in the coke plant at Inland Steel. It was a filthy place. Tell me about being inside a chimney.

"It's a dirty job and it always will be. But there is protection, whether it's a simple dust mask or an $800 respirator unit."

How many employees?

"Four in the field, including myself, and two in the office."

I'm sure you've been on some steep roofs.

"We have speciality roof scaffolding just for chimneys. We can set up on a 10-12 or 12-12 roof and work safely on a three-story chimney."

Do you guys wear safety harnesses?

"As needed. OSHA is a big part of it; there are a lot of rules and regulations that you have to follow. It's not the quaint idea of a chimney sweep dancing on a roof."

Dick Van Dyke's character in the film "Mary Poppins."

"Exactly. (The stage version of) 'Mary Poppins' is playing in Chicago now."

The chimney-sweep scene is your favorite part of the movie, I'm sure.

"Well, I tell you what, Dick Van Dyke actually did a public service announcement for the National Chimney Sweep Guild years ago. His voice and face will always recognized as Bert the Chimney Sweep. Whenever 'Mary Poppins' airs on television we get a lot more calls; it's like a reminder – 'Hey, we better get our chimney cleaned.'"

Wildlife in the chimney?

"Raccoons love to go into fireplaces. A raccoon can climb the side of a gutter, up the brick of a chimney and down into a fireplace and have their young there.

"Bats are another thing; they like to hang around inside of chimneys. Sometimes birds will sit on top of a chimney for warmth, but get asphyxiated from the fumes and fall inside. If you get enough of them in there they can block the system and cause carbon monoxide to come back in."

Chimney swifts?

"We get them in the spring and summer. The chimney swift is a migratory bird, and it's the only bird that can fly straight up a chimney. They'll build their nests right on the side wall. Chimney swifts are a protected species; we're real careful around them. They eat a lot of mosquitos."

* * *

Bailitz doesn't wear his stove top hat and jacket with tails on job sites anymore because his hat was continually blowing off rooftops and the tails of his jacket would catch on things; he almost fell off a roof because of that.

With our interview complete, Albert the Chimney Sweep and I shook hands and said our goodbyes.

As I drove away, I'll be darned if the voice of Bert the Chimney Sweep didn't start singing in my head: "Chim chiminey, chim chiminey, chim chim cher-oo! Good luck will rub off when I shake 'ands with you."

Augie Lamprecht *(Oct. 2010)*

"When it comes to getting things done, we need fewer architects and more bricklayers."
– Colleen C. Barrett

August Lamprecht, 81, is a Korean War veteran who was born and raised in Hammond and has been married to Virginia for 60 years.

They have raised three children: Jerry, Becky and Linda.

Lamprecht is a retired bricklayer who has lived in Griffith since 1956. And, yes, the Lamprechts live in a brick house that Augie built to last.

* * *

Hammond High School back in the 1940s?

"I graduated in 1947; there were 461 of us," he said. "A few years later, they graduated more than 500 students. Last year, Hammond High graduated 78. And they want a new school. You figure that out."

Did you start laying brick right out of high school?

"No, I worked for Fred Harvey in Chicago; it was a restaurant chain. He had all the restaurants on the Sante Fe line. I don't know if you ever saw the movie, 'The Harvey Girls' with Judy Garland. That was all about the Harvey restaurant chain."

What did you do for Fred Harvey?

"I worked in the main office in Chicago in the accounts payable department. While I was there, I went to Northwestern University after hours, studying to be a CPA, but I never finished. While working in Chicago, I got a 30-day round-trip pass on the South Shore for $11.20. Can you believe that? Things have changed. I went from there to the post office in Hammond because it was close to home."

Do you come from a long line of bricklayers?

"My dad was a bricklayer."

Your grandfather?

"I don't know; he came over from Germany. I'm not sure of the exact situation there. He came home one in evening, and said: 'Kids, we're leaving for the United States, I was in a fight and I think I might have killed a man.' So, that's how we got over here."

Back to your father.

"Dad was a strong man; he was 6-feet tall and weighed 275 pounds. He'd lay 80-pound concrete blocks with one hand."

Did you and your dad ever work together on the same jobs?

"Oh, yeah. I enjoyed those days. Dad was a great stone man. I laid stone on a lot of jobs, but my dad was the best; he had an 'S' on his union card signifying that he was a bricklayer and a stone mason. I never got that."

The early days of your career?

"I started my apprenticeship on July 21, 1950, for $1.45 per hour."

Tell me more.

"Things were kind of tough in the old days; the brick would come on a truck and they'd unload them by hand, 10 at a time. The blocks were unloaded by hand, too.

"I got a job for Bill Hasse in 1956; we were working on Harrison School in East Chicago. Bill wanted to know if I could figure out a way we could be faster and more profitable."

And?

"Hasse had a Pettibone bucket lift that could turn 360 degrees; I told him to put forks on it. Then I told one of the laborers I needed him to make 250 oak pallets 24-inches-by-32-inches. When the first load of brick came it was unloaded by hand. Then, we loaded the pallets on the empty truck for the next shipment from Canton, Ohio."

So the next load of brick arrived neatly stacked on those oak skids and the crane served as a humongous forklift that would set brick on scaffolds or wherever the material was needed.

"Yes – 500 pounds of brick per pallet. And when Lakeshore Brick and Block out of Michigan City delivered a load of block, we sent a load of pallets with them. The next shipment came back loaded with 60, 8-inch blocks per pallet."

You're idea was huge.

"We had been operating with four laborers to one bricklayer. They had to load everything on a flat wheelbarrow, put it on the hoist, take it up, wheel it down the scaffold, unload it, and do the same thing again and again."

What was the ratio after your idea was implemented?

"Just the opposite – four bricklayers to one laborer. Word spread about our method, and we soon had people from all over Indiana and Illinois coming to see what we were doing. As far as I know, we were the first gang to ever use a crane on a job."

Other memorable jobs?

"You don't remember Standard Forge."

Actually, I do.

"We went in there on a Friday and tore down 12 furnaces, turned the hoses on 'em because they were going to be tear-outs, pulled 'em off, and worked 'em out. They lit them off Monday. I made the boss $100,000 that weekend and he didn't even know what I was doing.

"I worked on the Purdue (University) North Central library building in Westville. A library is the best construction you can get. Because of all the books, the walls were 10 inches thick and the floors were 13 inches thick. We poured 500 yards of concrete every other day. I was superintendent on that job, but it was a sad deal because I lost a carpenter on that job – electrocution."

You ran jobs, but also were a member of the rank and file.

"Oh, yeah. I'm a member of the union yet. I have a gold card; my dad had a gold card."

Meaning you both were 50- year union men. Probably had to work up high in the sky a few times, huh?

"Oh, yeah. We had to tear out a bunch of glass-block windows at the top of Lever Brothers (in North Hammond). We were working from the inside of the building, but in order to finish up, we had to crawl out the opening and strike everything and close up the hole. We had mobile scaffolds up 110 feet."

That's getting up there.

"You know it. My son said, 'I'll go out there and do it.' Well, when it came time to do it, Jerry looked at me, and said, 'You wouldn't mind doing it would you?' I crawled out there and finished the job.

"Jerry is currently running a coke-oven job in Pittsburgh. When these outfits bid and get jobs they call up my son and ask him if he'll run it for them; that's how good Jerry is."

Augie, name just a few buildings you've worked on in Northwest Indiana.

"Hammond Tech High School (now the Hammond Area Career Center), Woodmar Shopping Center, Tiebel's Restaurant, Holy Rosary, St Edward's Catholic Church, St. Catherine's Hospital addition, Community Hospital, St. Sava Serbian Hall... ."

Did you work on residential jobs?

"When I was with Brant, we had 20 houses going at one time."

Your house?

"It has 18,000 bricks on the inside and 18,000 bricks on the outside. Our house has 8-inch thick walls."

* * *

Four years after Lamprecht came up with his fork-and-pallet method, the Masonry Institute adopted the 24-inch-by-32-inch pallet as the standard masonry pallet and started making equipment to handle the pallets.

Augie Lamprecht knows how to get things done.

The Diedam Bros. *(Feb. 2010)*

"...In the shadow of the steeple
I saw my people... ."
– Woody Guthrie

Herman Diedam was a German-born fresco artist who served a 12-year apprenticeship in his native land before emigrating to the United States in 1904.

He brought his brushes with him.

Eventually, Herman settled in Kentland and, by 1914, started his own company, redecorating churches and repainting statues.

He taught his son, John, the trade. John fathered 10 children, two of whom have kept the family business, Diedam Decorating Co., thriving. Mike, 50, and Jim, 49, graduated from South Newton High School. Mike still lives in his hometown of Kentland; Jim lives in Earl Park. The Diedam brothers also do tuck-pointing, exterior painting and steeplejack work.

Along with their aide de camp, Bill Patrevito, the Diedams currently are plying their Old World skills to make Cedar Lake's Holy Name Catholic Church look the way it did on Easter Sunday, 1940.

* * *

"Our younger brother Steve used to be with the company, but went out on his own," Mike began. "We travel a lot; he was tired of it. He has children; I can respect him for that."

Jim: "Our dad passed away about five years ago; my mother, Joanne, is the president of the company.".

You guys are third-generation Diadem Decorators.

"And we'll be the last generation of Diadem brothers painting churches," Jim said.

Why's that?

"Mike and I have three daughters each – no sons."

During the 1920s, your grandfather did the work on St. Martin Catholic Church in Cedar Lake before it was gutted by fire. What exactly is fresco painting?

"It's painting on wet plaster," Mike said. "First, you have to know how to plaster; that's a skill in itself. The painting is done while the plaster is still wet. You can only do about a 2-foot-by-2-foot area at a time. Then, you go to the next little section. We don't do it anymore.

"You'll have to interview me while on the scaffold. It's time to gold leaf the capital of that arch."

Do your thing, Mike, I can talk to your brother. Jim, how long did it take you guys to set up all this pipe scaffolding? It's amazing that they're still celebrating Mass here.

"Four of us set it up in about 10 days."

How far off the ground is that top tier of planks?

"About 26 feet. This is a little church compared to St. John the Baptist in Whiting. The ceiling of that one is about 70 feet from the floor."

God forbid, have any of you guys ever fallen?

"Never," Jim said. "As grandpa got older, he wouldn't climb around on the scaffold a lot. He'd stretch a canvas across an 8-foot-by-8-foot wooden frame on the ground level, and then prep it with whiting to make it a paintable surface. Then, he'd paint the murals, cherubs and angels. The younger generation would go up there and paste them to the walls.

"When my dad started getting older, Mike and I began pasting the murals on the walls or ceilings. Then, you blend in the filler or backgrounds while up there. Grandpa always said, 'You're not finished with a church until you put an angel on the wall."

Longevity rate for Diedam murals."

"They'll stand for 150 to 200 years," Jim said.

How many jobs do you guys take on in a year's time?

"Five or six."

Jim, name a few churches you've redecorated in Northwest

Indiana.

"The old Saints Peter and Paul in Merrillville, St. Mary in Crown Point, St. Mary in Griffith.... We just did St. Mary in Otis. My grandfather worked on that same church during the '30s."

Are churches the extent of it?

"Oh, no; Jasper County Courthouse was our pride and joy."

Let's walk over by Mike before he finishes the bottom of that arch.

"Wherever you put your size is where your gold leaf will stick," Mike said from the scaffold. "I was using three-hour quick-dry size."

Does size really matter?

"Oh, yeah," Mike said. "The basis of an oil size is a long oil varnish; it ranges anywhere from 1 1/2 to 3 hours."

Do you need to apply the gold leaf before the size dries?

"Yes, as soon as you get that certain tack. I checked on it just before you got here, but it was still a little too green – too wet."

Mike, that looks gorgeous.

"What I'm doing is called burnishing the gold. I use a quill and a brush."

Mercy, you also use both hands.

"I taught myself to be ambidextrous after cutting off my finger while tuck-pointing. I can tuck-point, paint and gold leaf as good with my left hand as I can with my right.

"Father Ed (the Rev. Edward Tlucek, pastor at Holy Name), showed me a Nativity set he has stored in the basement that he wants restored; it's an original Daprato. I looked it over and told him, 'My dad painted that.'"

Were you on that particular job?

"I wasn't even born yet. Your painting style is like your handwriting."

Mike, you mentioned the Nativity set was a Daprato.

"Daprato statuary is, by far, the Cadillac of wall statues. It's a pleasure to work on them. The company started out in Italy's marble country, but then expanded to New York and Chicago."

I can't get over how beautiful that gold leaf design looks against the snow-white background.

"Father Ed wanted green at the bottom of the arches," Jim said. "We told him that would take away from the gold leaf. We'll tell people if we believe their color schemes aren't going to work; it only takes one bad job to give you a bad reputation."

Mike: "I've told more than one priest, 'Father, you take care of my soul; I'll take care of your church.'"

Do you fellas specialize in certain aspects of the job?

"I do a lot of the fieldwork like stenciling and plastering," Jim said. "Mike does more of the statuary work, gilding and marbleizing."

Mike: "If you see us both up here, you know we're losing our asses."

Mike, explain marbleizing.

"It's where you do faux finish of a marble. A lot of churches used marble down low and then marbleized up above."

I'm sure you two have been inside some grand old buildings.

"In Fort Wayne, their Stations of the Cross are 12-foot-tall, quarter-sawed oak – beautiful carvings," Mike said. "This older gentleman came in while we were washing down the Stations. I told him they really needed to be completely redone; they were in bad shape.

"The old-timer told me, 'If you can put that German (lettering) back in there, I'll pay for it.' I told him, 'Sir, I don't think you realize, that would be like $70,000.'

"He replied, 'I meant what I said.'"

What did you say?

"You better go talk to my dad."

And?

"We stripped the stations down, refinished them and put them all back with English lettering at the top and German on the bottom. The old fella meant what he said."

* * *

The Diedam brothers are latter-day Michelangelos who still use their grandfather's antique stencils and designs.

As I left Holy Name, Father Ed entered the chapel. I asked him what he thought of the Diedams' work.

He said, "Our church will be like a diamond glistening."

No doubt Padre, but not before the grandsons of Herman Diedam put an angel on the wall.

Melting Pot

John J. Branley *(Mar. 2005)*

"Some do count it a misfortune
To be christened Pat or Dan
But to me it is an honor
To be born an Irishman."
– John F. Poole, "No Irish Need Apply" – 1862

John Joseph Branley lives just west of U.S. 41 and 129th Avenue in Cedar Lake. He was born in County Sligo, Ireland, nearly 80 years ago.

While living in East Chicago, he picked up a job repairing the old Hammond Times building. Branley also picked up a newspaper that day. In the classifieds, he spotted a house on four acres in Cedar Lake. The year, 1970. He's lived there ever since.

Although Branley will become an octogenarian this fall, he appears about as stout as a bottle of Guinness. The blue-eyed, ruddy-faced Irishman wears a size 13 shoe and has ham-like hands – bricklayer hands.

He's been a widower for more than 20 years and is the father of four. Both of his sons are bricklayers. One daughter is a nurse, the other a pharmacist.

Branley is a member of Holy Name Catholic Church and had just come home from Mass. He never misses bingo at the Knights of Columbus Hall on Saturday nights.

We took a seat at his kitchen table. Branley's brogue flowed and gurgled like the river Shannon.

* * *

"When I first moved here, a lot of people still called this area Cook," Branley began. "I watched a guy pull up in front of the house, get out, and put a couple a young guys in the trunk of his car. I was ready to call the cops. The next day, I told the neighbor about it. He laughed and told me they were just going to the outdoor movies next door and didn't want to pay. I thought it was a kidnaping."

So, you were born in County Sligo?

"Yes, I was. There's six cities here in the United States named Sligo, you know. I came to this country in 1952. Twenty-six, I think I was."

What happened to your hand?

"The bone is cracked; it's healin'; that's why it keeps swellin' up. It's fulla fluid, you know."

Have you been to the doctor?

"That I have, yes. I keep puttin' ice on it."

You're still working? With a broken hand and wrist?

"That I am. We've got a job going in East Chicago. Six days a week it is. I've always worked. Let me show you something.

"The union gave me this honorary gold-plated card for 50 years service. I've been a union man all my life.

"I've read about what they did to the kids in the sweat shops. And I tell you what, I think it's comin' to that again, if people don't look out. I remember back in the early 1950's, when bricklayer scale was $2.70 per hour."

Yeah, my dad worked as a second helper in the open hearth for Inland Steel during the '50s, except for two years heavy artillery in Korea. He said when they got up to $15 per day in the mill, they really thought they were in the money.

"The first helper had it made compared to the second helper. Your father had a tough, hot job next to those furnaces."

Do you ever enjoy a nip of Irish Whiskey?

"Oh, yeah. Care for a shot? I've got some Jameson!"

No, thanks; I'm working.

"Well, I don't mind if I do."

You actually came to the U.S. via Canada.

"Yes, I lived in Toronto for three years. I came here by motorcycle. The immigration guy says, 'Irish, you're travelin' light.' All I had was toothpaste, shavin' gear and a couple a shahrts in my saddlebag."

Sharhts?

"Sharhts lad, you know."

The weather was probably a little cool to be wearing a pair of shorts on a motorcycle up in Canada.

"Sweet Mother of Jesus – Sharhts mahn!"

Oh, shirts. I gotcha. Have you ever been back to Ireland?

"I was gone 41 years before I went back. My brother's there; he has a big family – one son and seven daughters.

"The thatch cottages are gone now. When I was there, I watched Dan Rather give the news; my brother had a satellite dish.

"We had open fires when I was boy. All the cookin' and bakin' and boilin' of the water on the open fire. I worked in the mines on top of Ben Bulbin Mountain. I hunted foxes up there. They'd give me a bounty of five shillings for each tongue I'd bring in at the police barracks.

"We had sheep dogs. They'd do the work of 10 men. Except for Ben Bulbin, the Ireland of my youth was gone."

Irish Protestants?

"The Orangemen were used by the English; they would get all the good jobs. The Catholics wouldn't get nothin'."

The IRA?

"The IRA was actually started by Protestants. Wolfe Tone, he was a Presbyterian about the time of the American Revolution. When Cornwallis was sent packin' back to England, he told King George III: 'We lost to America because of the Irish.'"

During the '30s and '40s, living in Ireland was probably a struggle.

"Oh, it was, you know. Ireland, at that time, was in real poverty. When you got out of school, you couldn't get no work in Ireland, you know. You had to go to England to get work. Today, in 2005, Ireland is advertising to get the English to help fill the jobs in Ireland."

Quite a change from "No Irish need apply."

"I've seen those signs many a time – in England. They'd have flats for rent. The sign would read, 'No Irish or dogs.' They had similar signs in Boston for quite a while, even after the Civil War."

No snakes in Ireland, thanks to St. Paddy.

"Brendan Behan, the writer, he used to drink a lot, he said all the snakes went to New York and became judges.

"We were taught that St. Patrick was born in Brittany, in France. But we find out now, the majority of the people believe he was born in

England. He was the son of a Roman soldier and a Welsh mother.

"Let me show you an old book I picked up when I was in New York; it written by Seamus McManus. See here, back in 432, St. Patrick came to Ireland expecting to find only pagans but there were some Catholics. Four bishops were already there, but they had divided up into clans and were fighting amongst themselves. St. Patrick converted King Angus to Catholicism, and the King's sons actually became missionaries."

* * *

Branley has remembrances of a hardscrabble way of life growing up as a child. "We had the country house dances on Sunday night; that's all we had."

Today, he listens to Irish-based radio stations and reads Irish newspapers on the Internet in Cedar Lake. But when he lays his tired head upon his pillow, a working man's best friend at times, he soon becomes a lad again... .

He's chasing after a fox as it flees off with one of his father's geese. With his collie at his side, he runs toward the base of Ben Bulbin. Fox, dog, boy, green mountain...

Irish eyes are smilin'.

Veronica Farrell *(June 2005)*

"England and America are two countries divided by a common language."
– George Bernard Shaw

Veronica Farrell, nee Smith, came to the United States June 9, 1968. She was 24. She grew up along the east coast of England, about 100 miles from London in the historic village of Norwich which is 15 miles from the North Sea. She met Jack, an Irish-American Catholic from the Bridgeport neighborhood of Chicago, while he was stationed in England during the Vietnam War. After Jack served nearly seven years in the armed forces he and his English wife moved to Alabama.

Jack and Veronica Farrell's daughter, Gerrie, sat in our conversation. I'd known her for several years.

* * *

That had to be a quite a culture shock moving from Merry Olde England to the Heart of Dixie.

"They couldn't understand me attall. I'd go to the store and ask for 'aff a pound of somethin' and they would always give me a pound. I could never get 'aff a pound of anything. They never 'eard the 'aff. Spot of English tea?"

Thanks, I take mine black.

"You don't puttin' nothin' in it!? Then you aren't drinkin' English Tea! I make my tea strong, You can stand your spoon up in it. You 'ave to 'ave milk and sugah. This is an English brand called Asda. We call weak tea donkey's eye water."

Pass the milk and sugar please.

"Too bad you don't have any marmite for Mr. Manes." (Says Gerrie with tongue in cheek).

Marmite? What is it, like marmalade?

"It tastes like 100-year old gravy that's been sitting out in the sun. We used to give it to our friends, 'Yummy, try this, it's really good...'" (Gerrie)

"Marmite's consistency is that of peanutbuttah," interjects Mrs. Farrell. "It's deep brown and very salty. It's from the grease of everything. You'd like it, it's lovely, you just spread a tiny bit on toast. You 'ave to put some buttah on it first. It tastes like... . "

"100-year old gravy." (Gerrie)

Does Jack like it?

"No!" (Jack)

Case dismissed.

"I'll get you some, Jeff," says the undaunted matriarch.

How about cockles and mussels, sweet Molly Malone?

"I don't care for mussels, but I like cockles. 'Ave you ever et winkles?"

You're makin' this stuff up.

"Oh, no. You'd buy 'em in a paper bag on a Sunday when the fishmonger would come 'round with 'is 'orse and caht. Winkles are about the size of your finger. They'd be in a shell. There's a little cap on the shell and we used to stick the cap on our cheeks for beauty marks. You'd take a hair grip, you call it a bobby pin, and hook it down into the shell and pull out this black wiggly thing and you'd eat it with a piece of bread and buttah and that was your dinnah."

Was the pea soup really that bad?

"Oh, yes. After work, somebody would 'ave a rope and a torch and we'd hold onto the rope while they'd lead us 'ome. Someone would also walk in front of the buses with lanterns to guide them."

Tell me more about growing up across the big pond.

"I was born in a bomb shelter. My mother went into labour during an air raid. Norwich has a market that's 1,000 years old and has beautiful cathedrals, too. That's why it got bombed by the Germans, because of all the 'istory. Of course, we did the same thing to them.

"By the time I was 15, I was out of school. When I did attend school it was only two days a week, maybe three. My stepfather wanted us earning money. He physically, mentally, and verbally abused us all. He was whacko. He would always say how stupid we were. That we'd turn out to be garbage, nothin'. He was unemployed. But I did become somethin': a wife, mother, grandmother – a person."

Did you ever meet your biological father?

"Once. When I was 14. He came to Norwich and was every bit a gentleman. He's what they called an English gentleman. He talked very well. He was raised with old money."

Why didn't it work out between him and your mother?

"My mother couldn't live that kind of life; she'd been poor all her life. When she married my dad, she had to be prim and proper. She couldn't adapt. He was from near the Scotland border, and my mother didn't want to be that far from her mother."

But look what she ended up with.

"You're right, Jeff. She walked away from my father. She could have walked away from that whacko. Something kept her there."

Is there quite a gap between rich and poor in England?

"There's more of a middle class now. Old money didn't even accept new money. You could win the lottery, and they'd know, because of the way you spoke. They speak like they have marbles in their mouth. They had no accent. It's called the Queen's English."

Tell me more.

"Every other 'ouse was English or Irish. They were adjoined. The government owned 'um. The English would shout out their windows, 'Get in your 'ouse so you can beat your wife and confess your sins.' And the Irish would say, 'Well, you English beat your wives and you don't get forgiven.'

"They'd all do that, you know. They'd beat their wives and in the mornin', the Irish woman would be sportin' a black eye, and the English wife, not to be outdone, would show 'ers off, 'That's nothin'! Look at the one I got last night.' It was very acceptable where we lived. Women would have big puffy lips. It was just... accepted."

What about all that King and Queen business?

"I like it. Even though I don't believe they should have all that money. But they also bring in a lot of money – tourism. The Tower of London is a fascinatin' place."

Kinda creepy, I 'eard. Ahem. Heard.

"Very evil. Look at the torture that went on. They say there's 15 feet of cement between the basement and the floor and you could still hear the screams of them people. Guy Folkes tried to blow everything up, the Houses of Parliament – everything."

Were you the first of your family to migrate to the United States?

"No, my mother's sister was actually one of the first GI brides. She married a Chippewa Indian from Michigan in 1946. They came back on the Queen Mary. He was a wonderful man. Personally, I hardly ever dated English guys. The Americans were so clean. They cleaned their teeth and washed their hair with shampoo and all this fancy stuff."

What do you miss about England the most?

"The countryside. If you took a walk down a country lane, it would be somethin' you'd never forget. It's truly breathtakin'. I miss the pubs. If you wanted a good night out, you didn't have to drink. They serve cups a tea and lemonade at the pubs. You've got sing song and good conversation. I miss that. I do miss the seaside."

Hard times?

"When I came over here and saw what was considered poor. I thought it was a joke. I never had a toy growing up in England. Nothing. On Christmas Eve, the movie houses would let us in for free because they knew we wouldn't be receiving anything Christmas morning. We were the poorest of the poor. We had a fireplace but no coal to put in it. Me and my brothers would take an English penny and rub it down on the cement floor of the kitchen until it was the size of a shilling and then put it in the meter, which would turn the gas on. Then we would get heat. Once a month they'd open up the meter and find it full of rubbed down pennies. Then we'd get fined."

* * *

"Ronnie" Farrell still carries a strong cockney accent, but loves country-western music, the First Assembly of God Church, anything pertaining to American Indians and Elvis. She's about as salty as a buttah knife plunged into a jar of marmite.

And she never drinks coffee.

Dave Kutanovski *(Jan. 2007)*

"Opportunity is missed by most people because it is dressed in overalls and looks like work."
– Thomas Alva Edison

Just east of Interstate 65 and Indiana 2, I pull into a place of business that truckers have been known to frequent in the wee hours of the night. No, not The Lion's Den, but Crossroads Service Center.

I find 50-year-old entrepreneur Dave Kutanovski reserved but friendly. At times he carries a slight accent. He also carries himself with dignity and class. Today, Kutanovski and wife, Lena, live in Crown Point. They have raised three children, Jennifer, Christopher, and Michelle. For nine years, Dave has owned and operated the service center. He has been in the truck-repair business for 26 years.

Today, Kutanovski is open for business from 6 a.m. until midnight, six days a week. "We're cutting back a little bit" he told me. "We used to be open 24/7. It wears on you after a while."

Today, the Kutanovski family owns hundreds of acres of prime real estate.

It wasn't always that way.

* * *

"My father moved to Gary from Yugoslavia," Kutanovski began. "My mother, siblings and I came a year later. I was 10 years old. We moved to Gary because of the mills. Dad went to work for U.S. Steel. I remember him coming home from the open hearth with burns on his face."

Did you have relatives already living in the States?

"Yes, my dad's sister was his sponsor. It was a big culture shock. We were from a village where there was no automotive. Poverty. To have a chocolate bar was like heaven."

What did your dad do for a living in the old country?

"Construction work, a lot of manual labor. He was also part of Tito's army.

The Germans and Italians could not get to them during World War II. Partisan soldier like mountain goat. Tito was a very wise man. Everybody tried to assassinate him, but somehow he outmaneuvered them. He kept the whole Yugoslavia together. Once Tito pass away, things kind of fell apart.

"When I lived there, we were still under the Russian regime – communist. They forced me to take Russian in school. I think every young generation needs to go to Europe for a year and see how other side lives. They would definitely respect this country more."

Tell me more about the village of your childhood.

"I wish I had a picture to show you. So much natural beauty. I grew up on Lake Ohrid. It is one of the deepest lakes in the world. If you tied a string to an unopened beer bottle and dropped it into lake 40 or 50 feet it would explode by the time you brought it back up because of pressure and cold. There were a lot of mountains. Bears and wolves lived there. We had watchdogs to protect us from them – big, strong mountain dogs. We lived near the border of Macedonia and Albania."

Dave, my grandfather came to Chicago from Italy. But 500 years ago, the Manes family lived in Albania.

"They're tough, very poor. Today, many of them are migrating over to Macedonia. The Albanians are very hard workers. They make some of the greatest walls from rocks. Miles of walls made of rock. They form them by hand. It is an art in itself."

Gary?

"We lived by 48th and Delaware. I remember my dad would buy bread from the store. We would go through loaves of those breads at a sitting. This bread it had no substance. Mom sent Dad out for flour. She made these huge breads. Our American neighbor loved the smell of Ma's bread. She would give the lady some. We were very fortunate to have good neighbors. They gave us shoes and coats that their kids had outgrown. These were American people. They were not rich. Some had Irish last names, some German. There were Greeks. Some came from the South. I remember the Goad family. They gave us whatever they can. And, to this day, I will never forget that. I treat people how I want to be treated.

"I went to Lew Wallace High School. My name is Dragan.

Americans interpret it as 'dragon.' Some people thought that was funny. There were fights. Dragan is my birth name, and that will never change."

All of your children have either graduated from or are attending Purdue.

"Yes; I am very blessed to have good kids. We live for them. If our kids don't succeed, we feel like we're failures."

Did you go to college?

"No, I went to trade school – Lincoln Tech in Indianapolis. Automotive. My younger brother got a football scholarship from Southwest Missouri State. Dad refused to believe it. He said to my brother: 'Son, nobody gives you anything for free. You have to sweat for everything you get.' He never went to any games. 'You call me when you graduate. I will come to that.'"

How long have you been married?

"Twenty-six years. Lena was born in Macedonia as well. My wife is a very intelligent woman. We met during church activities."

Macedonian Orthodox?

"Yes. My dad made a wise decision to come to United States. An open heart surgeon in Macedonia makes $300 a month. If your son is sick, doctor will not see him unless you offer some kind of payment. Fish, bread, eggs... I hope things will change over there with the free enterprise. I think it is for the better if people can be self-employed. Otherwise, there is no motivation or initiative to work hard. My kids loved visiting old country."

Do they speak the language?

"Little bit. I tell them: 'We are Americans, but don't forget we are Orthodox. Don't forget where your family came from.'"

* * *

Alimpije Kutanovski came to Gary back in 1966. He fed fiery furnaces with a shovel so his wife, Kota, could put homemade bread on her children's plates.

Dragan "Dave" Kutanovski was born in a country that had "no automotive," yet he has prospered repairing tractor-trailers.

Big and strong like a mountain dog, Christopher Kutanovski played football for the Crown Point Bulldogs. He is a senior at Purdue now. He will work with his hands as did the Kutanovskis before him – he will become a dentist.

And so it goes.

John Alessia *(Apr. 2007)*

"The olive tree never loses its leaves."
-Giovanni Alessia

John and Sue Alessia's beautiful home sits a pontoon boat's length from Cedar Lake. John does not fish, but he has fried his share of pollack.

* * *

"I came to South Chicago from Italy back in 1958; I was 18," Alessia began. "My mother came first with three of my siblings. She had to take care of my widowed grandmother, who was already here. Me and most of my brothers and sisters came with my dad three years later. We're a big family – 11 kids. I was right in the middle: five up and five down."

Continue, please.

"My first job in America was wash dishes. When you can't speak English, you wash dishes. As soon as I came to America, I went to night schools on my own. In a week, sometimes I would go to five different schools. The library in South Chicago had one class a week, St. George's on 95th, Chicago Vocational High School, South Shore Library, Fenger High School. I would sign my name on all of them. I had to take five buses to get to Fenger."

Which mill hired you?

"Wisconsin Steel in South Chicago. I worked there 21 years, until they shut the doors back in 1980. We had a meeting on a Thursday night. All the politicians were there. They said, 'Don't worry about it; International Harvester is helping to pay the bills.' Harvester used to own us. IH was on strike about that time. The next day, a guard tells me to call the union hall. 'The company is filing for bankruptcy – Monday.'

"Thursday, there was nothin' to worry about. The company asked some of us to come out that Saturday to help them shut the plant down properly, so things would go smoothly when they started back up. That was 27 years ago. Guess what? We're still waitin' for start up."

Did Wisconsin Steel employees eventually receive severance pay?

"I got a one-shot deal for about seven grand. My age and my seniority didn't add up to 65. The guys who had 65 points got 15 grand. I thank the Lord that I was able to get in at Amoco Oil Co. in Whiting three years later; I learned how to be an instrument repairman while I was in the mill.

"Amoco was the best company I ever worked for. I was there about 16 1/2 years. I get about $270 a month pension from Wisconsin. When they went bankrupt, the government took over the pension. At least it pays my insurance."

You are a member of St. Edward Catholic Church in Lowell.

"Yes; I'm a warden of the Knight's of Columbus. I like it. I also joined the Knights' fourth degree. We wear the regalia, hats, sword... ."

You guys fry fish once in while.

"Sometimes as much as 500 pounds worth. We fry fish at churches all over the area – all you can eat."

When I told your son, John Jr., that I wanted to interview you, he said: 'Please, get Dad to talk about Italy. He never speaks of it.'"

"He never asked!"

Adds Sue, "My husband doesn't think it's important."

"It's not important. I am not the only one who went through this."

Through what?

"The little town that I'm from is called Altomonte – high mountain. My dad was poor, but he put enough to eat on the table. We had a little farm. My mother, she would work in the fields the day after she gave birth to one of us. There were no jobs during the '50s in the part of Italy I came from, no industry whatsoever. The town didn't have no electricity, no paved streets."

When the famiglia sat down to the dinner table what kind of meat

–

"There was no meat. You eat your goat, you have no milk. You kill your chickens, you have no eggs. We did eat guinea pigs."

Guinea pigs. Those cuddly, furry... rats?

"Yes."

Meat's meat and a man gotta eat. John, there are Americans who enjoy the gonads of hogs and the legs of frogs. And we have a choice! Pesci?

"A guy would come from out of town with a buggy filled with fish. He would blow a bugle and then announce, 'The fish come to town!' He would also announce how much per kilo."

"When we built our house in Crete (Ill.), I wanted to do the downstairs family room in barnwood," recalls Sue. "That was the style in the '70s. John kept saying, 'I don't like it.' I could never figure out why. His brother went back to Italy during the '80s. He videotaped the inside and outside of the house John grew up in. I appreciated why John didn't like barnwood."

"It was a little house," reflects John. (With solemnity, he sips his coffee.)

Is John the name you were born with?

"My real name is Giovanni; I changed it."

Mr. Alessia! That's a beautiful sounding name.

"I know – excuse me. I shouldn't say, 'I know.' Years ago, nobody used that here. I asked, 'What's Giovanni?' They said, 'John.' I said, 'That's the name I want.'

"We were 50 miles from Sicily. We could see the Adriatic Sea in the distance. Italy is beautiful if you get out of the big city. My brothers and sisters have went back a couple of times. I've never been back.

"Right in front of the house we had fig, almond, pomegranate, persimmon, and olive trees. Olives everywhere. The olive tree never loses its leaves... I have an olive tree in my front room right now. I will show it to you when we're done talking. We used to make our own oil."

"He still makes his own wine," shouts Sue from the other room.

"I only make five gallons," says John. "Red."

Some say the Sicilians are a superstitious lot. The Calabrians?

"Even while living in Chicago, if a member of the family got a bad headache, my mother believed it was because somebody gave them the evil eye. She would mumble to one of the saints – to ward off the spell. I don't think that she was saying anything, just being melodramatic.

"Then, she would do this strange yawning thing when she was finished chanting. I would say, 'Ma, please. C'mon, Ma... Ma...' Then I would tease her by imitating her ritual. She liked that.

"We grew wheat because we had to have it for bread. We had an oven outside the house. My mother would put wood in there and get it hot for two or three hours. Then, she would bake the bread. There was a bakery in town, but we couldn't afford it. She made her own pasta. I will never forget the smell of my mother's bread."

Giovanni.

"Si?"

Let's have a look at that tree.

Tieh C. Wang, M.D. *(Feb. 2009)*

"An oppressive government is more to be feared than a tiger."
– Confucius

One of my trusty scouts, Lil' Joe Gutierrez, tipped me off about interviewing his acupuncturist, Dr. Tieh Wang.

Wang, 82, was the Laboratory Director at St. Margaret Hospital (now Saint Margaret Mercy Healthcare Centers in Hammond and Dyer) until he retired in 1997 at the age of 72.

He is the father of five adult children, all of whom graduated from Munster High School. Wang lives with his wife of 40 years in a small condo in Briar Ridge in Schererville.

* * *

"I was born near Beijing in 1926, the Year of the Tiger," Wang began. "My grandson was born the Year of the Rat; I told him rat is best – very alert."

Doc, as of Jan. 26, we've entered the Year of the Ox. Do you believe in Chinese astrology?

"No! But I wouldn't have told my mother that. Thousands of years ago, in China, people don't know that much except animals."

Tell me about living in China from the late 1920s to the late '40s. Did you have siblings?

"Only child. Too many Chinese. If a girl was born, parents would let it starve to death."

In "The Good Earth" a baby girl was considered an "unlucky child." When my twin daughters were about 12 years old, I paid them five bucks each to read Pearl Buck's novel, but they had to write a report on it when they were done. Have you ever read it?

"No; I saw the movie; it was done very well. Almost exactly like I grew up."

Religion?

"Chinese, automatically you were born in the culture of Buddhism, but the common people don't know the Buddhist bible, the theory or the history. The Buddhists don't have good organization. The temples are on top of the mountain. A few hundred monks live up there. All their lives, they practice martial arts.

"In the '30s and '40s, the nationalist army or government was based in the city. Mao Tse-Tung was the rebel; he lived in the countryside. His people cannot afford real doctor; so they went to the acupuncturists. Real doctor doesn't live in the country; he tends to the elite in the city.

"There was no doctor for the soldiers in the country. Chairman Mao killed many people, but he did one good thing; he decided there should be two kinds of hospitals for people to choose from. Acupuncture would be dead without Mao Tse-Tung.

"In 1937, the Japanese invaded my village; I became a refugee at the age of 12. At 13, I tried to join the army to fight the Japanese. While growing up, the Chinese, he feels himself useless. I felt angry."

Where was your dad during those chaotic times when you were a boy?

"My father worked in Hong Kong all his life. He was one of the minimum wage earners. He sold Chinese medicine like ginseng. He did not own the store; he just worked there. He would come home from Hong Kong once every couple of years; he couldn't afford it."

The Opium Wars or Anglo-Chinese Wars between Great Britain and China changed Chinese culture.

"Yes; for some reason, Chinese love opium. But after Chinese lose the Opium Wars, they realize how backwards China is scientifically. Eventually, Chinese in Hong Kong try to act like Westerners – they start wearing socks.

"Once young Chinese men go to Harvard and Oxford; they don't behave like Chinese when they return to China. They look down on backward Chinese medicine. American doctors feel the same way. I was just like them. That's how prejudiced your education can make you."

Chairman Mao eventually came out on top of the civil war. How did that affect you?

"When the communists took over China in 1949, I fled to Taiwan. The Red Chinese persecuted my father every day because I went to school in Taiwan. They threatened him; finally, he died young; all his teeth fell out."

When did you come to the United States?

"I graduated from medical school at Taiwan University in 1953; during the summer of '55, I did an internship in Rochester, N.Y.

"I stayed in Rochester for three years, then came to Chicago where I finished my training at Cook County Hospital and University of Chicago.

"I became a pathologist and worked at St. Margaret Hospital in Hammond from 1961 to '97, where I was in charge of laboratory and nuclear medicine. I was the person who started nuclear medicine at St. Margaret, St. Catherine and Community hospitals. You know, radioisotope work – before MRIs came to be."

Doc, I was the person who started in the bottom of a soaking pit at No. 3 Bloomer with a 90-pound buster, but eventually learned to connect six-inch schedule 40 pipe to a weld-neck flange using 6010 for a root pass and covering it up with low-hydrogen 7018 at about 160 amps. You know, steel work – please, proceed.

"When I retired from St. Margaret, I didn't know what to do with myself. I remembered a little office that dealt in Chinese medicine that was just 500 yards from the biggest hospital in Taiwan. I used watch people walk into it; I wondered why they would go there. It was an acupuncture clinic."

Yeah?

"At the age of 72, I went back to China to learn acupuncture."

How long did that take?

"Three months. Acupuncturist is easier than herbalist. Herbalist takes longer."

Doc, I've known quite a few herbalists through the years; most of them have been practicing since the late '60s. Let's stick to the needles; what happened when you returned to the U.S.?

"I knew all the doctors here; I wrote to them about my new endeavor."

And?

"Not a single reply."

They considered you a witch doctor, right?

"Still today, same thing; you're not going to change them."

What ailments can be cured or relieved by acupuncture?

"Just to name a few; carpal tunnel, sinus headache, migraine, sciatica, back ache and post menstrual syndrome."

Doc, in one way or another, I've suffered from every one of those maladies. And all I had to do, was come see you. How big are these needles?

"From one to five inches long. They are very thin, like your hair; you have trouble seeing them."

I realize most insurance companies don't cover acupuncture, how much would it run me to pay you visit?

"Eighty dollars for a half-hour; there is a $20 discount for seniors. Many people cannot afford that; it is cheaper for them to have their insurance company pay $60,000 for back surgery. If they would come to me, I could fix their backs in three weeks, they would never miss work, and the charge would be no more than $1,000.

"(President Barack) Obama promises medical reform – might change the standards, but it will be difficult because there are different interests."

I have a friend who is the athletic trainer at Lowell High School; he spells his surname Wong.

"Wong and Wang are the same. No one is named Wong in China; it was probably changed when his family came to San Francisco. Americans forced people to change their names. Americans pronounce Wang as if it rhymes with bang; Wang should rhyme with long."

Had Beijing changed much when you returned to study acupuncture?

"Oh, yeah. There is a golf course where my mother and I lived. I grew up right on the ocean. We ate lots of shrimp, scallops and noodles."

* * *

Change...

Actress Anna May Wong was touted for the role of O-lan in the film "The Good Earth." However, because Paul Muni (Wang Lung) was of European descent, the Hays Code's anti-miscegenation rules stated that his character's wife had to be played by a white woman. Dr. Tieh Wang's wife is of European descent.

Today, Wang has a one-room office just east of Cline Avenue on 15th Avenue in Gary. And he is content in semi-retirement plying the techniques his forefathers used 3,000 years ago.

Werner Riecken *(Apr. 2008)*

"I took a walk along the historic coast of Normandy in the country of France. It was a lovely day for strolling along the seashore. Men were sleeping on the sand; some of them sleeping forever. Men were floating in the water, but they didn't know they were in the water, for they were dead."

– Ernie Pyle

My plan was to focus on Werner Riecken's passion for woodcarving. He and his wife, Ursula, live in Schererville. Outside their front door is a mat which has the word "*Willkommen*" ("welcome") woven into it.

Riecken, 83, is a retired bricklayer. Come to find out, he also is a World War II veteran who spent two years in a prisoner-of-war camp – in Maryland.

Werner Riecken fought for Germany.

* * *

"Would you like some cognac?" Riecken began.

No thanks, Mr. Riecken. Where were you born?

"Uschi (Ursula) and I were both born in the same little village of Stolde, Germany. It is close to Denmark."

Lutheran territory.

"Yah. Northern Germany is mostly Lutheran; southern Germany is mostly Catholic."

School days?

"When I first started school in 1931 the teachers were still the old Democrats – good teachers. In 1933, things changed. All of a sudden, they took all the old teachers and sent them somewhere else.

"We got a new type of teacher – 100 percent, homemade Nazis. More and more pressure was put on the kids – the parents, too. But, at my home, I knew that my parents weren't impressed by what was going on. I had to join the service in 1935, just like the pope in Rome."

The service? You were only 10 years old.

"Hitler Youth. In 1938, I got out of school a year early because I made good grades. In Germany, you learn a trade. My dad took me by train to the city where he knew a contractor. My dad and brother were bricklayers. The boss looked me over; I'm 13 years old, 89 pounds. I couldn't lift a bag of cement, but the contractor hired me. I was an apprentice for three years. My pay was 3.72 marks per week.

"You had to know concrete work, how to finish, tile roofs, tuck pointing with long trowels. You had to know how to plaster – rough and fine. When I turned 16, I was making 72 marks per week.

"I was drafted before I turned 17. Actually, it was a work-force unit. You only stay in that for six months. Then you are drafted into the army."

What about the SS?

"The SS were the blond-haired, blue-eyed ones. They would ask for volunteers, but they would also force you to join if you fit their mold. The leaders of the SS would simply shoot their own if they didn't want to go forward. They wore black uniforms. On the sleeve was a lightning bolt."

Blitzen.

"Sprechen sie Deutsch?"

Very little. Donner and Blitzen were two of St. Nick's eight reindeer.

"Yah?"

Yeah.

"I became a machine gunner; the training was brutal. I was eventually sent to France. I dug foxholes along the coast until I got to Normandy. I also got 'flohes' while in France.

Flohes?

"Fleas. We dug dirt bunkers. Right next to us were guys running around having a good old time shooting at seagulls. They were White Russians who fought for Germany; they were from near the Black Sea.."

And then came the big day – June 6, 1944.

"Yah. One British plane after another it seemed passed by the moon – American 82nd Airborne, too. They also pulled gliders and when they got close to the coast, they unhooked them from the plane. There was no open space for them; it was all tall hedges. I felt sorry for them; many of them didn't make it.

"Toward morning, I came out of my foxhole and I could see parachutes hanging from trees. One of the parachutes had cube sugar and Pall Mall cigarettes in it. We were only issued three cigarettes a day. I ate the sugar because I was hungry. We were near Ste Mere Eglise, which was surrounded by 82nd Airborne.

"On the second day my buddy, Karl Heinz, joins me. We didn't know it, but we were the only two survivors of our company. It was just getting light in the morning, when Karl got hit. He asked for my pistol."

Why?

"He wanted to kill himself; he was in so much pain. Then, Karl closed his eyes... .

"I took off running along the hedgerows. Some were tall, some not. Shots were coming from all around. I'm laying behind a 3-foot hedge. Well, somebody saw me and I got shot. Here is where the bullet went into my neck, and here and is where it came out; it went through my spine.

"I'm laying down thinking, 'This is it.' I was bleeding. I started crawling. The Americans were so quiet. Our uniforms and boots – everything made noise.

"All of a sudden, there was two men with rifles standing above me – 82nd Airborne. I wished I knew what they were saying. They took me to the other side of the tall hedge. Every four feet sat an American soldier. I couldn't believe how they snuck up on us. All their jaws and mouths were moving. They were chewing gum. I didn't know what gum was.

"The medic bandaged me up. Then, a guy came up to me who spoke fluent German. He was an American interpreter who spent his childhood near my hometown. He told me to follow him to a farmer's gate and explained to me in German that the Americans had to climb over it when they first landed.

"He said, 'That was where we lost most of our guys,' meaning Americans. German sharpshooters had killed them from the apple trees. War... .

"I was eventually loaded onto a ship for England. The doctors were amazed that I was alive. I was taken to a hospital in Edinburgh, Scotland. They asked who caught me. I told them 82nd Airborne so I was sent to America. If I would have been captured by the British, I would have stayed in England.

"I stayed in Maryland for two years. I was here when (President Franklin D.) Roosevelt died and (Harry S.) Truman took over. I was well-treated. They let us drink beer. Read this."

"This certificate of achievement is awarded to Werner Riecken 31G128841 who successfully completed a course in geography and civic-history for prisoners of war conducted in P.W. Camp: Cambridge, Md. on this 15th day of November, 1945."

"Once released, I eventually made it back to Stolde. I went back to laying brick. Ursula and I married in 1950. I applied for papers to come to the United States. It took two years. We settled in Hammond in 1952; we moved to Schererville in 1958. After five years, we became American citizens. Our two sons attended Lake Central High School."

Woodcarving?

"I had to retire from laying brick because of a back injury in 1977. I took up woodcarving because I needed something to do while recovering from my surgeries. I couldn't walk.

"I started with a pocket knife. Then, I joined South Suburban Chislers in 1980. I am a lifetime member. I'm also a member of Duneland Woodcarvers. I've won four best of shows. Here is some of my work."

"You are welcome to come back to our home."

Willkommen.

"Yah, willkommen."

* * *

Bricklayers, Steelworkers and Autoworkers died on that beach in Normandy. Some guys made Fords. Some guys made Volkswagens. War...

.

Riecken never forgot how he was treated while a POW in Maryland. He returned to these United States, plied his trade, and helped build Jeorse Park, Omni Sports Center, Embers Restaurant, apartment buildings and churches.

While in France, he nearly was cut down for good. Disabled in America, he traded trowel for chisel. His carvings are magnificent. At 83 years of age, he is weathered like driftwood in the sand.

Werner Riecken has sculpted quite a life.

Sam and Cindy *(Oct. 2006)*

"Now I've been crying lately,
thinking about the world as it is.
Why must we go on hating,
Why can't we live in bliss?"
-Yusuf Islam (Cat Stevens)

Hosam and Cindy Ahmad lived in Shelby for 10 years. They just recently moved to Lowell. They have two daughters. Sameerah is a junior at Purdue and Sumaiyah is a sophomore at Lowell High School.

* * *

So, Cindy, you grew up in Riverdale, Ill.

"Yes, where the IC and Harbor Belt intersect. My dad worked at U.S. Steel in Gary."

What was your maiden name?

"Donohoe. I went to Thornton High School in Harvey."

Hosam?

"I was born in a small village in Palestine."

Bear with me, Sam. I've been to Palatine, but never Palestine. Fill me in.

"In the eyes of the Arab and Christian, it is Palestine. In the eyes of the Jewish, it is Israel. Same land. Two different names."

Donohoe. Were you raised Catholic?

"Yes. I went to Queen of Apostles in fourth, fifth, and sixth grades."

You gotta love the names of those Catholic Schools. Sam, how old were you when you came to the United States?

"I was 23 years. Half my lifetime I spend in Palestine. Half in America."

When you were a boy, did you have Jewish friends?

"Not really. I have more Jewish friends in this country. When Gulf War started, lots of troubles more and more."

Shelby?

"The day after we moved in, Sam went to take the garbage out and someone had put a cross in our yard. I was scared to death. Sam was standing out in the yard yelling.

"We must have had 30 people come to our house the next day and say, 'We heard what happened to you.' They brought jams and jellies. They also said things like, 'If anything like that ever happens again, you give us a call.'"

What do you do for a living, Sam?

"I'm a chef at new place in Beecher called Maxwell's Restaurant."

How did you fare on your realtor's exam, Cindy?

"I passed it."

Do you ever hear any derogatory remarks because you cover?

"From some people..." (Cindy)

"From a lot of people!" (Sam)

"In Dallas, I would have people approach me and talk real loud and slow, 'Where-are-you-from?' 'Chicagah!,' I'd blare back. After one of the Athletic Booster meetings in Lowell, I was talking to a friend of mine, she uttered a mild expletive. She looked at me wide-eyed and apologized. I said, 'I'm a Muslim. I'm not a nun.'

"When we lived in Dallas, Sam failed the test for his driver's license three times. Finally, I went in there, 'I don't understand what's going on. My husband knows this stuff inside and out.' I looked at the test myself. It was in Spanish. They gave him the Spanish edition all three times."

!Ay caramba!

"Sam was sworn in as an American citizen on Memorial Day back in '96. Right after 9/11, somebody stole our American Flag. The school heard about it. Lowell's freshman football team, they saw to it that we got another one."

Cindy, try not to do that. I don't want Sam to see me crying, too.

"Both countries I have lived in have too much killing," Sam said. "Over there, government probably handles it better. Over here, anybody can buy a gun. Over there, you have no right to carry a gun. If they catch you with it, you go to jail. If you kill somebody? It's over. You outta luck.. Over here, you kill 10 or 12, finally they might decide you're guilty." (Sam)

"But Sam, if you were accused of killing somebody, you would really appreciate due process. You know there have been people in your own family who have been taken away by the soldiers. They would admit to throwing a rock or something they were innocent of, because they were being brutally beaten. Our people fought hard for the rights that they have now." (Cindy)

"This is all true." (Sam)

"My mother was a military brat born in the Philippines. My grandfather went to West Point. My dad was from a small town in Iowa. He wanted to go to West Point but he had poor eyesight. He still did the ROTC thing." (Cindy)

The man from Munster who was killed at his restaurant, Aladdin Pita, in Merrilliville...

"My sister's husband."(Sam)

"Right after the funeral, Sam's niece walked into the house and answered the phone. It was a woman's voice. She said, 'You don't know who I am. I'm from Chicago. I just want you to know that I'm really sorry about what happened. It's a shame these type of things are happening. I am Jewish.'"

How did you two meet?

"My girlfriend introduced us. I'd been dating a 'nice' Irish Catholic boy, but she didn't approve of the way he was treating me. Sam asked me out for six months, finally we went on a date. He asked me to marry him on our second date. Jokingly, I told him to marry someone else, get a green card, and then divorce her. Then I'd marry him. I did worry that his family would say that he only married me to get a green card. I didn't trust Arabs."

"See, even my wife doesn't trust Arabs! I proved my love by marrying a woman for two months. I got a divorce, and then me and Cindy eloped the next day to Disney World. A lot of excitement, huh?"

Jiggers! How have the girls gotten along?

"Those daughters of mine, with Irish/Palestinian bloodlines? I don't believe my girls would ever submit to anyone. My dad's grandfathers fought against each other. Catholic versus Protestant. They... " (Cindy)

"From PLO to IRA! Geesh. I came to this country as an Arab to look for a better life. I find a home. I find a wife. Make a family. I did it myself. I worked one job. Two jobs. Three jobs! If somebody does some horrible thing in the name of Islam, it is not Sam and Cindy Ahmad. We just want to live our life. Still, people look at her funny because of the way she dress. Why? She is more patriot person than anyone I've ever met. 100 percent American!" (Sam)

“My grandfather’s job was to defend Chicago in case of a missile attack,” Cindy said. “It really hurts when somebody questions my loyalty.” (Cindy)

* * *

Interviewed a lot of good people down in Shelby. Some with names like Loretta, Eleanor, Babe, Chub or Coyote – one named Hosam.

Dwight S. Tyndall, MD *(Oct. 2010)*

"Emancipate yourselves from mental slavery,
None but ourselves can free our mind."
–Bob Marley

Dwight Tyndall grew up on a small farm in Jamaica before emigrating to New York City. Today, Dr. Dwight S. Tyndall, 46, lives in Flossmoor, Ill. with his wife Candace and their three children ages 9, 7 and 7 months.

Tyndall is a surgeon at Orthopaedic Specialists of Northwest Indiana in Munster. He had to cancel our interview the first time because of an emergency surgery. He has apologized about five times.

I told him it was ridiculous to apologize under the circumstances. The thing is, his apologies are genuine. He really feels bad about having to cancel.

Our interview took place at Orthopaedic Specialists of Northwest Indiana in Munster. The next day, Tyndall emailed me saying he enjoyed our conversation and how it felt like a couple of friends talking and less like an interview.

* * *

"I had the typical Jamaican upbringing," Tyndall began. "Jamaica is a Third World country; there is a different perspective than you see in this country. It's a different lifestyle; neither is right or wrong.

"My mother was the eldest of 10 kids; she moved to the United States eight years before I did. My grandparents raised me for those eight years. I came to the United States when I was 14."

What did your grandfather do for a living?

"He had a farm with cows and he raised cane."

Doc, I've known a few steel workers who've raised Cain – mostly on paydays and Saturday nights.

"I'm referring to sugar cane. We would sell the harvest to the factory which would make sugar out of it."

Nice and warm, all year in Jamaica?

"Hot; if it gets below 80 degrees in the winter, people get worried. If you moved to Jamaica you would acclimate to the tropical weather. There's a saying, 'When the mad dogs and the Englishmen go out in the midday sun.'"

That's from a song written by Noel Coward in the 1920s. It's also the name of an album by Joe Cocker. Speaking of musicians, Bob Marley?

"I'm a big fan. I saw him at his last appearance at Madison Square Garden. Bob Marley, for the longest time, was reggae music. The thing that is unique about Bob Marley is his lyrics and composition are complicated; it's not simplistic. The 'Redemption Song' is onc of my favorites. I love the line, 'Free yourself of mental slavery.'"

Popular sports in Jamaica?

"Soccer, cricket, and track and field. The amount of world-class sprinters who come out of a country as small as Jamaica is quite remarkable."

Was your family in Jamaica considered middle class?

"Probably lower middle class. I had a pretty good childhood; we got what we needed.

"The economic climate has gotten a lot worse in the last 20 years. There are just two classes now – rich and poor. This free-market economy idea doesn't really work that well for the working class. A lot of Americans are losing their jobs because everything is being made in China. As soon as the Chinese move up; everything will be made in Taiwan. The workers' labor is being devalued."

Doc, you're preachin' to the choir.

"Walmart boggles my mind. How can you buy something for $5 which was made thousands of miles away, shipped across the ocean, then shipped on a truck or train?

"The math, in my mind, doesn't add up unless the labor costs are extremely cheap. And if the labor costs are that cheap, those people are being taken advantage of. I don't like Walmart."

Doc, you're all right. Where did you live in New York City?

"The Bronx; I quickly became a Yankee fan."

Interview's over.

"Hey, the Yankees are good for baseball. ... I remember in '78, when the Yankees went from 14 1/2 games out in August to win the pennant and World Series."

Yeah, well, they wouldn't have done it without a couple of former Sox players named Bucky (Dent) and Goose (Gossage). Let's switch gears – college?

"I attended City College of New York."

Medical school?

"New York University; I went to Stanford University Medical Center for residency and The Hospital for Special Surgery (Cornell University Medical Center) for fellowship. Stanford only takes 64 medical students per year, and the program that I specialized in only took four students per year."

Did you think you'd end up a surgeon when you were in high school?

"No, I knew I wanted to be in medicine. In medical school, I did a surgical incision and one of my professors said I should consider surgery because I had the personality for it.

"Then, I had to decide what type of surgery. I liked orthopedics, so I chose that. Once I chose orthopaedics, I had to decide what specialty I wanted. I decided on the spine."

Doc, somewhere I read to be a great surgeon, you had to have the eye of an eagle, the hands of a woman and the heart of a lion.

"The job is demanding; it's like flying a plane. Take off is optional; landing is mandatory. It's the same with performing an operation. Starting is optional, but you have to finish it. There's no do-over.

"There's a lot of thought of what procedure you're going to do and why you're doing it. You have to be very precise and focused. It's strenuous; you're working 12-hour days sometimes. On my downtime, I just like to relax."

Talk a little more about your specialty.

"Spine surgery can be very delicate at one point and very aggressive at another point. I'm at a point in my career where I truly understand the science. I can recognize where the trends are going. The trend is toward minimal invasive procedures."

Explain, please?

"Small incisions, quicker operative times and quicker recoveries. I focus my practice in that direction. I use a lot of newer techniques. The understanding of the spine has evolved and our techniques have evolved with it. The danger is to not get stuck on the ways you were trained in school. Things change; you have to adapt."

How many Jamaican-born spine surgeons are there in the United States?

"The other one lives in Florida; I know him."

You're something else, Doc.

"Jeff, my profession doesn't define who I am. For some people, their profession goes wherever they go. If they go to a restaurant, they go as a doctor. Being a doctor is what I do, but being with my family, being a responsible person and being a productive member of society is most important."

* * *

Tyndall sponsors a Marion Catholic High School student through a program called LINK Unlimited. According to the website www.linkunlimited.org, the group "is a not-for-profit organization that provides four-year high school scholarships, mentoring and support programming to low-income Chicago high school youth who possess high academic potential and strong personal character."

Tyndall also is a board member of the Boys & Girls Clubs of Northwest Indiana. That's when he's just a productive member of society, a person his friends call Dwight.

George Kouimanis *(Dec. 2009)*

"The Greek who begins life in a new land, on the bottom step of society as a dishwasher, needs only to remember how Aesop left a legacy of poetry while cooking as a slave."
– Theresa Yianilos, "The Complete Greek Cookbook"

The outcome of many a Lowell High School football game has been predicted and or rehashed over a cup of joe and an omelette at George's Family Restaurant in town.

George Kouimanis, 57, recently celebrated his 25th anniversary owning the eatery at 1910 E. Commercial Ave.

He and his wife, Cally, have raised two sons. Johnny, the eldest, has remained in the family business. Steve is a chiropractor in Lowell. Both played football at LHS.

* * *

Wasn't this place called Jimmy's Coney Island before you bought it?

"Yes, in 1984, I took over for Jim Dimitroff," he said. "This is the last of seven Coney Islands he built in Northwest Indiana. Jimmy was from Bulgaria."

And you?

"A Greek village called Amades located on the island of Chios. Here is photograph."

Breathtaking. How many folks inhabit the island?

"About 70,000, but my village only about 100 people. Do you know Angelo from Twelve Islands (restaurant) in Crown Point? He's from same island."

How old were you when you came to the United States?

"I was 24."

Did you speak any English?

"Not too much. Cally was born on the same island. Her father, Stavros Fotinos moved to Gary in 1967 when she was about 7. She graduated from Merrillville High School, but then, she came back to the island after so many years and we met again. I married my wife and she bring me back to Indiana. Cally is a very sharp lady."

Education in Greece?

"I went to school until I was 12. My dad didn't have enough money to send me to high school; we are a big family. But there was a tycoon on our island who owned passenger ships. He wanted to produce waiters and cooks for his ships. I learned cooking at his school.

"At 14, I went to work with my Uncle George as his assistant cook on a cargo ship. By the time I was 18, I was the head cook."

Then what?

"When I'm 21, the military called me; we were having a little problem with Turkey. After 30 months in the Greek Navy, I came to this country. I started cooking at Ricochet Pizza in Gary. Then, I was grill man at The Patio (restaurant in Merrillville) for six years.

"A delivery man said, 'George, there's a restaurant in Lowell for sale, you should buy it.' I don't know where Lowell was at that time. For six years, it was just working. At 32, I take over Coney Island in Lowell. After a couple of years, I moved to Lowell."

Sell much Greek cuisine here in Lowell?

"I used to serve traditional Greek dishes like pastichio (Greek lasagna) and moussaka (eggplant casserole) with bechamel (white sauce) when I first opened, but it didn't move like it should. Now we just do American kitchen. We have a Greek omelette with a gyro, feta cheese and tomato inside."

Was you father a restauranteur?

"My dad was a butcher. He taught me how to clean up the cow."

You mean cut meat?

"Cut meat, yes."

George, what is the secret of your success?

"We have a nice atmosphere and good food. We keep the place clean the best we can. Customers want to see the owner. And I agree with them. That's why I'm here 12 hours – use to be 16 hours.

Your days off?

"Christmas; I work seven days. I do go to Greece most summers for four to six weeks."

Is Labor Day, with Lowell's big parade, one of your best days?

"Not so good. Lot of people in restaurant, but they eat and then sit and wait for the parade – no turnover."

Is breakfast your best crowd?

"Weekends, yes. My son Johnny finished the culinary school in Chicago for kitchen management and hospitality. He gives me some new ideas. We try to fix the menu a little bit better. Johnny was here bussing tables when he was 12."

The same age his father began learning the trade.

"Same age, yes."

* * *

Kouimanis used to catch catnaps underneath a blanket and the stars behind his Lowell restaurant between "shifts" during those first two years before he moved from Merrillville. It was common for a Lowell police officer to give him a nudge and say, "George, it's time to open up."

And maybe, while under the spell of Morpheus, the Greek god of dreams and sleep, Kouimanis briefly returned to the foothills of Pelinneon Mountain and the olive groves and cherry trees of Amades. There is a beautiful beach nearby.

The stuff of which dreams are made.

Mary and Wally Kasprzycki Jr. *(Nov. 2009)*

"I know an Irishman who married a Ukranian girl and he was crazy about her mother's cooking. When he later learned the truth about czarnina, though, the shock was severe. He even went to his priest to ask if he had done something wrong. The priest told him that as long as the blood was from a duck and not a Protestant, it was OK."
– Mike Royko

Consonants remain a constant when it comes to Polish surnames. Remember boxer Bobby Czyz? Italian names are more vowel voluminous. Lido "Lee" Iacocca and Joey "Doves" Aiuppa come to mind.

Wally Kasprzycki Jr., 52, and his mother, Mary Kasprzycki, own the Cavalier Inn in North Hammond. The Kasprzycki family has operated The Cav, as regulars call it, since 1955.

Wally and his wife, Nora, have two sons who attend Bishop Noll Institute. Wally graduated from Noll ('75), where he was a three-sport standout. Kasprzycki, a tight end/defensive end, was named to the prestigious Parade magazine All-America football team and played tight end for Northwestern University. He earned a degree in economics from NU and, in 1989, served as defensive coordinator on Noll's Class 3A state-championship football team.

Mary is a widow; she and Wally live in Hammond.

The Cav is a vintage neighborhood bar-restaurant. Polish-made hand-carved wooden eagles are displayed with ethnic pride. The juke box offers everything from Sinatra to The Temptations – and plenty of Polkas.

* * *

"My dad started in the business in 1949," Wally began. "That establishment was located in Indiana Harbor – 3800 Main Street. I'm told it was close to Main Sporting Goods, possibly even the same building. In 1955, Mom and Dad opened the original Cavalier Inn on Johnson (Avenue in North Hammond). They built this place in '63 (at 735 Gostlin St.)."

Added Mary: "We are very fortunate, we have good customers. They might not come back for a while, but they always come back.

"My husband and I worked liked workhorses, you know. He was 36 when we got married, I was 21. He was 92 when he died; he lived a good life."

Wally said, "Dad passed away two years ago on Nov 16."

Mary, ahem, my readers will want to know your age without having to do the math.

"I'm 76."

Added Wally: "You are a brave man; Mom must like you. I wouldn't have asked her that."

Memories of Europe?

"I was a child in the work camps just after World War II. We were hungry many days. The Jewish girls would give us sausage. I will never forget what they did for us. I came to the United States in 1951."

Added Wally: "My dad sponsored more than 500 Polish immigrants. He found all them jobs. Every once in a while one of their children will come in here, and say, 'Your dad sponsored my dad.'"

This area, especially North Hammond, is the epitome of the Great Melting Pot.

"You got it. We have all makes and models around here," Wally said. "St. Caz (Casimir Catholic Church in North Hammond) was the Polish church. St John the Baptist (in Whiting) was the Slovak church. Further to the east, just north of the Hoosier Theatre, was St. Al's, I think that was Croatian."

Do you speak Polish?

"Oh, yeah," Wally said. "Growing up with immigrant parents, Polish was my first language. We're lucky, we still have a lot of Polish customers and friends. Polish is spoken here daily."

Wally, tell me about the culinary part of The Cav.

"This place was designed as a bar with a hall. People could rent out the hall; we'd have fish fries. Over time, it evolved into a restaurant with a bar."

Added Mary: "From the beginning, we always had good fish," Mary said. "Always fresh lake perch, hand breaded."

Mary, I interviewed a lady down along the Kankakee River for this column by the name of Venus Lukes. The Cavalier Inn is Lukes Restaurant

North.

"I used to go to a Lukes Bakery in Chicago years ago. They had a good business. I loved their cake."

I believe that bakery ended up in a place called Sumava Resorts.

Added Wally: "Mom, my cousin and a little Polish lady down the street, still hand prepare everything. Two nights a week they stay up to the wee hours making pierogi. We can never stockpile enough because as fast as we make them, people eat them."

Wally, what's your favorite filling?

"I like kraut pierogi the best, but that's easily the least popular with the clientele; potato is the best seller. Around Easter, everyone wants cheese pierogi. My Italian buddy Al Gandolfi will come in here and order a dozen cheese pierogi and have me put tomato sauce over it. Al calls it Polish ravioli.

"Our traditional favorites like golabki (stuffed cabbage) are all Mom's homemade recipes. The kapusta (sauerkraut) is homemade. We have no trucks delivering boxes. We shop at every grocery store in Hammond for our ingredients. We don't make our sausage; but we get it from a local butcher, Misch, in Calumet City, Ill. Even our soups are still homemade everyday."

Duck blood soup?

"We import the blood – we don't kill the ducks. We sell out of czernina every week. Most people take it home in half gallons."

Polish beer?

"We carry Okocim. There are various Polish beers, but due to laws in Indiana, it's tough to get right now. If you cross the state line, you could probably have about five choices."

Added Mary: "My husband used to tell customers if they drank enough Polish beer they would end up speaking Polish."

Really.

"I've served quite a few newspaper writers through the years."

Guys with surnames like Sweeney, Jefferson, Garcia and Schmidt who, by closing time, enunciated perfect Polish, no doubt.

"There's not many places like this left," Wally said. "Everything is getting very corporate – franchised."

* * *

With my work complete and taste buds ready to explode, I ordered the Polish Platter for $16. When in Rome, right?

I figured Wally was eating with me when the waitress brought two heaping plates of kielbasa – smoked and fresh – potato pancakes, mashed potatoes, green beans, sauerkraut, three or four kinds of pierogi and a stuffed cabbage. Not to mention the rye bread, kidney bean salad, cottage cheese and cole slaw that preceded it. Amazingly, it was a single order. And it was real food, done right.

As a half-starved girl in post-war Europe, Mary Kasprzycki was shown kindness by those who were nearly annihilated. She has never forgotten that and has fed folks sausage for six decades.

No one leaves The Cav hungry.

Mike Salinas *(Apr. 2009)*

"Labor is prior to, and independent of, capital. Capital is only the fruit of labor, and could never have existed if labor had not first existed. Labor is the superior of capital and deserves much the higher consideration."

– Abraham Lincoln

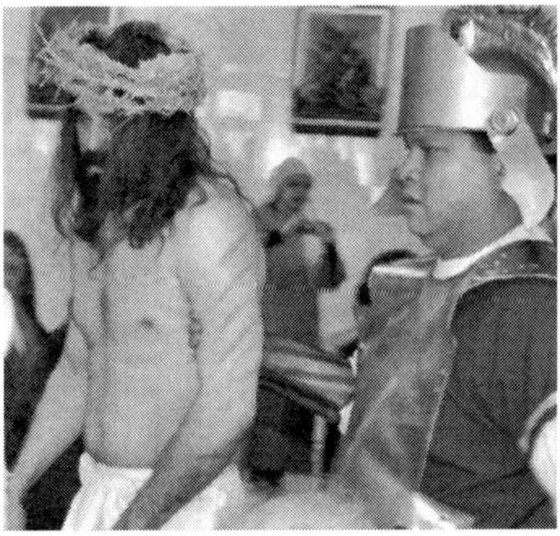

It was still March when I interviewed Mike Salinas at Our Lady of Guadalupe Catholic Church in East Chicago.

Sixteen days later, Salinas, 54, had a cross to bear. Good Friday marked the 29th consecutive year Salinas has portrayed Jesus Christ.

He was born Miguel Salinas in Mexico. In 1965, at the age of 10, his family moved to Fresno, Calif. By the time he was 14, Salinas was working full time alongside his brothers, sisters, mother and father in the San Joaquin Valley.

Today, he lives in Hobart with Marissa, his wife of 32 years. They have raised three children.

* * *

Mike, let's start with California.

"We worked from 6 in the morning until 6 in the evening," he said. "At that time, we probably make about $1.60 in an hour. We picked peaches, plums, grapes – you name it."

Benefits?

"Nothing. They would not provide water for us to drink. We were very poor, you know. We didn't have anything – no unemployment, no nothing. That's why we worked so hard."

What job did you dislike the most?

"Cleaning up the cotton; some of the fields were a mile or two long."

Education?

"I went to the fifth grade, but only for a few months each winter. In summer, I worked to help my family make money. The hardest part was going to school and not knowing how to speak English. Everybody makes fun of you. That's why a lot of kids don't want to go to school; it's embarrassing."

Who made fun of you, the white boys?

"No, I went to school with American-born Hispanic kids."

You also received a little schooling from the late, great labor leader Cesar Chavez.

"Yes, he was one of the best men around. When Chavez and his people came, they helped us a lot. They demanded portable bathrooms in the fields for us. Thanks to God for these men, we got a little more, you know?

"When we stood on picket lines near the fields, Chavez was there with us. Sometimes we got arrested and taken to jail. They would say we were trespassing."

Women and children, too?

"Yes, my mother she went to jail with her six children, but the union people would bail us out. Every day was like that."

Was a family member the connection between California and Indiana?

"Yes, my oldest brother got a job with Local 41 out of Hammond. When I moved to East Chicago in 1974, I got a job with the Laborers' Union, too. I returned to California one time and got married.

"As a boy, I had a green card while living in California; I became a U.S. citizen 25 years ago in Indiana."

What is the job description of a laborer?

"We do everything. We clean out flumes of casters, bust out concrete at basic oxygen furnaces. We uses lances and torches, too. Metal going to the scrap yard is considered laborer's work.

"Most of the time, I work at ISG or Inland (ArcelorMittal – Indiana Harbor Works). But right now, it's real slow; they don't have anything. All the contractors are out right now because the mills have had to lay off some of their own people."

Do you work at US Steel?

"U.S. Steel is Local 81 territory; they're out of Valparaiso. I'm a general foreman, so I can go out there with people, but they have to be from 81."

General foreman? Have you become a salaried employee?

"No, I like to be paid by the hour. I'm still a member of the union."

How long have you been a member of Our Lady of Guadalupe?

"For 30 years. When I was 25, the priest was leaving for Peru to do some missionary work. Before he left, he asked if I wanted to portray Jesus for the living Stations of the Cross. I said, 'I don't think so.' It was hard for me, you know?

"The priest said, 'Think about it for two weeks.' In two weeks, I said, 'OK, I'm going to do it.' Since then, I have continued doing it. Last year, there was a big crowd. We walk like two miles. Sometimes it is raining. One time, it was like 10 or 12 below zero and snowing. Last year, it was cold."

Did you wear a coat?

"No, I wear a white robe and sandals. I take the sandals off when they hang me up in the parking lot."

Corona de Jesus?

"Yes, I got the crown of thorns from the Holy Land."

You've been to Israel?

"About 10 years ago; I've been to the Vatican, too. I love Italy; I'd like to move there."

I've never witnessed one of these Living Stations of the Cross re-enactments. Are other characters involved?

"We have it all when we start walking on Deodar Street. Mary, the mother of God; Simon, the one who helped Jesus with the cross; Veronica, Barabbas, the thief on the cross. In Spanish, I say the seven different things Jesus said while being crucified."

Phrases such as, "Father forgive them, for they know not what they do" and "I thirst"?

"Yes."

How long will you continue to do this thing?

"I was going to retire for about 10 or 12 years, but nobody else wants to do it. As long as the Lord keeps giving me my health, I will continue. The Lord wants me to do it. Whatever good I have done was because of God. Jeff, most of the guys I work with don't know the story of my life."

My brother, that could change Easter Sunday.

* * *

As a laborer in East Chicago, Salinas has been paid a decent wage when finding himself on the working end of a 12-foot burn bar or a 90-pound buster.

As a young man in California, he thirsted on his hands and knees while those in power washed their hands of it. He was unjustly jailed. Yet, he is one of the most humble human beings I've ever met.

Forgiving, too.

Gerrie Maxwell *(Mar. 2007)*

"Storytelling... The oldest form of education."
– Terry Tempest Williams

She was born Geraldine Clancy in Limerick, Ireland, a cobblestone's throw from the River Shannon. Today, Gerrie Maxwell lives in Lowell, a half mile east of State Line Road. Art and Gerrie Maxwell were wed the year Neil Armstrong did a little moon walkin', and the Miracle Mets had Cub fans squawkin'.

Gerrie works at Jo-Ann Fabrics in Schererville a couple of days a week at the cutting counter and in the quilting department. She is an avid reader. And yes, Gerrie has beautiful red hair.

* * *

You lived the first 12 years of your life in Ireland. What did people do on St. Patrick's Day on the Emerald Isle?

"Everybody was out in the fields digging up shamrocks," she said. "The bigger the shamrock you had, or the more lush it looked, the better an Irishman you were. St Patrick's Day was more about appreciating your Irish heritage."

The countryside looks enchantingly picturesque in books and postcards.

"It is. The east side is comprised of green fields and pastures. It's comparatively flat in regards to the west side which is rocky with high cliffs. It's blustery with a lot of gales; it rains ever 15 minutes. That's why it's so green."

I've heard it can be a hardscrabble way of life.

"Growing up in Ireland makes you very appreciative of what you have; it also makes you tough. We had no heat except for the open-hearth where mother cooked. When we got up in the morning she would place our clothes in front of the fireplace to warm them. We took a bath on Saturday night. We had to go out and get the water.

"My mother and I would walk to the farmer's house with three eggs; he would give her a bottle of milk for my lunch. He had cows. Everybody exchanged what they had. It was survival. A big treat was to get an apple or an orange. I would opt for the apple; it lasted longer. I had never seen nor heard of corn."

Cabbage was probably a more common vegetable.

"My mother would peel leaves of cabbage and place it between two pieces of bread; that was my lunch. In the morning, if the chickens hadn't laid any eggs, she would take a slice of bread, put it in a cup and pour hot water on it with a little bit of sugar; she called that American Goodie. For dinner I would get a boiled potato, two if I was lucky. On Sundays we had meat."

Corned beef?

"I never heard of corned beef until I came to America. We had boiling beef, somewhat similar to pot roast. I was anemic when I came to America. I had malnutrition.

"We did have socialized medicine over there, but no one ever saw a doctor. We were born at home and we died at home. For three days, they would hang a black wreath on the door. It was like an open house. Anyone could come in and see the casket. It was a party for three days."

They like their dark beer over there.

"I got Guinness stout for everything. Sore throats, aching gums when teething... When you were sick – you got stout. My Uncle Bat owned a pub. He lived above it."

Entertainment?

"We had no television; the radio would come on for one hour at night time. People would tell stories. They wove wonderful stories. They would embellish the stories, you know." (With smiling eyes, Gerrie leans toward me from across the kitchen table and whispers with a delightful brogue, "'Let me tell you this one. Let me tell you that one.'")

Education?

"Have you read Frank McCourt's novel, 'Angela's Ashes'? McCourt attended Christian Brothers. I attended Presentation Convent, across the street. You start school when you're 4 years old. It's called Babies. When I was in first grade, my younger sister was in Babies. I remember my mother telling me to peek in the window to see how she was doing. Parents were afraid of the teachers and nuns – they ran everything. I looked in on her. Blood covered her white blouse. She had fallen asleep; she was used to taking a nap. The nun meant to hit her hands with a ruler, they said, but hit her in the nose.

"We didn't receive report cards. You knew what you were supposed to know – you were beaten if you didn't. You had to knit a perfect pair of socks and sew a perfect patch to get into 6th grade. They expected you to speak the Irish (Gaelic) fluently by fifth grade."

What did your father do for a living?

"He drove a wool truck from Limerick to Belfast. He received an offer to move north to Belfast. Every Sunday the family would gather to debate whether he should move to Belfast or emigrate to the United States like his older sister. He decided on New York. That was 1957. My mother, sisters, and I came to the United States a year later, once he'd saved enough money.

"My mother sold the house and everything in it. She gave the key to someone. In the morning she locked the door. I knew when I went to school in the morning I'd never be in that school again. We were only allowed 26 pounds of luggage when we came over here – three bags. A car took us to the Shannon Airport where we boarded a Pan Am airplane with a propeller. Everybody threw up. The biggest disappointment I had was when the pilot circled the Statue of Liberty. I had seen a few movies in Ireland. At the beginning of some of these American films they would show a glorious woman. I thought she was the Statue of Liberty. I had this vision of... ."

You speak of Columbia Pictures' Torch Lady.

"I had never had American History, science, geography... I didn't know what they were talking about. All I knew was Irish history and geography. I knew how to sew and knit, and I knew the Gregorian chants by heart.

"I couldn't believe milk came in cartons. Vegetables came in cans! My two younger sisters fell right into New York. For me, it was a culture shock.

"After I got out of high school, I worked downtown for a year on 3rd Avenue, about a block away from the United Nations. I felt I needed to get away from New York and I figured LA was about as far as I could get. I met Art out there. When he decided to move back to his home in Chicago, I went with him. The Midwest was the first place where I felt comfortable. We married and settled in Illinois. We've been in Lowell since 1989.

"Jeff, I want to show you something. From the time I was 2 years old, my mother would re-sew this doll from a pair of my father's old socks. Every Christmas, she would cover it with a different pair of socks so it would look like a new doll. This was my Christmas present each year. It started out so very small.

"I've always wondered how my life would have turned out if my father would have decided to move to Belfast with all that was going onup there. He would be so proud if he were alive today. His dream has been fulfilled. All three of our children have graduated college. Like my father, I love Ireland. But this country has given me my life, my husband, my children."

* * *

I Googled the history of Columbia Pictures' logo after my interview with Gerrie. The Torch Lady has been modeled by several different women featuring various looks since the 1920's. The latest is a redhead. Her chin is up. Her head's held high. Words came to me... .

A colleen by the name of Clancy,
Her county 'twas green but not fancy;
She brought with her a doll,
And that was about all,
This brave lass by the name of Clancy

History Books

Ella Wietbrock *(Jan. 2006)*

"So if you're a walkin' down the street some time
And spot some hollow ancient eyes,
Please don't pass 'em by and stare
As if you didn't care. Say hello in there.
Hello."
– John Prine

When Ella Wietbrock was born, the average life expectancy was 47 years. Theodore – not Franklin – Roosevelt was the president of a country whose flag wore but 45 stars. When Ella was old enough to vote, she had a choice of either Coolidge, Davis, or La Follette. The previous election? No woman had a choice. But Susan B. Anthony had a say in that.

Wietbrock resides at Lowell Health Care Center now. Her eyes are pale blue. Her hands, a pair of threadbare silk gloves. Resting wearily upon the backs of those hands are thin violet veins which have tunneled well-traveled lifeblood. She is hard of hearing, but Ella Wietbrock has her wits about her.

Wietbrock's daughter, Marlene Adam, sat alongside us during our conversation.

* * *

Can you tell me about your childhood?

"After grandpa was gone, my dad's mother lived with us in a little apartment next to the house," she said. "After a while, my parents said there was no need for her to be cooking. So she had her meals with us, but she still had her own bedroom, living room, and kitchen just to the north of the house."

Did your parents come from Germany?

"No. My father, Frank Schmidt, was born in Chicago. He was a farmer. I can still understand German, but can't speak it very well anymore. Mother was born in, oh, what's the name of that place? I've been there; it's southwest of here. Kankakee!"

So was I, a few generations later. What a memory you have, Ella.

"People ask me, 'How do you remember all that stuff?', I say, 'Well, you just write it down in your brain.'

"I remember going to Minnesota when I was 5. I also remember going to church by horse and buggy on Christmas Eve. Mother warmed bricks in the oven to keep our feet warm while we rode to church. Didn't do much good on the way back."

Were you always a homemaker?

"I went to Chicago when I was 16. There was a lady who was expecting and needed help. They were a nice Jewish family. They paid me $10 per week. I was only getting $2 per week doing the same type of work around Lowell."

Siblings?

"I had two brothers; they're both deceased. Both my sisters are still living. Gertrude is 90; Mildred is 95. They both reside in Grant Park. They call us 'The Three Musketeers.' I also had one sister who only lived four hours."

Ella, I'm told you were born in rural Will County in Illinois, but moved to Lowell when Herman Wietbrock asked you to marry him. What did your husband do for a living?

"Herman worked as a jobber for Standard Oil. He passed away 33 years ago."

Did you attend the World's Fair in Chicago, back in, um, '37, I believe...

"1933. Yes, Clyde was just a baby; it was the only time my mother kept one of my kids."

First car?

"It was an Overland. I had a sister who died when she was four hours old."

Do you remember the Great Depression?

"You can say that again. We'd tell the kids, 'You can't have this or that because there isn't enough money.' Maybe that was good. Today, a lot of children in this country ask for the world – and get it. We were happy to have something to eat. But we lived through it.

"The Depression was something else, though. You'd butcher a pig, and have the meat with potatoes and vegetables the one day, and you'd eat the juice and the soup from it the next. I haven't seen a piece of meat since I've been here."

Added Marlene: "Now, Mom, yes you have, they just grind it up because you don't have strength to cut it."

"We had a freezer down at the Royal Blue Store here in Lowell when the kids were little. I'd pluck 50 or 60 chickens, pull the innards out, cut them up, and package them."

Added Marlene: "I remember when there was half a hog laying in our basement. Mom butchered the hog herself, then made soap from the fat. She'd add a little cologne, so it would smell good. She did all the sewing, baking, and cleaning. She was quite a worker and was the – "

"Who's telling this story, Marlene? I've got every original tooth in my head since I was a child except for one, and that one was replaced when I was 17. That's a long time. When they fixed a tooth back then, they fixed it!"

Democrat or Republican?

"Depends on the person running for office. I had a sister who was born two-and-half years after I was. She only lived for four hours. I remember when we took her to the cemetery. A couple of months or so later, my dad took me to town. He said, 'We have to get a stone for your little sister.' I was only about 3 years old then."

Church affiliation?

"I've been a Lutheran all my life. Used to attend the old church down on the corner by Burnham Street. Herman and I waited to get married; we didn't want to start out with a lot of debt. I've worked hard all my life. But I usually didn't get paid. What is, is; no matter what you do."

"Tell Jeff about your headstone, Mom."

"When they made me and Herman's gravestones they got the birth dates correct, but the first two digits on my departure date are of the wrong century! They're going to have to change that, I suppose. Won't matter much to me; I'll be dead. And Marlene, don't you kids spend a bunch money on a casket. I'll turn over in my.. ."

Ahem. You raised three children; was Marlene you're only daughter?

"Clyde was the oldest, then Marlene, and then Ron. There were so many boys on both sides of the family. I remember Herman running up to me; I was just coming to from the anesthesia, 'We have a daughter! We have a daughter!' That was the day you were born, Marlene."

I've heard you were quite a pinochle player in your day. Which do you prefer, double or single deck?

"Either one. Here, they play a lot of bingo. I've grown tired of it. I won a prize once; I thought it was tooth paste. It was dental adhesive. I've got all of my teeth, you know."

* * *

God willing, on Jan. 20, 2010 they'll place 106 candles on Wietbrock's cake. She had a sister who was on this earth for four hours. Ella's never forgotten. There's something poetic about all that.

While gathering up my stuff to leave, Ella had more visitors.

"Mom, look who's stopped by to visit you. It's your nephew Brian and Reverend Phulghoeft."

"Hello, Aunt Ella."

"Hello, Ella."

Ancient blue eyes liven as Wietbrock looks up from her wheel chair... .

"Why, hello."

Charlie Smith *(Feb. 2006)*

"Age is a case of mind over matter. If you don't mind, it don't matter."

– Leroy "Satchel" Paige

I picked up my buddy Greg Marshall in Merrillville. We were off to visit his maternal grandfather, Charlie Smith. Mr. Smith lives in an apartment complex no more than a beach ball's toss from Lake Michigan in Miller.

He has been a widower several times. He has been married to his wife Comella since 1994.

On Friday, someone will have the daunting task of fitting 103 candles on Charlie Smith's cake.

Greg told me that Charlie still drove while past age of 100 and didn't wear glasses until recently. Charlie suffered a stroke several months ago which slowed him down a bit. Remember, he's 102.

The 'two' must have confused him somewhat.

When Comella admonished her husband regarding some foible a while back, an exasperated Charlie muttered, "You'd think a man who has lived 200 years could do whatever he wanted!"

* * *

I'm going to sit real close to you, Mr. Smith. I worked in the steel mill most of my life with your grandson. I don't hear so well.

"I have that trouble, too."

You worked on trains?

"Oh, yeah. I welded on steam engines for Combustion Engineering over on Railroad Avenue in East Chicago. They wanted to ship me to Canada when America went diesel. When diesel come in, I retired."

Were you born in Northwest Indiana?

"I was born in Mississippi, March 9, 1904. I moved up here back in '26. I can't forget Mississippi. My daddy, he was a farmer."

Probably used mules in the fields, huh?

"I plowed with Ol' Beck. Gee, Beck! Haw, Beck! Whoa, Beck! Ol' Beck smart. She do whatever I say."

Were you close to the Delta?

"Yeah, near Vicksburg. People get they whiskey in Arkansas. The river cut right down into Louisiana. My people come from Bolton. That was the closest town from the farm. One man owned the whole county. That's the way they was down there. My uncle, he gin the cotton. He used to let me run that thing – I liked that."

What about the boll weevil?

"I remember a year when that boll weevil ate up everthin'. Farmers suffered that year. Locusts eat the corn, too. They get in the cornfield and go right through it! Boll weevil, he get in that cotton patch and knock them blooms off."

Do you remember what kind of pay you received for working in the cotton fields?

"Dollar a hundred. If you could pick a hundred pounds you get a dollar. Never could pick two hundred pound. I tried."

Did you receive much public education?

"I went to the fourth grade."

What do you remember about your mother?

"She was a church lady. 'Love God, son, and he'll give you 100 years. If you mind your own business, take care of yourself, the Lord will let you live!' I did what I was told. I give my mother credit. She taught me how to live."

What religious denomination was your family?

"Church of God – the crown and pillar of the truth! My daddy was a 33 mason, you know. Thirty-three, high as they go. But when he got broke and hungry? He become a Baptist preacher!"

(*The old-timer belly-laughs with a slap of his lap.*)

Charlie, a man's gotta do what a man's gotta do. Let's see, you were already up here during the Great Depression.

"Mr. Roosevelt, he was all right. He said, 'Give a man some money.' I helped build Highway 20 for $27.50 a month – WPA. Started over there in Hammond and worked all the way to Michigan City.

"I had a boss from Hammond named H.P. Downey. Work was scarce. There was some guys who said they was gonna run us out of this county. This foreman of mine, he wouldn't hire those men, you know."

He liked you.

"Oh, yeah. I liked him, too – because I got my money! Mr. Downey wasn't afraid of nobody. He say, 'Boys, all of you that got a gun, bring it tomorrow!' They wasn't gonna run H.P. Downey nowhere. I didn't bring no gun, though."

Were you involved in World War II?

"Oh, yeah. I helped make shells and tanks. I got off the train in Mississippi and there was all these people hollerin' and shootin' guns. I didn't know it was peace they was celebratin'. There was a boy who had a shoeshine, he say, 'The war is over!'"

First car?

"A secondhand T–Model Ford. Paid $35 for it."

What do you attribute to your good health? Probably never smoked.

"I smoked, chewed, and dipped snuff most of my life. I'd get into my mother's snuff bottle when I was a boy. The ballplayers all chewed Red Man. It started givin' them cancer. That broke me from chewin' tobacco."

Were you a baseball player?

"When I was young, that's all I knowed to do, baseball. I was a left-handed pitcher, a flame thrower, but it was my curve ball they couldn't hit."

What team do you root for? The Sox?

"The Dodgers. They whup the Yanks back in '55. Henry Aaron played for the Braves. He broke Babe Ruth's record."

* * *

Thelma Smith Marshall stepped into the conservation... .

"Jeff, I would like to say that my father was stern but kind. He raised eight of us children on a meager income. We were never hungry and we always had proper clothing. He saw to it that we all finished school. He was a wonderful father. He was always there."

* * *

Before I took Charlie's photograph, his son-in-law, the Rev. Marshall, retied his tie for him. After the photo, the good reverend protected Charlie's suit with a sheet so he can cut the old fella's hair.

"This man is not only my barber, he's my pastor," Charlie said. 'Where He Leads I'll Follow' is my favorite hymn."

Pointing to Greg: "This is my grandson – he can SING!"

It's been an absolute pleasure, Mr. Smith. I learned a lot.

"That big ol' steam engine sittin' on 4th Avenue – my work is in that."

* * *

Charlie Smith, a man who has left quite a legacy from the cotton fields of Mississippi to the concrete of Highway 20 by the Big Lake.

Prof. James B. Lane

"Mommy's alright, Daddy's alright,
They just seem a little weird
Surrender, surrender
But don't give yourself away"
–Cheap Trick

Just typing his official title, James B. Lane professor emeritus of history, Indiana University Northwest, Gary uses up a good portion of my allotted word count. But when Lane e-mails me, he always signs off, "Cheers, Jimbo."

I like that.

Lane, 67, is from Easton, Pa. He graduated from Bucknell University in Lewisburg, Pa., in 1964 – the year the Civil Rights Act became law. He earned his master's degree from the University of Hawaii and his Ph.D. at the University of Maryland in 1970.

Lane and his wife, Toni, have raised two sons both of whom graduated from Portage High School and Indiana University in Bloomington.

Although retired since 2007, Lane continues to serve as a co-director of the Calumet Regional Archives which are preserved at IUN's library. He is still the editor of Steel Shavings magazine and has recently published Volume 40: "Out to Pasture, but Still Kickin': A Retirement Journal, 2007-2008."

* * *

You grew up in suburban Philadelphia during the '50s, attended college during the '60s, then taught in Northwest Indiana throughout the '70s, '80s, 90s and well into the 21st Century. Has it been a long, strange trip?

"My parents were bourgeois," he said. "Dad was a corporation man who commuted to Philly by train. He sort of epitomized that Eisenhower era.

"When I graduated from the University of Maryland, the campus was under martial law because of riots that took place along U.S.1 in association with (President Richard) Nixon going into Cambodia. It was a tense time."

What about IUN in 1970?

"There were protests going on at this campus, too. At the time, all the history faculty were young and pretty radical or at least left of center. Anti-war, certainly. This was a great place to teach."

The melting pot of Northwest Indiana.

"When I moved here, I found this region to be the most blue-collar area I'd ever been in. I loved the cultural diversity – eating pierogi with the Slovaks on 11th Avenue and Harrison Street.

"Most of my students' parents or least grandparents were immigrants. Their families' stories are that of coming to Northwest Indiana, looking for a job, adjusting, maybe starting nationality clubs, going bowling. That's the kind of stuff I like to catch in Steel Shavings.

"Jeff, I have your philosophy. I want to write history from the bottom up. I try to find out about people who aren't normally in history books – everyday people. Talking about politics, economics and war is important, but I'm a social historian first and foremost."

You were hired to teach urban history.

"Yes. Right away, I wanted to make Gary a dimension of the class, especially, after I learned how rich and interesting Gary's history was."

Your history courses basically covered 20th-century America.

"Yes, I tended to take what some people call an American studies approach; I'd study a period in all its dimensions. I actually taught a course on the 1980s shortly before I retired."

How did that one go?

"Well, I thought I was pretty fair to old 'Dutch' Reagan. For a long time, I thought I couldn't be. Reagan was a good ceremonial president."

Elaborate.

"He could give a speech."

Yeah, go on.

"He could dedicate a ship."

Name some great presidents.

"Abraham Lincoln and FDR. The more I read about Lincoln, the more impressed I am by him. Franklin Roosevelt had a lot of weaknesses, but he basically saved the country during the Depression and then during World War II."

Other people you've admired?

"Martin Luther King, Cesar Chavez and women who fought for

social justice."

Authors?

"Studs Terkel is one of my heroes, but Jean Shepherd is my favorite writer. He coined the phrase 'shards and midden heaps.' From the shards and midden heaps of the past, you can find nuggets that will tell you what life was really like. Shepherd's books do that. And that's what I want my magazines to do."

Let's talk more about Steel Shavings.

"It was actually (fellow IUN professor) Ron Cohen who came up with the idea of publishing student articles dealing with local family history and putting them into a magazine. He and I did about two or three issues together; then, he went on to other things. I've kept it up ever since. I consider Steel Shavings the best thing I've done as a historian."

Any recurring topics that appear in more than one volume of Steel Shavings?

"Ethnicity, cultural diversity, race and labor history."

Volume 40 is a journal.

"Yes, it's not the first issue of Steel Shavings to appear in journal form. I'm calling it my retirement journal. It has a lot of local history. I'll comment on stories that are in the news or some of the research or book reviews that I have done. I'm in touch with several former students and some of my e-mail correspondents – you're in Volume 40."

Really? Jimbo, I wanna buy five copies for my mother.

"Jeff, if more funds were available, I'd do a special issue of Shavings on your Salt column; it represents the people of Northwest Indiana as well as anything out there. That's why we've stored all them here at the Archives.

"Another feature I've added is what I call a Calumet Region Master Names Index for the first 40 volumes on my Steel Shavings site that is linked to the Calumet Regional Archives website."

What's on the cover of "Out to Pasture but Still Kickin' '?"

A photo of me in front of Hawthorn Hall the day I retired."

Surely a somber shot of you shuffling through IUN's parking lot for the last time with slumped shoulders, while dragging an ancient attache case.

"Actually, I'm standing in front of a microphone along with my son's band Voodoo Chili while covering Cheap Trick's 'Surrender.' And I'm really bringing it. We jammed for hours. Earlier that day, IUN had a retirement ceremony for me. They gave me a clock, of all things."

* * *

James Lane was born and raised nearer the part of Pennsylvania known for making bars of chocolate than bars of steel. But he came to this region, rolled up his sleeves, and has recorded our stories for nearly four decades.

And he did it by sifting from the bottom of the midden heap up.

Gloria Dosen *(Jan. 2010)*

"The man who dies rich dies disgraced."
– Andrew Carnegie

Like an Iditarod contestant, I recently mushed my Ford Fusion through a foot of lake-effect snow and the 38 stop lights along Indianapolis Boulevard between Indiana 2 in Lowell and Kosciuszko Park in East Chicago.

Gloria Dosen, 80, has lived on Olcott Avenue, a snowball's throw from the park, since 1951. She was married to her husband, Edward, for 50 years before his passing. They graduated from Whiting High School in 1947. The couple raised two children who graduated from Bishop Noll Institute in Hammond.

I was searching for old photographs of the Inland Steel Christmas tree when I first met Dosen about 10 years ago at the East Chicago Public Library on Columbus Drive. She is quite the history buff and presided over what is known as the library's East Chicago Room. Dosen is retired, but worked at the library for 40 years. Inland Steel Co. donated the land for a dollar.

She stays active by helping run a food pantry at St. Stanislaus Catholic Church in East Chicago, where she's a member. Dosen is one of the most pleasant people I've ever met. And she's a diehard Chicago White Sox fan to boot.

* * *

"Isn't living in the Midwest great?" Dosen began. "We have all four seasons."

You're telling me. Gloria, you're also a member of the Whiting Historical Society. Tell me about Whiting during the 1930s and '40s.

"Simply walking through the streets of Whiting and experiencing the friendliness of the people was so nice. I have fond memories of going to the Whiting Beach to swim. And, oh, the Hoosier Theatre and Capitol Theatre.

"On a Saturday, for a quarter, you could watch a feature-length film, a Western, a serial, a comedy and coming attractions. The Hoosier is still there. The White Castle at Indianapolis Boulevard and 119th Street was one of the first around here."

Did your family attend church in Whiting?

"Yes, we belonged to St. John the Baptist Catholic Church. My mother still lives in Whiting with my sister; mother is 102.

You're the daughter of a steel worker.

"Yes, yes, yes. My dad, Mike Lengyel, started at Inland Steel when he was 16. His first job was shoveling coal into the steam engines. He ended up driving the last steam engine at Inland.

"I remember Dad taking us to see the Inland Steel Christmas tree. Then, when my husband worked at Inland, it was his job as a member of the Field Forces Department, to help erect the framework for the tree."

It was actually many trees made to look like one gigantic tree. My father used to take us to see it, too. Did your husband retire from the mill?

"No; when Edward had 13 1/2 years of seniority, he quit Inland to become an East Chicago Policeman. His father was quite upset with him."

Talk to me about living in East Chicago.

"We became members of Immaculate Conception Catholic Church down the street. It was Father Campagna's parish. This was an Italian neighborhood when we moved in here. Being Hungarian-Croatian, we were 'foreigners.'"

I.C. is a Baptist Church now.

"Yes, but it originally was made from the discarded bricks when it was decided to repave Indianapolis Boulevard. At the time, the Italian-Americans were using a funeral parlor in the Harbor for a church.

"You see, East Chicago was divided by the canal; there were two sides – Harbor and East Chicago. There were Catholic churches for the Irish, Slovaks, Hungarians, Romanians and the Hispanics. We had Jewish synagogues and Baptist churches as well.

"When we first moved here, our newspaper boy, Ray Castillo, lived down the street. The Castillos were the first Mexican-American family to reside on this side of town. Today, Ray lives directly across the street from me. John and Joe Flores also delivered my newspapers. They became principal and superintendent of the schools."

My buddy, Joe Gutierrez, grew up a few blocks from here.

"I know Joe; his family lived on 147th (Street) and Olcott.

Joe's written a book about his childhood called, 'The Neighborhood." It's great – full of nostalgic and ethnic tales of Italian shoemakers and Chinese laundries.

"Yes, yes, yes. Does he mention the chicken store on 147th ?"

Something tells me you're not talking about a KFC or Popeye's.

"The chicken store was on the 4700 block. You'd pick out your chicken, and the chicken man would chop off the chicken's head for you, unless you wanted to take it home live and do it yourself."

Tell me more about your city.

"Jeff, the history of East Chicago is phenomenal. That's why I enjoyed working in the East Chicago Room, which is the history room.

"Because of working at the library, I've met so many people of all ancestries. We had 52 different ethnic groups here in East Chicago at one time, yet, we're all so close. We can all get along; we just need to accept one another as we are.

"We also need to keep the children informed. Most of them have no idea how this city started or about the people who came here to work in the mills. Today's children don't read enough; that's too bad; the great thing about the library is, it's free – unless you lose a book."

What about losing old buildings?

"Once they're gone; they're gone forever."

For instance?

"I'm on the Carnegie Arts Board. They wanted to tear down the Carnegie Library in the Harbor. That was ridiculous. We're the only city in Indiana that has two Carnegie libraries."

I've been to the one on Chicago Avenue, where's the other one?

"It's at 3601 Grand Blvd. We're making it into an art center. First, we got it on the state historical registry. Then, we got it on the national registry. Once we did that, they couldn't tear it down.

"I feel real bad I couldn't help save the First National Bank building; I didn't have enough clout. The marble, the carvings on the walls... ."

You're still asked to solve family mysteries from the long ago.

"Yes, yes, yes. I get calls quite often. Just the other day, I was asked to look over a bunch of photos. I recognized at least one person in every photograph. I don't know why I can remember so well; maybe it's because I take gingko (biloba)."

You love the north end of Lake County.

"Jeff, I've walked the Great Wall of China; I've been to England, Scotland, France, Canada and Mexico. But there's no place like home. Neighborhoods change, but there are still good people here in East Chicago.

"I walk three miles a day. Walking is good; it's a way to get to know your neighbors. I have good neighbors; they look out for me.

"My son and daughter know they'll never get me out of here. I want it this way. I'll stay here 'til they wheel me away."

* * *

Gloria Dosen is a living history book. While riding in the family automobile as a 8-year-old girl, she witnessed picketers at Republic Steel on Chicago's East Side running from police gunfire in 1937. Ten unionists were killed.

Today, Gloria Dosen is on the committee of the Northwest Steel Heritage Project that hopes to build a steel museum in the region.

Beth Bassett *(Aug. 2010)*

"We've uncovered some embarrassing ancestors in the not-so-distant past. Some horse thieves, and some people killed on Saturday nights. One of my relatives, unfortunately, was even in the newspaper business."
– Pres. Jimmy Carter

Beth Bassett entered this world in 1957, 21 years after the birth of her oldest sibling – same parents. She grew up on a 60-acre farm in Morocco, but has lived in Brook for the past 26 years.

Bassett, 52, has never married. She was a classmate of mine at North Newton High School. We hadn't seen each other for almost 35 years until last winter; she was giving a presentation to the Newton County Historical Society in Morocco.

Beth enjoys gardening and listens to outlaw country and classic vinyl.

* * *

We both ended up working for newspapers. Who woulda thunk it?

"I've been with AgriNews for 17 years," she said. "It's a family-owned publication based out of Illinois. There's an Indiana and an Illinois edition of AgriNews. I sell advertising."

Life right after high school?

"I lived in Indianapolis for five years and attended Professional Careers Institute there; I earned a degree in medical office management. I stayed with that career for those five years. Then, Dad became ill; I returned home in '81.

"Donna LaCosse was the editor of the Morocco Courier at the time; she knew I was back in town and offered me a job selling advertising. I eventually became the sales manager at the Rensselaer Republican, a daily newspaper."

You were a Democrat working for the "Republican."

"That's right. I worked for them about 13 years. There was a lot of unrest in '93; they were cutting back to the basics, people were being let go. I was very fortunate to be offered a job with AgriNews.

"The next year, two of the other folks who worked at the Republican called me up and wanted to know if I'd be interested in starting a publication of our own. So, in '94, we launched The Guide, which was basically a free weekly publication that circulated to almost 35,000 in the area. We had that for five years. We ended up selling The Guide to the Rensselaer Republican. I work out of my home for AgriNews."

Let's back up a little. Tell me about your family.

"I have two sisters; my brother passed away of mesothelioma. He worked in Crown Point, mainly with asbestos brake pads for tractor-trailers. He was 36 when he died and left two young children behind. But they're doing well, and now have children of their own."

Besides farming 60 acres, what did your father do for a living?

"Several things. He worked at the Gaff Ranch, which was a cattle ranch near Morocco. Then, he went to work at Newton County Stone Quarry."

The quarry in Kentland on Indiana 24?

"Yes, it was supposedly created by a meteorite hitting the earth. Instead of the walls being in the usual limestone formations, these are at an angle. So, in other words, something very heavy fell on that piece of ground and actually made the sides vertical to where they are north and south instead of east and west. That's an anomaly for the type of soil and rock that is there."

You traced your roots several years ago.

"Mom had always talked about her family history. The Zoboroskys, in 1857, emigrated from Prussia (Poland) to Ellis Island on The Dr. Barth.

"Then they took the Monon Railroad all the way to Remington. They ended up settling in Newton County. My great-great-great-grandfather, Joe Zoborosky, was 92 when he sailed across the ocean. He's buried in North Star Cemetery near Mt. Ayr; he lived to be 108. One of his sons, Martin, was shot in the knee with a mini-ball and bled to death at the battle of Iuka (Miss.) during the Civil War."

Local history?

"While researching the Bassett side of the family at the Resource

Center in Kentland, I just kind of got attached to the place; that's when I became interested in local history.

"The president of the NCHS, Janet Miller, found out I had a newspaper background; she asked me if I'd put together a newsletter. 'The Newcomer' has been around for 10 years now."

So-called because Newton County is Indiana's youngest county.

"Correct; in 2006, the NCHS opened a facility in Kentland that is air-conditioned and air-controlled to store artifacts. It's a beautiful site."

The book you're helping create?

"It's entitled, 'Roselawn, Thayer and Shelby: The First 100 Years (1882-1982).' I'm doing the layout and design.

"Jeff, the articles in this book are just amazing. There's information on the dredging of the (Kankakee) river, the first railroads, family histories... . We used a lot of Lowell historian Richard Schmal's articles. It's wonderfully done."

How big is this tome?

"Almost 800 pages; the picture gallery itself is 20 or 30 pages – the index is 75 pages. It's priced at $50, and we hope to have it available to the public by Sept. 1."

Can't wait.

"I have a question for you, Jeff."

Sorry, I'm the question asker.

"Why do you think it's important to preserve the histories and write the stories of everyday people? Why do we do what we do? Do you really think that someday, somebody is going to give a damn?"

Beth, the folks I interview fascinate me. They don't usually get into the newspaper, with the exception of their obituaries, maybe. Yet, I learn so much from every one of them.

"Jeff, I'm hoping that ours isn't the last generation that cares about things like that. And I hope the preservation of old things continues after we're gone."

* * *

Beth Bassett is an incredible worker who volunteers countless hours with the NCHS. She's as good-hearted as they come. We keep in touch several times a week now, but never via cell phone.

We write.

Richard Schmal *(Dec. 2006)*

"...I am to represent, therefore, those men and women, venerable in age, a few of whom yet remain among us..."
-Rev. Timothy H. Ball, 1889

Today, Lowell youngsters might Roller Blade past places of business like Burger King or Family Video. But when Richard Schmal, 93, was a boy, he roller-skated past Lowell's blacksmith shops and livery stables.

At the southeast corner of Jefferson Avenue and Clark Street, a talking picture entitled "The Jazz Singer" appeared at Lowell's Grand Theatre. There were several hotels, one of which served chicken dinners for $1.

Schmal is Lowell's town historian and authored "Tales of the People and Places of the Olde Kankakee River" and "Memories of Lowell, Indiana." He also is a fellow columnist and a good friend of mine.

Daughter Mary was busy decorating the interior of her father's home for the yuletide season while Dick and I began our fireside chat.

* * *

You're of German ancestry, aren't you?

"Actually, my paternal grandmother was a Rasier," Schmal began. "She migrated from France; that's where I get my dark hair. Other than her, German. There's an old saying, 'All the Germans' horses drank out of the same tank at some time or another.'

"Our families were intermingled by marriage. That hill on Commercial Avenue just south of the grocery store was known as German Hill. Schreiber, Schmal, Schutz, Heiser... ."

What was life like in town when you were growing up?

"Lowellians had more public transportation in the 1920s than we have today. Twice a day, you could take a Model T bus to Crown Point and hop on the street car to Gary, which was quite a shopping Mecca.

Bought my wedding suit in Gary back in '47.

"Chicagoans would ride the 10 o'clock train from the city to The Schmal Hotel for our chicken dinner on Sundays. Huge platters of chicken, and mashed potatoes piled high in big bowls were served family style. We charged $1. The hotel had a huge dining room. Everybody sat at long tables. After they'd eaten, patrons would relax in the parlor or music room, then go back on the 4 o'clock train."

Continue, please.

"The city folk would take jugs of our sulphur water back with them. They claimed Lowell had the same water they were accustomed to paying big money for when they took the Monon (Railroad) down to French Lick. 'Drink Nature's Tonic: Lowell's Sulphur Water!' The old-timers would congregate out in the sunshine where Nellie Jayne's Cafe is located."

Spittin', whittlin', tellin' lies... .

"They'd spin interesting yarns. Some of them were Civil War veterans. The Grand Army of the Republic was here yet in the 1920s. That was the veteran's group from the Civil War. I can remember them in the parade."

Lowell's Labor Day parade?

"No, the Decoration Day Parade. Memorial Day was called Decoration Day back then; people would decorate the graves."

Education?

"I attended St. Edward's two-room school through eighth grade. The two rooms were up above the church in the same building where the health center is located. I went to high school where the middle school is now. Did you know there was a high school in Shelby for a couple of years?"

No. Who's the first President of the United States you remember, Benjamin Franklin?

"Franklin was never president. Harding, maybe.

Tell me about the old opera house. I remember it being Fry's Department Store when I was a kid.

"The churches would hold bazaars up there. They had graduations there. And there were plays, of course. Lowell High also played their basketball games at the opera house because the 1914 school on Oakley Street didn't have a gym. There was no football team at the time."

No football in Lowell? You've always spoken with great admiration of the circuit rider-historian Timothy H. Ball from this area's pioneer days.

"Without Timothy Ball, a lot of us wouldn't have anybody to copy from. At one time, Rev. Ball lived in a house out on Parrish (Avenue). My wife was born in that house."

Your father had an interest in history as well. Is that where you get it?

"Could be; when he related stories back to me, he'd make me sit down and listen twice. He'd say, 'Now, this time when I tell you the story, I want you to listen.'

"Excuse me for a second, Jeff. Mary, don't unbox too much. You'll just have to put it back. Personally, I think we should keep the pine trees in the woods where they belong."

Mary replied: "Dad, you're the one who complained last year, 'Is that all you're putting out?' Remember? Hey, look what I found inside this small box. There's a note."

"What's it say?"

"Ornaments from 1905. First used in the Schmal Hotel."

* * *

On Dec. 7, Schmal received the prestigious Hubert Hawkins History Award from the Indiana Historical Society in downtown Indianapolis.

It was while stationed in Honolulu during World War II, that a homesick Staff Sgt. Richard Schmal of the Army Quartermaster Corp. stumbled upon a used book entitled "Lake County, Indiana, from 1834 to 1872." It was published in 1873. Schmal was fascinated by the tome; his grandfather and great-grandfather were mentioned in the book.

The author?

The Rev. Timothy H. Ball.

Anne Zimmerman *(July 2006)*

"What is past is prologue."
-William Shakespeare

I visited Anne Zimmerman at The Lake of the Red Cedars Museum; she is director there. In its glory days, the monolithic manor was an upscale 60-room hotel. We sat upon the museum's sprawling veranda. Like dots on a treasure map, bungalows peeked through a wooded horizon to the west.

* * *

Were you born and raised in Cedar Lake, Anne?

"No, I moved here from the south side of Chicago when I got married," she said. "I met my husband in Cedar Lake and moved out here for good. My parents followed suit about a year later. My dad had already bought the property back in 1947, so I was no stranger to Cedar Lake. We had been spending our summers here forever."

How I spent my summer vacation?

"We did a lot of swimming, hiking, biking and cookouts. The roller rink was still open back then. We spent a lot of time doing the summer things. We didn't have TV back then – not out here."

What was your maiden name?

"Aanerud. My father was of Scandinavian descent. He worked for US Steel in Chicago. We lived about four blocks west of the mills.

"Dad had always wanted to own some type of business that he could count on in retirement. His original intention was to build a resort. Unfortunately, right after the war, the resort era waned here. We did have a picnic grove for a number of years; we charged all of 50 cents per carload."

You went to high school in the early '50s.

"It's OK, you can ask me my age. My children are going to have a birthday party for me. I'll be 70."

Was your husband a native Hoosier?

"No, his family was also Chicagoans. The Zimmermans bought land and a summer cottage here in the'20s, eventually they built a house in 1927."

Tell me about some of the early times regarding this site once known as The Lake of the Red Cedars.

"Cedar Lake's history starts out with the Balls back around 1836. Jane Ball taught school here out of her home."

What about Rev. Timothy Ball?

"Timothy was her oldest son. I read his book, 'Cedar Lake, Will it Live?' A fascinating read. Some people might find it boring – no car chases.

"Jane also practiced dentistry. In those days, women didn't have careers other than schoolteacher, maybe. One of Jane's sons died in the Civil War from infection."

That would have been during the1860's.

"In '61, war begun. In '62, bullets flew. In '63, slaves were free. In '64, war was o'er. In '65, Lincoln died. Actually, the war didn't end until '65.

"By the 1860's, we had a hunting lodge here. According to the records, it was built by European noblemen; the cabin still exists on the north end of the lake. Hotels started being built in the later 1800s. The resort era really began to flourish at the turn of the century. During the '20s, this part ofour building was dragged across the lake. It was originally a boarding house for the ice workers."

Continue, please.

"Beatrice Ewer Horner Castrogiavanni was our designated town historian. Bea actually had an office in the town hall. She spent a great deal of time doing research and writing articles. She was quite an artist as well.

"Hi, Millie. Oh, my; where did you find that?" (Millie and Anne work at the Museum together every Friday.)

"eBay,"says Millie.

"We've been looking for one of these for a long time."

What is it?

"This 12-inch by 12-inch card was placed in people's windows. It let the iceman know how much you wanted, 100, 75, 50, or 25 pounds."

Icebox. I remember my grandma using that term when referring to the refrigerator. Sort of like old fishermen calling a plastic bobber a cork.

"The only reason the Armour brothers cut ice here was for their meat packing business. The other ice cutting companies in Cedar Lake were here strictly to harvest ice. John Shedd was one of the men in charge. He ended up owning Consumer. Consumer and Armour shared the same conveyor."

I always figured Shedd was a Jacques Cousteau type – not an iceman. Why did they name the aquarium after him?

"Because he gave them $3 million. If you had given them 3 million bucks, they would've called it the Manes Aquarium."

Nice ring to that. I have been in the tank a few times.

"I also work at Buckley Homestead; I'm on their payroll. Here, we have no paid staff. "

Do you work the World War II re-enactment at Buckley Homestead?

"Yes, the homefront aspect of the war – the rationing, scrap drives, rubber drives... . I try to explain to the younger generation how a person couldn't buy a new pair of shoes, even if they had money. I told a little girl about giving up my rubber doll; I thought it was the right thing to do. The poor dear burst into tears.

"History is not hearsay. We need to get the facts straight. People often approach me with, 'Well, I always heard that... .'

"I'll say, 'What you've heard is possible, but I don't have documentation.' Even facts get distorted. And if something has been in print – it has to be gospel! Not necessarily so."

I always heard there's a grave site of the last known Potawatomi who lived in this area; legend has it the tombstone is hidden somewhere around this lake. They say she was married to a voyageur and... .

"You're probably referring to LaRose Surprise. And no, she is not buried along the shores of Cedar Lake. LaRose rests in a cemetery in Creston. And she was not a Potawatomi – but she was Native American. LaRose and her husband, Peter Surprise, who was of French descent, were married up in Canada. Bea was a direct descendent of LaRose Surprise.

"The Potawatomi were in fact the last tribe in this area, until (President) Jackson forced them out. You must remember the times. LaRose Surprise was allowed to live around here only because she was married to a white man, and she dressed in 'white people's' clothing. It wasn't popular being an Indian back then."

Sounds like it wasn't popular being a woman back then.

"You don't remember, but there were two Surprise brothers who owned businesses across Morse Street from each other. They didn't look anything alike. One was slight and fair-skinned; the other brother was a much larger man, dark complected, high cheekbones."

Took after LaRose.

"He was a very cordial individual. He ran Surprise Hardware. Actually, I know more history regarding lifestyles and events than I do about people; I'm not as good as Richard Schmal (town of Lowell historian) with names."

Well, Dick's been around longer, plus he lived his entire life in this area.

"And he's done a lot more research, albeit I've done quite bit of reading myself – particularly diaries. A person can get some real truths, there."

What church do you attend?

"Holy Name. I sing in the choir. I'm not that good. I'm just that tenacious, and won't leave. When I first moved here, Cedar Lake was known for its churches and taverns. Do you know how neighboring Cook got it's name?"

No, but I've known a couple of old-timers who were quick to correct me if I said they were from Cedar Lake and not Cook.

"Tact... . Some of the people from Cook felt that because this was a resort area, with all its resort activities, that Cedar Lake was somewhat unsavory; they didn't want to be associated. And, there also were the rough-hewn ice cutters who stayed in the boarding house at what was known as Armour Town. They were men who were brought in from Chicago. Men who were out of work. Men who were..."

Anne, no need to soft soap it. Some of my best interviews have been hobos and winos.

"...itinerant workers. Come on inside, Jeff. You might find

something that piques your interest."

Sure, Anne. You know, a person could get lost in here. Lost in reverie. The stories this place could tell. The stories this place does tell! Wasn't ever a house of ill-repute, was it?

"No. It was not. I could probably point out a few buildings that were. That is a part of our history that we are not proud of, but we can't deny it."

What do you think of the pastel-colored condos now gracing the lake?

"Well, there are those who have taken a negative attitude toward them. I like them. I think it helps Cedar Lake resemble the resort area it once was."

Will you look at the time? And we haven't even touched the tip of the glacier that formed Cedar Lake! The Dr. Scholl exhibit! Rumor has it the good foot doctor's brother, Father Scholl, was a priest at St. Augusta in Lake Village.

"Rumor?"

A wooly mammoth bone! I always heard we had wooly mammoths around here. That proves it!

"Mastodon. Jeff, I would like to show you something in this particular room. Close the door behind you."

Kinda dark back here. Whattya got for me, Annie?

"This is where we store the ice picks... ."

Ahem. Maybe next time. Gotta go.

* * *

Anne Zimmerman and her historic Lake of the Red Cedars Museum. Visit them both; you'll be glad you did.

And that's a fact.

Hettie Abbott *(Mar. 2011)*

"No sane local official who has hung up an empty stocking over the municipal fireplace, is going to shoot Santa Claus just before a hard Christmas."
– Alfred E. Smith (American Governor 1873-1944)

Hettie Abbott was raised a farmer's daughter in Newton County near Lake Village and Roselawn. In 1964, she and her second husband, Bill Abbott, moved into and opened up a mom-and-pop grocery store called The Farmer's Market on U.S. 41 in Sumava Resorts. Sadly, Bill is now deceased and The Farmer's Market sits empty.

For the last 18 months, Abbott, 91, has lived with her daughter, Lois, in Rensselaer. Hettie has raised four children. She doesn't drink beer any more, but still smokes. The staunch Democrat says smoking is what keeps her going.

* * *

Hettie, bear with me, I jump all over the place with these interviews.

"That's the only way I can talk," she said.

I remember when you were the justice of the peace for Lake Township in Newton County. Probably married a few couples during your tenure, huh?

"Oh, yes. Lots of people."

Did you ever meet Fern Hale, the JP who lived in Enos?

"Many times. Fern had a bunch of motorcycles in one night, maybe 30 or 40 of them. I don't know what the charges were, trespassing, probably."

Fern made a great homemade ham salad sandwich at her tiny grocery store. Yeah, Sumava was the Big Apple compared to Enos. Your store was a little bigger than Fern's, too.

"Yep, Fern dealt with the bikers. I took care of the truckers."

Truckers? What were they charged with?

"Visiting a house of ill fame. I had 29 of them stop in; it took all evening to mug 'em and fingerprint 'em."

Where was this house of ill repute?

"The nudist colony in Roselawn. It made national headlines in the newspapers at the time; I believe it was in the early 1970s. I know it was a Friday night because I'd eat fish at Lukes Restaurant on Fridays and they messed up my dinner plans."

Hettie, Roselawn has had nudist colonies for close to a century. Why did those truckers get fined?

"Because they weren't there to worship the sun. Two 'waitresses' were brought to me as well. I found all of the truckers and one of the women guilty."

But Roselawn is Lincoln Township, why did they bring the truck drivers to your office in Sumava?

"You take whoever the police bring you. Ralph Knapp, the JP of Lincoln Township, might not have been available at the time."

Knapp – wasn't he the original owner of the nudist colony back in 1920s?

"You're thinking of Alois Knapp. The nudist colony started about the time I started school – 1927."

The year Babe Ruth swatted 60 homers. You mentioned Lukes Restaurant. You must remember the place in the early days.

"The first time I ate there was in 1931; there was a big rally going on. Al Smith was hoping to get the Democratic nod in the primaries against Franklin D. Roosevelt."

Smith was a Catholic, wasn't he?

"He was an old drunk."

During part of your childhood, you lived east of Lake Village near the area known as Bluegrass.

"Yeah, Bluegrass was known for bootlegging. Annie Duchler ran a bootleg place near Indiana 10 and Old (U.S.) 41."

Did you go to Mount Ayr High School?

"For three years. I graduated from Morocco High School."

Ever bump into any of your classmates?

"I'd have to go to the cemetery to do that."

Life on the farm?

"Dad farmed 40 acres. We raised corn, potatoes, strawberries... .

Truck farming more or less. We lived off the land. There were 12 of us kids – two died. We were poor, but we didn't know we were poor. It was the Great Depression."

Let's talk more politics.

"My father was a devout Republican. And you know what? My father and I never saw eye to eye."

I knew you were a Democrat because I remember you and my ma representing the party when you worked the polls together on election day.

"Your mom and I were talking astrology 50 years ago. She knew how to do charts way back then."

Yeah, I remember when the Baptists would knock on our door and warn her to change her ways, that astrology was evil.

"And what would Karen say to that?"

Ma would remind them the Magi were astrologers and close the door. What year did you first run for political office?

"I started in 1960, when John Kennedy was elected president. I was the Democratic county chairman for eight years. I also was vice-president and district secretary."

Let's switch gears. Do you still like to gamble?

"Oh, yeah. My sister and I used to go down to Arkansas every year and bet the horses. We had a lady friend who tended bar in the hotel. She invited us for a couple of beers after the races."

A bar is a logical place to have a beer.

"It was Election Day. All of a sudden about 15 men came in through the back door and ordered drinks. Soon after, the Feds came in and asked what we were doing in the bar on Election Day. I told them we were thirsty. One of the Feds said, 'I'm going to have to haul you all in.'"

Then what?

"Well, one of those 15 guys who was drinking at the bar said, 'I don't think so; I'm running for Governor of this state. These are my friends and we're going to have a few drinks.' The Fed said, 'What about these two women?' Soon-to-be Gov. Bill Clinton said, 'They're with us.'"

* * *

The Farmer's Market was a place where you could buy a quart of blueberries, a can of yellow wax beans or a box of red worms. And every riparian ragamuffin who stepped foot in that store always received a free piece of gum or candy from Hettie Abbott.

Later, when we got to be in our teens, The Farmer's Market was where we'd pay our speeding tickets. Most of the time, Hettie would let us off the hook.

Hettie Abbott has always maintained, "When you go out on the town, wear red and sit in the middle of the room."

That's comin' from a beautiful, progressive woman who was born in 1920, the year the 19th Amendment was passed.

Carl Deering *(Sept. 2011)*

"Tell them to be patient and ask death for speed; for they are all there but one – I, Chingachgook, – last of the Mohicans."
– James Fenimore Cooper

Prohibition began in 1920. Carl Deering was 10 at the time; he turned 101 in June.

Deering was born in Hegewisch, Ill.; his family moved to Hammond when he was 3. He was one of 13 children and he graduated from Hammond High School the year the stock market crashed – 1929.

Deering didn't get married until he was 50. His wife of 47 years passed away five years ago. They never had children.

I met with Deering at the Hammond Mohawks Athletic and Conservation Club, Inc. at 4040 Calumet Avenue. He is a charter member.

Deering was sitting at the bar, enjoying a jigger of brandy with a can of Dr. Pepper for a wash. He never has smoked, but has dipped snuff for about 85 years.

* * *

Carl, what did you do for a living?

"I was a boilermaker at Graver Tank in East Chicago, but I started at a wallpaper mill," he said.

Where was that at?

"In Hammond, it was called Commercial Wallpaper Mill. I worked my way up until I became a printer. Then, I went into the service. After the war, I went back to my old job for three or four years. I didn't like the job of a printer."

Why not?

"Because I wanted to keep all my fingers. You had to stick your hand in a machine and it was nothing but gears."

Talk about the Great Depression.

"You could go to Calumet City (Ill.) and buy a 32-ounce glass of beer for a dime and a shot of booze for a nickel. You don't have a depression today. Back then, you couldn't buy a job."

Do you remember prohibition?

"Oh, yeah. It was repealed in '33. When I was a teenager, I lived on Grover Avenue. There was a place on Gostlin that used to handle what we called 'Yonkey Doc.'"

What's that?

"Homemade liquor; they could sell beer legally if it was 1 percent alcohol or less. The Hammond cops came into that joint and drank.

"When the proprietor would get a call from City Hall that the feds were going to raid the place, he'd say, 'Boys, c'mon, take this booze next door and hide it in the basement. He'd give us ice cream cones for our efforts. He sold ice cream, too."

Anything else?

"I remember when Hammond Dairy delivered their goods with a horse and a sled during the winter. Nowadays, you don't even have a milkman.

"I delivered ice on Saturdays when I was in high school. People had signs in their windows: 25 – 50 – 75."

To let the iceman know how many pounds they needed?

"That's right. I was paid $1 a day. I remember when gas went up to 18 cents a gallon; that was high."

Let's travel to the 1940s; Do you still remember your dog tag number?

"Oh, yeah – 35575472."

Where were you sent during World War II?

"The South Pacific. I went in at 32 and came out at 35. Once I was drafted, they asked me if I had a problem with fighting in Germany because both my parents were German-born."

Your reply?

"'I don't give a good goddamn, they'll kill me in either place.' I became a foot soldier in a weapons platoon. We hit those islands before daybreak."

We?

"The 111th Infantry. We had a recon outfit with us; they led us in.

Our job was to protect them. I was on a 50-caliber machine gun. When the fighting stopped, all the Japs was killed but two. We hollered for those two to surrender; one just sat there, crying, and the other one started to run away. He didn't get too far. We took one prisoner out of the whole bunch. We had to feed him; it was the rules of war."

Did you get hit?

"No, but I was awarded two Bronze Stars. A kid from Whiting was killed – shot in the back. The Japs mutilated him... then opened up his mouth and stuck a stick in it. We buried him on what we called Cemetery Island."

Carl, lets switch gears. Tell me about the Mohawk Club.

"It actually began in 1938; it was just a bunch of guys who got together and started a hockey team. We used to go to the old glue works in Calumet City when the big ditch froze over. We made our own sticks and used tin cans for pucks."

"After the war, in '47, the Mohawk Club got chartered as a not-for-profit organization. We used to have bowling and softball teams, too."

So, the Mohawk Club isn't just hunting and fishing.

"Hunting and fishing came way later. We are Hammond Mohawks Athletics and Conservation Club. That's why we bought the island."

I know where you're talking about, Mohawk Bayou on the north side of the Kankakee River. As a boy, I used to fish that area – still do. Mohawk Bayou is the one with the bridge.

"We put that bridge in there. We got the steel from Standard Oil. We just got rid of the property last year"

Why did the Mohawks sell?

"Because we got a bunch of young punks who aren't interested in that type of thing. There was no expense to it. We used to pay $5 or $6 per year taxes. I used to catch a lot bass and pike in that bayou – big bluegills, too. "

When did the Mohawks purchase that land?

"I can't remember the exact year."

How much did the Mohawk Club pay for the land surrounding Mohawk Bayou?

"We paid $25,000 and sold it for $45,000. I hope they're happy. There aren't any old guys in here no more, see? We had more than 10 acres on both sides of the river."

That means the Mohawks owned land in two different counties.

"Absolutely; we had to pay taxes to Lake and Newton Counties. When we first bought the place, the bayou wasn't connected to the river. We had a guy come in with a crane and open it up to the river; that's when we really got the fish. I used to love that place."

This is really a nice building.

"It used to be a steakhouse. We remodeled it not too long ago. I liked it the way it was. They tried to take the kitchen out, but I said, 'Nothin' doin' – that kitchen – you leave it alone.'"

How many club members are there?

"We used to have more than 600. Today, I don't think we have 100."

How's your health?

"I feel real good. If it weren't for my knees, I'd still be golfing and bowling."

* * *

As a young man, he fought on the atolls of the South Pacific. Later, like Civil War Gen. Lew Wallace, he found serenity on the bayous of the Kankakee River.

Carl Deering, last of the original Hammond Mohawks.

WARRIORS

Dorsey Ruley *(May 2006)*

"And I'm proud to be an American,
where at least I know I'm free.
And I won't forget the men who died,
who gave that right to me."
-Lee Greenwood

Carl Dorsey Ruley, 85, is the great-grandson of Jonah Thorne, one of Lowell's founding fathers.

As a hobby, Ruley restored antique automobiles including a 1929 Packard seven-passenger touring car. He also restored steam-engine popcorn wagons which he sold to a chap by the name of Redenbacher.

Ruley is deaf as a post and blind in one eye. He suffers from work-related asbestosis.

A bricklayer by trade, he built the house he lived in. The foghorn-voiced octogenarian possesses a firm handshake and can recite "The Cremation of Sam McGee" in it's entirety.

* * *

"The Ruleys came up from the South," Ruley began. "When I was a boy, growing up in Lowell, the old opera house was still standing; I fell from the ceiling trusses through three floors – all the way to the basement.

"I remember when the army came through town; they ended up spending three days in Lowell – contracted diarrhea from the sulfur water."

I buy my water from Wilco.

"When we got picture shows, I'd hang posters and deliver handbills of coming attractions to people's doorsteps all over the neighboring towns of Brunswick, Shelby, Hebron, and part of Cedar Lake. A Model A would drop us off, we'd thumb rides home. My pay was three passes to the show, but I couldn't use them on the weekends. It only cost 10 cents to see the show; I didn't have a dime. My dad moved clear across town to save a dollar-a-month rent."

Were you a union bricklayer?

"Darn right, I was; 50 years in the hall. I got a watch that don't work and a gold card to prove it. Ain't real gold, you can bet on that."

You graduated from Lowell High School back in 1940.

"Yep, I saved up my money and bought a brand-new '41 Ford – $678. When the war broke out, I was just a young kid, laying brick. On the way home from work I heard the Japanese had hit Pearl Harbor. I went to Chicago and enlisted in the Navy. I received three weeks of training at Great Lakes. I was always a sailor at heart. Even in high school, I owned a sailboat. I'd take it out on Cedar Lake.

"We was sent straight to the Pacific where we took the 2nd Marines to Guadalcanal. I was aboard a ship that had been hit at Pearl Harbor – a light cruiser called the Helena."

You were on the Helena?

"We were in pretty good shape out there. Most big ships only have nine guns in their main batteries; we had 15. We prided ourselves on how fast we could fire. A scheduled bombardment was 1,000 rounds of 6-inch and 400 rounds of 5-inch. When we got a hold a somethin', it looked like we was a burnin' when we were firin'.

"The first battle we were in was at Guadalcanal. We were trained in on the enemy; we kept asking for permission to open fire. The admiral was on the Salt Lake City. When the signalman received our message, he uttered, 'Roger.' We took that as permission; we gave 'em a dustin'.

You were in several engagements.

"Yes; we bombarded Munda on the 4th of July. We got back to Guadalcanal before the airplanes came; we did all our fightin' at night. We got word that the Japanese were comin' up the slot. We turned around and went back; tangled with 'em again."

Were you on the Helena when she went down?

"Yes; we were fightin' a bunch of ships. When we got torped it took the entire bottom of the ship out; went right between No. 1 and No. 2 turret. The next torpedo we took was right between the smokestacks. The third torpedo we took was in the same hole; cut us in three pieces."

What happened then?

"The raft was gone from my abandon-ship station. I took off my hat and shoes, set them on deck and jumped in the drink. When the torpedoes ruptured our fuel tanks, it created what was similar to a thin layer of tar on the water. I started swimming. I'd look back and there was the Helena, following me, drifting. Finally, she just went down.

"We were in Japanese territory. When it started getting light, there come a string of Japanese Zeros just above the water. The first guy was firing his machine gun, just the first one. Right after, came a Navy Privateer; it's like a DC-3. They threw us three rafts. We got two of them inflated. They were only four-man rafts."

How many guys in the water?

"Nearly 1,000. Commander Chew was in one of the rafts; officers and those wounded the worst rode in the rafts. Guys were yelling for help. It's not easy to inflate your vest when you're in the water and injured.

"I left the raft and swam to a couple of my buddies, Pepper and Little Joe Summers. Pepper was trying to pull Little Joe along. I told him about the raft I'd been holding onto. We never found it.

"I told Pepper, 'I think Joe's dead;' his face was in the water. We let him go. Luckily, we found the second raft; it held other officers and a guy who was hurt real bad, but he died and they tossed him.

"Twenty-seven of us hung to the sides of that four-man raft. All you had to hold onto was a thin cord draped around that raft. I had scars all over my fingers and hands. The guys were getting disoriented, crying... After three days and nights, only14 of us were left. One by one, they just drifted away..."

Sharks?

"No sharks – that was the (USS) Indianapolis."

What happened next?

"An island appeared; I decided to swim for it. I made it and then conked out. Chew had already gotten in. The Japanese had a stronghold on the island; I was on Vella Lavella Island for eight days."

Then what?

"Chew called us all together. He said: 'You guys got it tough. It's gonna get worse. There's a Japanese column comin' this way. It's gonna be every man for himself.'

"I couldn't even walk. I had raw gaping sores all over my legs and groin from being in that salt water so long. They were turning all yellow, rotting. As luck would have it, our planes from Guadalcanal came up and bombed the daylights out of the Japanese and all their motor launches.

"Manes, I've enjoyed myself in retirement; that's why I'm broke."

. *Dorsey, what good is it to die rich anyhow?*

* * *

The USS Helena helped destroy 15 Japanese warships in 13 different fire-filled engagements.

Japanese propaganda radio broadcasts claimed the U.S. Navy had a new secret weapon, a 6-inch machine gun. But it wasn't a machine gun; it was the rapid fire of Helena's gun crews.

While battling numerous enemy ships, sinking all of them, she was torpedoed from two miles away. Like a pair of boxers knocking out each other simultaneously, Helena sank the ship that sank her. She received seven battle stars for actions in World War II.

When Ruley finally returned to Lowell for good, he recalled American Legion Post 101 waiting for him when he got off the bus.

On Memorial Day weekend, this column is dedicated to the 168 men who died when Helena went down. And to a salty bricklayer with baseball mitts for hands who lived long enough to tell me about it.

Cipriano Gamez *(June 2010)*

"...33 days of action without relief, without replacements. Every mission accomplished. No ground gained was ever relinquished."

– from the post-battle report of Maj. Gen. Matthew Ridgway regarding the 82nd Airborne Division and its part in the D-Day invasion of Normandy on June 6, 1944.

Cipriano Gamez's day began as early as it gets on June 6, 1944 – 12:01 a.m.

Pfc. Gamez was a pathfinder with the 82nd Airborne Division's 508th Parachute Infantry Regiment.

Under cover of fog and darkness, Gamez landed in a tree about 10 miles behind enemy lines in Normandy, France.

Today, Gamez, 87, lives in Highland with Hope, his wife of 23 years.

* * *

"I was born in Belmond, Iowa," Gamez began. "There were 14 of us kids. At the time, the sugar-beet farmers needed laborers. My parents had originally gone to Texas from Mexico to look for a better life.

"While in Iowa, my dad would communicate with his compadres who had come directly from Mexico to the (Indiana Harbor section of East Chicago). One of them wrote to dad saying there was a lot of work in the steel mills and at Atlas cement plant in Gary. So, we migrated to the Harbor in 1924.

"My dad started at Inland, but left there to work at the cement plant. During the Depression, the plant shut down."

Then what?

"Back to Iowa. I was about 11 by then and old enough to work in the sugar-beet fields from sunrise to sunset. A year later, we returned to the Harbor. I didn't like working in the fields and gladly shined shoes or sold newspapers to help out the family."

You ended up in the mill.

"Yes; I got a job at Inland Steel, but was drafted in January of '43."

You became a paratrooper.

"I got paid double, $100 per month, when I joined the paratroopers. It was considered hazardous duty. We were taken to Nottingham, England."

Cipriano, what was going through your mind on the evening of June 5, 1944?

"At about 9 p.m., there still was a lot of hooting and hollering going on. We were paratroopers; we were invincible... .

"Nobody is bulletproof. As we were flying over the English Channel, the noise subsided. Reality set in. You're looking around and you know some of you aren't coming back. Maybe all of you aren't coming back if the plane gets shot down and there's no chance to jump. There were 16 of us in that C-47."

The duties of a pathfinder?

"We preceded the main body by about an hour or so to set up lights and what they called a Eureka. It was a gizmo that sent out high-frequency waves. The lead plane in each echelon had a receiver called the Rebecca."

You guys jumped at night.

"Yes, we painted our faces with soot. When the planes hit the coast of France, there was a heavy fog; the pilots took evasive actions. They're supposed to throttle back to 90 mph when we're getting ready to jump. But when the pilots hit that cloud bank, they scattered; it was pedal to the metal. When they dropped us, they were doing 200 to 250 mph."

What happened?

"The opening shock was terrific. The pouch that carried my light, plus my canteen and entrenching tool, were all torn off."

Your rifle?

"I hung on to my M-1. On my third oscillation, I hit a dwarfish apple tree. It was a soft landing. The Germans had flooded the areas where we were supposed to jump.

"I weighed 140 pounds back then. By the time I got on that plane, I weighed about 250 pounds with all that equipment. We were scattered all over hell's half-acre, 10 miles behind Utah Beach. The 101st (Airborne) jumped about four miles behind the lines."

Then what?

"At first, I was all by myself in that orchard. Eventually, seven of us found each other in the dark. Then, we joined up with a makeshift group; there was no single unit. But we were a fighting force – about 70 of us from different outfits."

Was it daylight yet?

"Yes; the first time I heard those German machine guns it scared me bad. They threw out a lot of lead in just a fraction of a second. The

Germans had heavy artillery, too. We fought with what we carried: rifles, hand grenades, bayonets and knives.

"After about five days of fighting with different units, I finally joined my unit at Hill 30. We were almost out of ammo. Our main objective was to keep the Germans from reinforcing the beaches by taking out bridges and railroads.

"Of the 36 guys in my platoon, only six of us made it back to England. But we held Hill 30."

Mr. Gamez, I can't imagine.

"There is something inside of you, in spite of the fact there is death and destruction all around you, you keep going. You don't want to remember seeing your buddy drop beside you, but you don't want to forget it."

What happened after that 33-day battle?

"Holland; we got torn up bad. We jumped on Sept. 17 at about 11 p.m.; I immediately was out on the point leading C Company that night. By the grace of God, I spotted a (German) recon patrol an instant before they saw me. I killed two of them before I got hit in the arm. Once I got hit, my Thompson (submachine gun) was of no use to me."

Then what?

"I spent two weeks in a field hospital recovering. I was still sore and I couldn't bend my arm. The major who ran the hospital said, 'You're going back to your outfit.' I said, 'Sir, my arm still hurts.' He said, 'You'll be surprised how quickly it's going to heal once you get back over there.'

"I remember when Harry Muhme got shot in the stomach. The last time any of us saw him, he was laying on the side of the dike with his guts in his hands. You see things like that, but there are times when you can't stop to help.

"At one of our Army reunions, in walked Harry. It was like Lazarus had risen from the grave. We all thought Harry had bought the farm. They put wire mesh in his stomach to hold it together."

Was The Netherlands the extent of it for you?

"At the Battle of the Bulge, we not only had to fight the enemy, we had to fight Mother Nature. It was so cold. I prayed to God: 'If I get hit, make it a good one. I don't want to lay in the snow and slowly bleed to death before anybody can get to me.' I never got a scratch in Belgium; I was lucky.

"I got back to the States on Nov. 19, 1945. On June 6 last year, 38 of us received an all-expense-paid trip to France; we were awarded Legion of Honor medals."

* * *

During the Great Depression, Gamez wielded a machete in the sugar-beet fields from sunup to sundown. Later, alongside my father, he helped feed the fiery furnaces of No. 2 Open Hearth.

The 82nd Division was nicknamed "All-American" because its initial members, back in 1917, hailed from all 48 states. Sgt. Alvin K. York and Chief Dave Bald Eagle (the grandson of Sitting Bull) were 82nd Division.

And so was a pathfinder from Indiana Harbor named Cipriano Gamez.

‘Sug’ Bailey *(Nov. 2006)*

“There were six vestal virgins chosen by the high priest. Vestals served for 30 years, 10 as students, 10 in service, 10 as teachers.”
– Wikipedia

West of U.S 41 near the state line on Belshaw Road in Lowell sits the Bailey homestead. In Josiah Bailey’s day, there was no Belshaw Road. But there was the remnant of an Indian trail.

Josiah’s great-grandson, Don Bailey, lives there now. I usually interview a veteran for this column in early November. I chose Don Bailey’s wife, Sug (short for Sugar).

Sug Bailey, 87, was born Vestal Dean Williams down in Cajun country. The Bailey’s have been married for 64 years and have raised four children.

The Bailey kitchen is a cornucopia of homegrown goodies filled with pecks of peaches and apples, bottles of herbal vinegar, a bowl of hazel nuts, and jars of jams and jellies.

* * *

I love all this kind of stuff.

“Jeff, I know that; give me a hug,” she said. “Don’t you remember when I used to come to your booth at the flea market? I’d use your dried flowers for my wreaths. Let’s have a seat out on the porch.”

Wow, I’ve never seen a clematis so thick and sprawling.

“Isn’t it beautiful? Don cuts it back to nothing every year. It’s very old.”

Sug, I haven’t known many native Louisianans. Tell me about that.

“I spent most of my childhood in Winnfield, La. There’s a museum in Winnfield made from a train station. In that museum hangs the portraits of four people who hailed from Winnfield. Three of them became governors – O.K. Allen, Earl Long and Huey Long.”

The Kingfish. Was Huey as crooked as some folks claim?

“Crooked? A lot of my father’s friend’s held jobs like ‘smoke chaser’ – anything to get on the payroll. I moved to get away from all that corruption. And where do I end up? Lake County, Ind., right next to Chicago.”

Who's the fourth portrait of?

"Me – in my uniform."

We'll get to that. Do you have any French blood in you?

"No, my grandfather, William Williams, was from Wales. He was a horse and buggy doctor down in the Cajun country where my dad, Burton Williams, was born. Just before my grandfather died, he told grandmother to burn all the books."

Burn books?

"A lot of poor people owed him for his services. He'd bring a baby into the world for a dozen eggs or a chicken. That was the way of the horse and buggy doctor. They really served the people.

"My grandmother opened up one whole wing of the house just to rent to schoolteachers.

"My maternal grandfather was a sheriff. He also raised goats. After he died, I found out why. He'd take the goat meat and goat milk to wherever people were undernourished. At his funeral, people came up to us and said, 'This man saved my life.'"

What did your dad do for a living?

"He was a paymaster of a railroad; he also served on a repair ship during World War I; The USS Vestal. The Vestal was hitched to the Arizona when it was bombed at Pearl Harbor. My father loved that ship."

So much, he named you after her.

"Yes. Here's a picture of the Vestal. This is Don when he was a flight instructor during World War II. We were on the same base for three years in Pensacola."

Whoa. Who's this babe? Looks like Gene Tierney.

"Why, that's me. Still today, I don't gray. It's a family trait. I became the youngest WAVE officer in the United States. I gave up a good job to join the service. (Navy WAVES were Woman Accepted for Volunteer Emergency Service.)

"I was the only one of our group from New Orleans who passed all the tests, both mental and physical. I had earned an athletic letter in college as a tennis player and archer. I also marched with the Cajun Red Jackets. I had to eat bananas to get into the service; I only weighed 99 pounds. You were supposed to weigh at least 100.

"When it came time to swear me in, they realized I wasn't of age. They had to defer me three months until I became 21. I was a senior in college, but had gone there at 16."

Where did you go to school?

"I attended Smith College in New England when Nancy Reagan was there. She was known as Nancy Davis back then. But it was Mount

Holyoke College where they taught us coding and encoding.

"I became an air traffic officer at Pensacola. We learned to break codes and to encode because we would have flight plans that came from Europe and South America. During the war, many flight plans were secret. And everybody kept the secret. They didn't blab like they do now."

Loose lips sink ships.

"That was our motto. My unit controlled seven outlying fields. It was very difficult when we had fly-aways, because you had to stay up the whole time. There were six of us who were trained in intelligence and communications. We were there to take the place of the men. Some of us were the traffic duty officers. It was really intense, but we were young – that's why they took us.

"They also assigned me as personnel officer over a big unit of sailors. Here I was, a 21 year-old gal, in charge of these hardened yeomen. But I had the authority. I was their parole officer; the one who would go to their court martial and bail them out if they got into mischief. They knew they had to depend on me. I loved the time that I served. I don't regret it."

Do you still volunteer your time at the Methodist Church's Resale Shop?

"Yes; I've been service-oriented all my life. I read from a book of devotions every day. Jeff, read what it says for today's date. 'Remember to serve all. Be ready to prove yourself by service, look at all you meet as guests in your Father's house.'

"I wanted to be a missionary when I a young girl. I prayed for it. And you know where the Lord finally sent me? To be a teacher, because that was a mission in itself. I still see some of my students and we always have a hug. It's a wonderful blessing, being part of other people's lives."

What did you teach?

"Home Economics and English. Now, they don't even have a home economics department in the school, and that just floors me.

"I went to college (before Smith) at the University of Louisiana-Lafayette, but I got my Master's at Purdue. So, I went to two Lafayettes."

* * *

For four score and seven, the lady called Sugar has proved worthy of her salt. Day by day, serving others along the way.

Bob Hoycus *(May 2005)*

"Under a spreading chestnut tree
the village smithy stands;
the smith, a mighty man is he,
with large and sinewy hands..."
– Henry Wadsworth Longfellow

We honor our fallen soldiers on Memorial Day. Lt. Robert Hoycus of the United States Marine Corps didn't fall in Vietnam. He was staggered, but did not fall.

Hoycus, 63, lived in Roselawn with his wife, Jackie, for 38 years, but they recently moved to Waveland in west-central Indiana. They have raised five children.

At 6-feet 3-inches and 225 pounds, 'Big Bob,' still is a rock. He also is retired from ArcelorMittal where he worked as a machinist.

* * *

"Hey, I've got an interesting nature story for you, Mr. Manes," Hoycus began.

Bob, I love your interesting nature stories.

"What do you know about the American chestnut tree?"

Not too much.

"At the turn of the century, do-gooders wanted to cross the Chinese chestnut with the American chestnut. The Chinese variety brought a blight that infected the more flavorful but smaller American chestnut. The American chestnut once ranged from Maine to Georgia. It was a dominant tree in the eastern American forests. They were wiped out in 50 years."

That's too bad.

"I was squirrel hunting and spotted something on the ground that looked like a sea urchin. They were green and had prickly things all over them, about the size of a billiard ball."

Yeah?

"I looked up; they were falling from a tree. I did some research and happened to find a National Geographic containing an article about the American Chestnut Foundation trying to breed a resistant strain of chestnut tree. The photos of the burrs in the magazine looked identical to the burr I held in my hand.

"I tried to grow some trees from the nuts, but didn't realize I was planting infertile nuts – they fall first. The fertile ones don't fall until the end of September.

"Eventually, I got in touch with a member of the American Chestnut Foundation. He was leery: 'I get a lot of calls like this. It's always a wild goose chase.'

"Finally, he showed up; one of those scientist guys, with a big floppy hat and a vest with lots of pockets."

Yeah?

" I took him to the tree; he looked up, and said, 'Oh my God,' about 10 times while walking in circles around the tree.

"Turns out it's the largest chestnut tree in Indiana. There were actually four of them in the area. How they got there nobody knows. He came back with pollen from trees he's growing and then bagged the flowers in the top of the biggest tree; it looked like a woman with curlers in her hair."

Then what?

"He returned in the fall and harvested them. The Hardwood Tree Improvement and Regeneration Center at Purdue has Chestnut trees now growing from our Roselawn tree."

Great nature story, Bob. Let's switch gears. Tell me about Gary during the '60s?

"I grew up in the Brunswick neighborhood of Gary and a little enclave called Cudahy; it was right on the Grand Calumet River by Cline Avenue. There were a lot of Mexican-Americans in the area at that time; we all got along great. Our fathers worked together in the mills; it wasn't like two different levels of society. Everybody was in the same bucket."

Bob, most people don't know you're a biologist.

"One of my teachers at Gary Edison was former House of

Representatives member Adam Benjamin. He had a twin brother, Myron; they took a liking to me.

"They said Austin Peay was a good school and it was cheap. I told them, 'I don't wanna go.' Myron made me fill out an application; he sent it in. It came back accepted. I thought I'd better give it a try. So, I went and I enjoyed it".

What happened between college and the mill? I know you were an officer in the Marine Corps. How did you get into that, ROTC during high school?

"Are you kidding? In Gary? They didn't have that kind of stuff for us. The Marine Corps has a program called the Platoon Leaders Class. College students can go to Officers Candidate School during their summer vacation. I did that between my sophomore and junior year and my junior and senior year. PLC is unique to the Marine Corps."

What happened next?

"People were getting drafted. Hell, I didn't want to get drafted. That's why I figured if I got through OCS, I could avoid the draft. Once you enlisted in the program, you were untouchable. By the time I graduated college in '68, Vietnam was red hot."

Bob, my dad fought in Korea; they drafted him right out of the labor gang of Inland Steel's No. 2 Open Hearth.

"For generations, it was the poor white guys. Later, we got enough poor black and Hispanic guys. You look at the surnames on that wall in Washington D.C.; there's a whole lot of Jeffersons and Garcias. But that's America, I suppose."

Care to talk about getting hit?

"We were checking for mines when we got ambushed. When it was over, nine Marines were wounded; three Marines were dead. I was shot in the groin. The bullet ended up in my leg. Smashed my femur pretty good.

"At first you don't feel a thing. You know what happened; you just don't feel it. By the time they got me to the field hospital via helicopter near Dong Ha, the closest town to the (demilitarized zone), I was shaking pretty bad.

"They flew me to the hospital ship Repose, then they flew me to the hospital ship Sanctuary off the coast of the South China Sea. I ended up in a Naval hospital on the island of Guam. Six weeks later, I was back in the bush. Limping, but back in the bush."

You've, um, you've fathered children... .

"One is all you need. What else do you want to talk about?"

What about when you got out of the service?

"Well, I had married the colonel's daughter out in California. I needed to get away from it all. Jackie went with me to Minnesota, where we lived in a shack deep in the woods. I was a wild man for a while. Then reality set in; I needed a job. I brought her back home to the Region. Ended up at Inland, like my old man and my grandfather."

You're quite an outdoorsman.

"Whatever happened to you? Your dad, brother, Uncle Joe... . You're the only 'Preying Manes' I know who doesn't hunt. It's in you though; I remember the night you killed that rat in our lunchroom in the mill – with an apple! That was a heckuva shot, Lefty."

Bob, that was a heckuva rat; I've seen smaller woodchucks.

* * *

The Union Pacific used chestnut railroad ties; there are 100-year-old chestnut fenceposts in the Appalachians – hardwood that dies hard.

The folks at Purdue are about seven or eight years from a trial reforestation of disease-resistant American chestnuts.

Since Hoycus' discovery, one of the Roselawn chestnuts was killed by a lightning strike and one was snapped in half by a falling snag (dead tree). The big one still survives and has become state champion at 90 feet tall and 32.64 inches in diameter. Thirty-eight young chestnut trees have sprouted up near the remaining two.

As part of Newton County's sesquicentennial commemoration, the Newton County Historical Society recently placed several markers at sites thought to be of historical significance. One such marker is dedicated to the rare Roselawn chestnut grove.

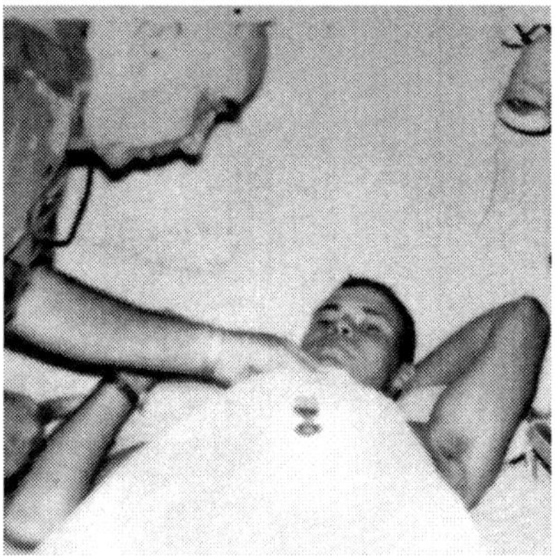

Although once dominant, the American chestnut, like Lt. Hoycus, came close to extinction.

They were staggered, but did not fall.

John Keithley *(Nov. 2005)*

"...When you pop, your speed brakes; the MiG flashes by you. Quickly closing the brakes, you slide onto his tail and hammer him with your '50's.'"

– Col. Harry Thyng, USAF (10 victories, World War II, Korean War)

West of U.S. 41 in Lowell, I turned off Belshaw Road into the driveway of John Keithley. Cream-colored barns match a cream-colored farmhouse. Kept nice, the place resembles a Norman Rockwell painting – Midwestern style. Grant Wood, perhaps.

Keithley, 91, was married to his first wife, Ruth, for more than 50 years before her passing. They raised five children. He has been wed to Mary Jo for 12 years.

* * *

"Won't be much of a story," Keithley began. "As a youngster, I grew up along the Grand Kankakee Marsh, this side of the Singleton ditch. Come springtime, it was rough back then. Water is worse than fire; you can't stop it.

"Mother died when I was 14. There were seven of us kids. By the time I was 16, I was pretty much on my own.

"Back in '33, it was a drought year, the sky was a reddish-gray, full of dirt all summer long because of the Oklahoma dust bowl. That year, the corn had no ears. My dad realized what was going to happen. We had horses and a slip scraper. He dug a trench and we laid the stalks down into it for silage to feed the cows for the winter."

You were one of the stars of an undefeated football team for Lowell High School.

"We had moved to just west of Parrish Avenue by then, but it was still a five-mile hike back home every night after practice. When I did get back to the farm, there were plenty of chores to do. I'd eventually eat a cold supper and then hit the hay. Lowell has a pretty good coach out there right now."

What do you think one of Coach Kirk Kennedy's favorite pastimes is?

"What's that?"

Reading about World War II.

"Is that right?"

You're a World War II veteran.

"Yes."

John, this book, "Penetrating The Great Northern Shield," there's a sentence that's circled: "Sept. 11th, 1943 – the 11th Air Force suffers the loss of seven B-25s and two B-24s, the worst in its history."

"I was a 1st Lieutenant of the 11th Air Force and 77th Bombers."

Care to talk about it, Lt. Keithley?

"All who went down in those nine planes perished. We had a B-25 in the water with seven guys on the wing. Four or five Japanese Zeros strafed them. A B-25 would float six or seven minutes. You could only live 40 minutes in that water.

"Our flight would be the longest over-water mission ever attempted by twin engine airplanes at that time. We flew across the Bering Sea to bomb the Japanese off of the Aleutian Islands.

"The 24s were going to go in at 20,000 feet. In the briefing, they told us, 'The Zeros have a very small fuel tank and they'll be up there with the 24s. Bombers, you'll be 10 minutes behind, because the Zeros will be out of gas.'"

The Zero was their fighter plane?

"Yes; they were made out of plywood. We were skip bombing their ships and destroyers in the bay. We went in at deck level, when we were a couple hundred feet from the boat, that's when we'd drop our bomb which would skip over the water into the sides of the ships. But the Japanese had shore batteries on both sides. It was almost impossible to get through."

Sounds like an American version of Kamikaze.

"It was; trying to get through those narrow straits with the enemy having big guns on both sides of us – not to mention all their ships having gun decks.

"We got shot up. A 20mm shell went through our auxiliary gas tank. In order to fly that far, half your bomb bay was taken up with a rubber gas tank. We had to make a force landing in Russia. The Russians thought we were spies.

But the Russians were our allies?

"The Russians were very suspicious people. We were treated as prisoners of war. You see, they weren't at war with the Japanese at that time. After we dropped the atomic bomb, Russia realized we were going to beat Japan. That's when the Russians jumped into the fray – so they could get a piece of the pie.

"There were 62 of us captured in that particular raid from various planes that were forced to land."

How long were you held prisoner?

"Six months. Even though we were deloused every night, the bedbugs were brutal. Heads of cabbage were thrown into three big iron kettles. After the cabbage boiled for awhile, all the dirt and worms came to the top. We'd ladle it off. Occasionally, unwrapped black bread was delivered in a horse-drawn manure wagon. We preferred the crust.

"All 62 of us survived the six months. Some died soon after though. Diarrhea had weakened them so badly; they just couldn't regain their health. Some became alcoholics. We weren't declared POWs until 1987. A lot of the guys thought we would be killed. But I kept telling them, telling myself, the Russians wouldn't be feeding us if they were going to shoot us. Food was too scarce.

"There are only two of us left now; the other fella lives in Hawaii. They want us to remind people about what took place along that 'Great Northern Shield'. It's called the forgotten war because it was just days after Pearl Harbor.

"The worst part was that it was directed by generals in Seattle who couldn't understand why we weren't winning faster. They didn't know what tundra was back then. When the tundra thawed, we were literally knee-deep in mud. The Japanese were in the mountains. The Americans were in the valleys. Percentage-wise, we lost more men in that campaign than any other.

"Mary Jo and I have a little place down in Ft. Myers (Fla.). It's not much. We like it. I stay busy and warm. I do a lot of woodworking."

* * *

While gathering up my stuff, I glanced out Keithley's back window. It was late October. Purple cosmos persisted along the edge of his garden – sentries guarding withered tomato plants. Erected in the middle of the garden was a handcrafted weather vane that just happened to be pointing south. It was a wooden replica of a B-25 Bomber.

Head for that trailer park in Florida, Old Soldier.

And stay warm.

Harold LaCosse *(Aug. 2011)*

"The quality goes in before the name goes on."
– Zenith slogan

The Japanese bombed Pearl Harbor on Harold LaCosse's 16th birthday.

On Dec. 8, 1944, the day after his 19th birthday, he arrived in Europe with the 63rd Infantry Division, also known as the "Blood and Fire Division."

LaCosse, 85, was born in Lake Village and raised in Fair Oaks. Today, he lives in Morocco with Donna, his wife of 63 years. They've raised three children; the youngest, Gina, graduated from North Newton High School in 1975. We were classmates.

For 55 years, LaCosse owned an appliance store in Morocco. Harold and Donna are members of the Newton County Historical Society.

* * *

"My parents came from the Momence (Ill.,) area," LaCosse began. "At one time our surname was spelled La Quiox,"

There still are quite a few people of French ancestry from that neck of the woods. What high school did you attend?

"Mount Ayr."

After being discharged from the Army, what did you do?

"Thanks to the GI Bill, I attended Coyne's Electronics in Chicago. In 1948, I opened up an appliance store – repairs, sales and service."

Television was in its infancy back in '48. I imagine, even after going to school in Chicago, you had to keep up with the latest technological advances.

"Absolutely."

Making contact with one of those old television tubes could sure could wake a guy.

"You had to watch where you put your hands; I've been knocked off of more than one stool."

Me, too, Harold. But it was usually in a place like the Hilltop Tavern, just down the street.

"I've also fallen from a few roofs in the wintertime while putting up antennas."

Did you sell items like refrigerators?

"No, I didn't do any white goods – all electronics."

Which included?

"Radios, TVs, stereos ... ."

Harold, I remember my mother working as a waitress for a buck an hour so she could buy a stereo. That behemoth was the size of a sequoia.

"They were a piece of furniture back then."

What kind of TV set sat in the LaCosse living room?

"I liked Zeniths."

Electronically speaking, what's one of the biggest changes you've seen between the '50s and '60s and the 21st Century?

"You used to be able to repair things; nowadays, you can't afford to repair things. It's a throw-away world now. It's cheaper to buy a new item."

Are you a member of Morocco's American Legion?

"Yes, but I've never been to a meeting."

Who's the oldest World War II vet you know from the Morocco area?

"Vane Harrison; he's well into his 90s."

You're kiddin' me. Speed Harrison is still alive? That rascal has defied all laws of science and nature. When I first hired in the mill, "Speed-o" was still working as a locomotive engineer.

"'Speed' was a pilot in the war."

In which parts of Europe did you fight?

"Southern Germany and southern France; I wound up on the Danube River."

You were probably involved in several battles.

"Absolutely. We went through the Siegfried Line and the Maginot Line. Both of those lines were nothing but pillboxes and dragon teeth."

Harold, bear with me, I know what a pillbox is. Dragon teeth?

"Dragon teeth were cement blocks about 3-feet square and about 3-feet tall scattered out on about a 20-foot-wide pad. They were tank obstacles."

How did you overcome them?

"The Allied Forces would take bulldozers and push dirt up against them, and the tanks would go right over the dragon teeth."

Harold, I can't imagine the chaos and horror you guys endured.

"It's unexplainable; you have to experience it."

What kind of weapon did you use?

"I carried an M-1 (rifle)."

What about a Thompson machine gun?

"I carried a Thompson for a little while, but they're too doggone heavy. It wasn't a good gun for where we were at."

Were you awarded any medals?

"I received some medals. It lists them on my discharge papers."

Can I take a look at those papers?

"I suppose; they're in the other room somewhere."

Among several other decorations and citations it says you were awarded not only the Bronze Star, but also the Silver Star. Harold, they don't get much higher than the Silver Star. Do you care to talk about what you did to earn that?

"I'd rather not."

* * *

This is the 63rd anniversary of 63rd Infantry Division Association. The association's annual national reunion will be held from Aug 18 to 20 at the Crown Plaza in Indianapolis.

Donna LaCosse is secretary-treasurer of the association and editor of "Blood and Fire," which is the association's newsletter. The publication comes out three times each year.

Some guys expound upon their battle experiences and some don't. Former Sgt. LaCosse wouldn't go into a lot of detail, at least not with someone like me, who wasn't there. I never push it.

Most folks from northern Newton County who know Harold probably think of him as the polite, unassuming man who repaired their TVs. They probably don't realize he's also a former GI with a Silver Star boxed away in a back room. And that's just the way he wants it.

Harold LaCosse is a lot like those old, American-made Zeniths he knew inside and out – the quality was within.

They don't make 'em like that anymore.

John J. Latko *(Dec. 2008)*

"...December 7, 1941 –
a date which will live in infamy..."
-Franklin Delano Roosevelt

John J. Latko's home sits due west of Hammond High School on the Indiana side of State Line Avenue; he's lived there half his life.

On June 19, 1919, Latko was born in the section of East Chicago known as Indiana Harbor. On Sunday, Dec. 7, 1941, Marine Corps Pvt. John J. Latko was aboard the USS West Virginia in Pearl Harbor.

* * *

"East Chicago and Indiana Harbor were called the twin cities back when I was a boy," Latko began. "I was raised on Alder Street. Both my parents were born in Czechoslovakia. My mother was living in Czechoslovakia when her brother was killed while digging trenches in World War I. While still in my teens, I wanted to enlist in the service; she wouldn't co-sign for me."

What did you do?

"I went to work for Youngstown Sheet and Tube as an ironworker. As soon as I turned 21, I quit and joined the Marines. It was 1940. I didn't know what I was getting into.

"I had mess duty for the first six months. We would go out to sea for 10 days. Then, another group of ships would go out and we'd go on liberty for 10 days.

"On Thanksgiving of '41, I remember asking one of my buddies, 'What the hell are all these ships doing in the harbor?' In boot camp, we learned you don't put all your eggs in one basket."

Why were all the eggs in one basket?

"I don't know if chiefs of staff back in Washington or (President Franklin D.) Roosevelt had anything to do with that decision or not. I voted for Roosevelt, but a general or admiral wouldn't have kept all those ships in Battleship Row simultaneously."

John, if you don't mind, tell me about Dec. 7.

"We were waiting for colors; it was about five minutes before 8 a.m. It was a Sunday; some guys planned on playing baseball when they went ashore, some were going to attend church. It was peacetime; we were sitting ducks.

"When we saw the first ship across the harbor getting bombed, fire and rescue was sounded. When we saw they were coming for us next, fire and rescue was delayed. The call went out for general quarters – protect the West Virginia.

"We lay moored outboard of the Tennessee; we couldn't fire our guns without hitting her.

"Planes were dive bombing us; going for the stacks. The (USS) Arizona blew up. I could see the (USS) Oklahoma, those poor fellas were clinging to the propeller; she was sinking.

"Some of the planes were torpedoing us. After our ship took a few torpedo hits, we started listing to the starboard side. I was thinking about my mother who didn't want me to join the Marines.

"Our captain got killed. A piece of shrapnel flew from the Tennessee to the West Virginia and cut his gut open."

What happened next?

"After being bombed, torpedoed and strafed, we were ordered to abandon ship. She was on fire. I jumped into the water and began swimming behind the Coffey twins; then they started climbing up the hawser of the Tennessee.

"Did you ever try to catch a greased pig? The twins' clothing was drenched in oil. While attending (East Chicago) Washington High School, I could never climb the rope. I climbed an oily rope all the way to the top of a battleship that day.

"When we got to the top deck, the Japs were machine gunning everything that moved, but me and the Coffeys were able to hide in the Tennessee's paint locker."

What did you do then?

"After the first wave of bombings, those of us from the West Virginia who were able-bodied went back aboard our ship to fight fires and search for wounded men.

"A motor launch hauled the wounded from the West Virginia to the Tennessee. I spotted a guy in the water; he must have been a sailor aboard the West Virginia – I didn't know him as a Marine. I threw him a rope and pulled him out of the flames.

"While I was aboard the West Virginia, the coxswain running the motor launch said he wasn't coming back again. I told him to wait, that I was going into the casemate. I wanted to make sure there wasn't anyone in there still alive.

"I'm not going to call the Navy chickenshit; they were OK, but that coxswain was, I have to say, chicken.

"Dougie was a Marine and my closest buddy; he stepped onto the motor launch. When I returned from the casemate, the motor launch was already18 to 20 feet from the West Virginia. The water was still on fire below me. I ran as fast as I could behind the 16-inch guns at midship and broad jumped toward the motor launch; I was saying the Our Father while I did it. I barely made it. I injured myself when I landed on the edge of the motor launch and would have to be operated on later.

"I told the coxswain, 'Hey, there's two more guys over there.' I saw their heads bobbing in the water. He said, 'No, I don't want to catch fire.' He took me, the sailor I pulled in, and Dougie to shore at Dock 1010."

Was there any doubt what was happening when you saw the first planes?

"I knew those were Japanese planes bombing us because I could see the red Rising Suns painted on them. The first person I saw was a Japanese worker. Our eyes met. I'm thankful that my weapon sank with the West Virginia. I would have shot him. And I would have killed an innocent man. Many times, I have thought about that."

What did you do then?

"Although I could've got a month's liberty while they raised the West Virginia and started repairing her, I was through with seagoing. While in the slop chute, a Sgt. Carter asked me if I wanted to join the 2nd Marine Division and serve with the engineers."

Slop chute?

"That's where you get your beer. I was shipped to New Zealand, but eventually ended up in Saipan. I tried to look up Dougie while I was there. The guys from his outfit said he didn't make it. He hadn't been home in four years... ."

When did you get out?

"August of '45; I made Sergeant."

Then what?

"I went to work at Inland Steel's 76-inch mill, but I had trouble standing for any length of time. The people at Hines (Edward Hines, Jr. Veterans Administration Hospital in Maywood, Ill.) said to ask my boss for a lighter job, but even a janitor has to be able to stand on his feet – I bought a tavern on Deodar (Street) in the Harbor.

"When Russia developed an atomic bomb, I moved my family to Hammond, La.; I figured the Calumet Region was a prime area to be bombed. I didn't want anymore of that. In 1955, I moved to Hammond, Ind. I've been here ever since."

Did you purchase another tavern?

"No; I worked at Mercantile Bank on Calumet Avenue for 30 years."

You've been back to Hawaii.

"Yes, but it took 50 years before I did. That was the first gathering of Pearl Harbor survivors. I bumped into a guy named Bill Moore. He saw that my amulet read USS West Virginia. He said, 'You're a Wee-Vee? So am I.'

"Then, he showed me a photograph of him being rescued from the water; it appeared in Life Magazine.

"I looked him in the eye, poked him in the chest, and said, 'See that guy on the other end of that rope? That's me, you son of a bitch. You've lived 50 years longer than you should have. You owe me a drink.'

"He said, 'What'll you have?'

"We became good friends. Moore was a California boy, but moved to Hawaii later in life."

Mr. Latko, thanks for sharing your story.

"I still play it in my sleep. I relive it over and over again."

* * *

Pvt. Latko jumped for his life from the West Virginia onto a motor launch. His best buddy, Dougie, took his life by jumping off a cliff in Saipan. Bill Moore, the man Latko saved, suffered burns over 80 percent of his body. He was hospitalized for one year. At Moore's bequest, his ashes were spread over Pearl Harbor.

A ceremony is scheduled at 10:55 today at the gazebo in Main Square Park on 5th Street and Ridge Road, Highland. That's 7:55 a.m. Hawaiian time – when all hell broke loose 67 years ago.

If you get a chance, stop by. Say hello to John Latko.

And shake his hand.

The River

Coyote Larson *(Nov. 2007)*

"...We can skin a buck; we can run a trot line
And a country boy can survive... "
-Hank Williams, Jr.

Fifty feet east of where Highways 55 and Harrison come to a T in Shelby is Bayou Road.

At the south end of that gravel stretch is the Kankakee River and the home of Tom Larson. He and his wife Cathy have lived there for 23 years. The Larsons have raised three daughters. Tom is 55 years old.

It was late October when I interviewed Larson. He had just finished up work for the year. Larson is a pipe fitter by trade and a member of Local 597. By choice, he has not worked a winter as a fitter in more than 20 years. He also is a trapper. Larson's nickname is Coyote.

A man in a jon boat could be seen drifting by Larson's picture window as we sat down to talk. There was a full moon.

* * *

"I got into the fitters September of 1977," Larson began. "I've been trapping for 43 years. During the '80s, there was (pipefitting) work in Louisiana. Cathy and I lived down there for about 3 1/2 years. I chose that location because I wanted to extend my commercial fishing and trapping knowledge.

"We lived near Bayou Nezpique. The Cajuns kind of adopted me – took me right in. The fiddle player in the movie 'Southern Comfort' was my daughter's school bus driver. I think he also appeared in the film 'The Big Easy,' too. Quite a guy. He also owned a furniture store in Basile."

How's trapping this season?

"I just waxed up my traps and put out 19 coyote sets. Caught three opening day. Caught six more today and a fox. Coyote, fox, and skunk are the only thing open right now. They prime up a little bit sooner."

How many coyotes have you trapped in your career?

"Six more and I'll be at 1100. Caught my first one in '77. Then there was a dead spell until the mid-eighties before any more showed up."

What do you use for coyotes?

"A No. 3 coil (jaw trap). They're a little more sturdy than the old No. 2s that were used for fox."

Do they pay you bounties for coyotes?

"No, I sell the pelts. They use them in coats – collars and trim mostly. My best year was '01, I caught 126. I use road kill for bait. Gary Airport hired me to trap coyote about 10 years ago."

They're very intelligent animals.

"A coyote is much harder to catch than a fox – and a fox is smart."

Do you consume any of these fur bearers?

"I don't eat as much beaver as I used too. Cathy and I are getting older now; we eat out a lot."

Muskrats pretty tasty?

"Oh yeah, the hams. 'Rats are vegetarians – clean animal. We've had years where we caught as many as 3,000 muskrats – 150 to 200 per day. I had a partner back then, Jimmy Gatlin – phenomenal trapper.

"I make my own muskrat traps. It's like a tube they swim in – they drown. I can skin 60 'rats per hour. I was Northwest Fur Company's first fur skinner. They were located up by Ramsey's Landing. They'd pay me a penny for fleshin' it and penny for stretchin' it.

"I've caught more than 2,000 beavers – 171 in one year here in Indiana. I use snares for beaver."

A beaver can do a lot of damage.

"I have to do a job for a lady next week. She doesn't believe in hunting or trapping of any kind. All of a sudden beavers are damming up her ditch and all the trees are disappearing. Now the beavers have to go. It would have been a sin to kill those beavers if they were chewing her neighbor's property. But the beavers set up shop on her land. I see that all the time."

You're kind of a mercenary at times.

"I contract out for different counties. The farmers have formed a conglomerate that all their money goes into.

"I also trap beaver, otter and bobcat out of state. I'm paid a bounty for every beaver tail I turn in. I've done some removal work for the state of Arkansas."

What was the highwater mark for fur?

"The late '70s. Ninety percent of the fur in the world is fur farmed now. The Scandinavian countries are huge on fur farming. Most of the fur sold in the world is ranch mink."

How much do you get for a mink nowadays?

"A large buck mink will go for about $15 – $10 for a good female. It's all speculative as far as the prices right now. Hopefully a good blanket beaver will go for about $25."

You mentioned commercial fishing.

"I kept a commercial license for about 10 years on the Wabash River down by Attica. Gill nets, trammel nets, hoop nets, trot lines. I'd fish commercially on weekends. Catfish, dogfish, carp, buffalo, shovelnose sturgeon – rough fish are all you're allowed to take out of fresh water."

As a kid, I speared a few buffalo. They look just like a carp, but have a bluish-gray tint to them. They're served in fine restaurants, correct?

"Oh, yeah. Jewish people eat them a lot. They say a 10-pound carp in England is worth a huge amount of money – big sport fish over there. I put out 20 fiberglass bank poles the other day for channel cat. I fish the surface with the hook half out of the water. I bait the hooks with catalpa worms or minnows."

Can you fish commercially here on the Kankakee?

"No; you can run trot lines and limb lines, but not commercially."

Tom, the first time I ever met you was at a Friends of the Kankakee River meeting held at the Grand Kankakee Marsh a few years back.

"Most hunters and trappers love nature. I'm a past president of the Izaak Walton League.

"I'm also the proxy for Lake County surveyor George Van Til on the Kankakee River Basin Commission – I go to every meeting. If it wasn't for the hunters and trappers there would be species that would go extinct."

Explain, please.

"Jeff, a pair of fox stay within a square mile. The adjoining square mile? Another pair of fox. They'll wipe out every rabbit there is in that square mile.

"Coons, possums and skunks would wipe out the eggs of ground nesting birds like pheasants and wild turkeys. The areas that don't have a predator control program? Up to 99 percent of the eggs get destroyed every year.

"The difference between us and an animal activist? We are biologically sound. We have proof that you need to depopulate. The animal rights people have nothing biological behind them – strictly emotional. They don't want to see the animal killed because their heart bleeds for it."

A wildlife rehabilitator friend of mine mentioned oral contraceptives as possible solution.

"Purdue University tried that in Wheatfield. They experimented on deer. They found out a year later if an animal came by and fed off the carcass of one these dead deer – they'd become sterile. It went right on down the food chain. They had to destroy all the tagged deer, called them white buffalos."

You're saying if a hunter ate one of those deer, he could be shooting blanks in the future?

"It's quite possible."

* * *

As a young man Coyote read Jack London. One of those tales featured a fellow named Wolf Larsen. Tom says he enjoyed London's Alaskan stories the most. "To Build A Fire" being his personal favorite.

Here in Indiana they made a drainage ditch out of the river the Potawatomi referred to as Aukiki. The dredgers had ambitious thoughts of doing the same on the Illinois side. French-blooded trappers bearing guns and knives convinced them it wasn't a good idea. Today, the Kankakee River remains its serpentine self in Illinois. Wildlife abounds.

I do believe the Billedeaus and Boudreaus of Bourbonnais, Momence and Kankakee could have counted on the rugged Hoosier standing amongst them, watching their backs.

But as fate would have it, Coyote Larson was born a century too late.

Venus Lukes *(Apr. 2005)*

"Pivo prosim." (A beer, please.)

As I parked in front of the Sumava Resorts post office, I stared at the small apartment sitting above it. Memories.

Behind the post office is the home of Venus Lukes. She lives beside Lukes Restaurant & Tavern. Three generations of Lukes have owned and operated the establishment for nearly 70 years.

Always a fine-featured, slender lady, Lukes, 84, looks remarkably the same as she did 45 years ago. Her pleasant voice and polite manner of speaking remain as well.

She and her late husband, Jimmy, raised three sons: Tom, Bob and Jim. Tom, the eldest, continues to run the family business.

* * *

Venus, tell me about some of your earliest memories.

"I was born on the southwest side of Chicago," she said. "My parents were immigrants who had come to Ellis Island from Czechoslovakia; they met in New York, married, and eventually moved to Chicago.

"When I was 3, my parents were forced to move back to Europe. It was the early 1930s. But my father moved back to the U.S. a year later. When he saved up enough money, he sent for us. I was 5 by then. I spoke only Bohemian when I returned to America.

"I graduated from grade school in Chicago, but my father had tired of city life and found a farm outside of Schneider. We moved to the farm in 1941. Then, I went back to Chicago and got into the cadet nurse corps; it was run by the government."

When did you meet your husband?

"I knew of him and his family when I was in high school because I would buy rye bread from his parents' bakery – I'd walk along the railroad tracks from Schneider to Sumava. Jimmy's family were also Bohemians who migrated to Chicago; they were some of the earliest settlers of Sumava during the 1920s.

"I'd take the bus from Chicago to visit the farm; Jimmy was in the Navy at the time. His mother would always let me know when he was going to be coming home."

Sounds like Bessie Lukes was a bit of a matchmaker.

"Yes, she kind of hooked us up. Jimmy and I started writing each other. He came home and gave me an engagement ring in '46. It was about the time of V-J Day; I remember people celebrating the Japanese surrender. In Chicago, they didn't want me to leave nursing, but I told them I was getting married."

Decided to become a restauranteur instead.

"Yes, my in-laws opened the restaurant in 1940; we took it over in 1948. Jimmy did the cooking. Whatever he needed, I was right there. I was his 'right-hand man.'" .

I remember, Venus. I remember Doris Hendryx and Adrianna Havlicek, too – darting into the kitchen. Gracefully weaving their way through tables while toting platters of walleyed pike fillets, frog legs, fried mushrooms and cold sweaty bottles of Stroh's Bohemian-style beer.

You mentioned Jimmy's family was here before yours. I'm sure they told you about Sumava during the late '20s; fill me in.

"From what has been handed down, in 1925, a group of real estate agents – all Czechs from Chicago: Kral, Kucera, Dvorak and Koutny came upon the land. They formed a company named Sumava Forest Resorts Inc.

"They subdivided it with streets, beaches and parks. All the work was done by big scoop shovels drawn by horses. They put in deep wells for the people. In June of 1927, the first lots were put up for sale."

Continue, please.

"By 1928, a chartered train brought hundreds of prospective customers to Sumava. Women would get dressed up in native Bohemian attire and greet the people as they spent the day looking at lots. Later, they bought buses to bring the people in. Many Chicagoans bought lots and built summer cottages. They would stay for the weekends in these little bungalows, most of which had no insulation.

"Jimmy's parents had been successful bakery shop owners in Chicago. He said his father spotted an ad in a Bohemian newspaper about

Sumava Resorts. At first, Jimmy's parents built a small cottage way back in the woods, then, as did some of the others, they built a house suitable to live in year around. It is still standing near the old Sumava Hotel. Then came the Depression in 1929. By 1930, they lost the house."

Hard times.

"The Depression stagnated the growth of Sumava. When the country finally started to pull out of it, Sumava started to make a comeback, too.

"Then, in 1950, the Kankakee River overflowed causing a 75-foot break in the dike. The entire community was flooded; everyone had to leave. I was expecting, so I went to stay on my parents' farm in Schneider.

"Jimmy and his mother were the only two people from Sumava who remained; he got around town by boat. It lasted six weeks. Volunteers from the Lake Village Grange and American Legion loaded up more than 9,000 sandbags into wagons and pulled them with tractors to Sumava. Men in boats transported the sandbags to the break."

Other years when Sumava flooded?

"The floods of '67, '76, and '93 were bad, but nothing like what happened Easter Sunday, 1950."

Final thoughts?

"Jeff, I can still see my brother running down the deck of the ship that took us back to Czechoslovakia. He was playing with paper airplanes. I was known as Venuska (pronounced Ve-NOOSH-ka) Zamazal back then. I was 3 years old."

* * *

Venus Lukes also was the postmaster for 32 years. A post office that served, simultaneously, as Lukes Bakery for many years.

She baked her share of kolachkies, waited tables ad infinitum, and made sure our letters got mailed – all the while raising three sons.

Venus still runs the cash register and washes down tables at the restaurant. She'd feel out of sorts not to.

Jimmy Lukes was my parents' landlord when we lived above that tiny bakery-post office almost 50 years ago. My dad said he had to fork out 30 bucks a month rent, but the utility bills weren't bad in the winter living above a bakery. I remember when we moved.

I was 3 years old.

Flip Phelps *(Feb. 2006)*

"Give a man a fish and he has food for a day; teach him how to fish and you can get rid of him for the entire weekend."
– Zenna Schaffer

I don't have time to fish anymore, so like some pathetic grouper groupie, I decided to interview a fisherman. What the heck, listening to and telling fish stories is the best part.

Dick "Flip" Phelps has been on the payroll at the Grand Kankakee Marsh County Park for about 12 years, but the weatherbeaten outdoorsman volunteered his services ever since the park opened up in '78.

Phelps, 69, is a living legend. He's "The Man" when it comes to landing the elusive walleye from the murky logjams of the river the Potawatomi called Aukiki .

* * *

"I was born in Hammond," Phelps began. "We moved to Cedar Lake when I was 10."

Flip, I once heard you say at a fishing seminar that you've never fished a drift (logjam) in the Kankakee River without catching at least one fish.

"That's true to this day. If you use live bait, you can get it down underneath the drift without hanging up where you'd get snagged using artificial bait.

"I'm fishing for walleye when I fish a drift, but I catch largemouth, smallmouth, rock bass, blue gills, crappie, carp, dogfish – everything hits crawlers.

Got any tips for novice river fishermen?

"If you let the worm set, you'll catch a lot of carp. I don't let the worm set. You gotta keep it rollin.' If you keep 'er movin,' you have a better chance for game fish instead of carp or suckers."

Ever eat carp or sucker?

"I've ate it all. Hog-nosed sucker is good eatin.' Meat's sweet, but bonier than heck. I used to cut 'em up in strips, and then score 'em 'til the meat just about fell apart. You just fry 'em up and eat the bones and all – like eatin' potato chips."

When I think of the river, I think of catfish and walleye.

"There's big crappie and bluegills in the Kankakee. If more people would fish the timber, they'd catch a lot more fish. But folks are afraid of hanging up, so they leave those spots alone."

Where exactly did you catch your 13 1/2-pound walleye?

"In the Kankakee River on Oct. 6, 2004. She was a big female, almost 32 inches long. Caught her on 4 lb. test (line) using a weedless jig and a minnow. She was down in a hole with a lot of debris."

But where did you –

"I've fished the Illinois side, but all the big fish I've caught were in Indiana. Thing is, guys find out the good spots, and most of them can't fish it right. They hang up with heavy line. They yank on it, break it off, and then you can't fish that drift because all that line down there. My light line will hook up with all the other line and go right to where it's hung up – then I'm hung up, too."

But where –

"I hook crawlers Texas style with a small No.6 light wire hook. It's the best way to fish the river without hanging up."

Flip, they say 90 percent of the walleye are taken out of the Kankakee by 10 percent of the fishermen. I've tried. But usually ended up going to Lukes Restaurant for the fillet. Mrs. Paul's fish sticks are pretty good.

"Oxbows, neck downs, drifts, jams, drop offs, where a creek or bayou comes into the river, are all good feeding areas – any time of year. The higher the water the better. When the river gets real low you'll find walleye in holes or undercut banks or drifts because it's dark.

"A guy should know when the water goes up or down the holes fill in. Drifts move, too. If you get a lot of ice in the winter it'll pull out a lot of drifts. One year a hole will be really good for fishing and the next year that hole is gone."

You mentioned the depth of the water. What about water

temperature?

"Above 50 degrees, I use nightcrawlers. If the water is below 50 degrees, I'll use a jig and minnow, Rapala, twisters, or plain jigs.

"If I'm in an area full of hang ups I'll use a weedless 1/16th-ounce jig with no paint on it or nothin'– with a minnow.

"Walleye will hit crawlers when the water temps are 30 degrees, but they'll just kind of hang on to it. They won't suck it down like when the water is warmer. I guess there's more protein in the minnow than the crawlers. They don't normally get crawlers in the winter because there's no run off. That's how fish usually get crawlers."

Best month for catching walleye?

"Late March. Spawners. They're more vulnerable. Your darker hours and overcast or windy days are best. Although there are times in late August you can catch 'em in the middle of the afternoon with a crank bait and the sun shining."

The state record was caught out of the Kankakee, right?

"Yep, 14 pounds, 4 ounces. I'll usually sit in one spot if I'm after big fish. I've also caught a lot of big fish from shore. Since 1967, I've caught 26 walleye over 10 pounds, five over 11 pounds, and two over 12 pounds. That's not easy. That's hard fishin.'"

I know you're semi-retired, what did you do for a living when you wore a younger man's hip waders?

"I was a union laborer. It was right up my alley. I've never worked a winter in my life. I'd take the winters off so I could ice fish and regular fish."

Got any final words of wisdom for future river fishermen?

"Light line sinks quicker than heavier line. If more people would drop their poundage, they'd catch more fish because you get down to where the fish are sooner."

Ever fly fish?

"Sure."

You know who the greatest advocate of fly fishing is, don't you?

"Who's that?"

The nightcrawler.

* * *

Flip Phelps is a lifetime bachelor and a friendly cuss. He's just kinda murky about where he caught the 13 1/2-pounder.

Kathy Voyles *(Oct. 2012)*

"Those who dwell among the beauties and mysteries of the earth are never alone or weary of life."
– Rachel Carson

Kathy Voyles, 52, lives a bullfrog's leap from the Kankakee River near Marti's Place in Hebron. She has been married to Bill Voyles for 29 years.

Our interview took place in Kathy's backyard, which included a fantastic herb garden, no less than a dozen humming birds darting around inches from us, a greenhouse and plethora of gourds growing from trellises and pine trees. She has a business known as Nature's Bounty.

Kathy paints, burns and etches delightful images on gourds.

* * *

You've lived near the Kankakee River all your life.

"Yes, I grew up in a community in extreme southern Lake County known as Pons," she said. "It's just west of Schneider and U.S. 41. It's old Kankakee River bed. This place also is original Kankakee River bed."

Wouldn't you have liked to seen the river before it was straightened and dredged?

"Oh, my gosh. All the islands, animals and the Indian tribes that lived around here."

Tell me more about your childhood in Pons.

"I ran the woods like a wild child. It was wonderful back then. The bayous were full of playful muskrats and quacking ducks. There were actually swans back in there. And there were big fields of wild strawberries and a creek full of crayfish. We used to rake them out."

Crawdads are great bass bait.

"My brothers were the fishermen."

Siblings?

"I'm the eighth of nine kids. By the time my parents got to me, I was lucky if I was even looked at. I probably changed my own diapers. My oldest brother was born on Christmas morning right on the river."

What is your maiden name?

"Radaszewski

Did your parent's place in Pons ever get flooded?

"One time; I think it was in '78. One of the dikes broke and we got about two feet of water in the house. We actually had to leave.

"I remember my conservation teacher at Lowell High School was real interested in the situation. He came over and we took him for a boat ride all through the subdivision."

Did you like art in school?

"Oh, yeah. All the classes that could get me out of just sitting around. You know, the boring ones like typing and stuff – couldn't handle it. I was either in art class, shop class or the greenhouse.

"We used to have to walk to Studer's gas station to catch the bus. On those beautiful spring mornings with the sun coming up and you could smell that grass growing, I'd purposely miss the bus. I'd rather help my mother hang laundry outside than sit in a classroom."

Great garden. You have everything from cherry tomatoes to tropical hibiscus.

"Oh, gosh, I have all kinds of herbs out there like oregano, sage, tarragon, lemon thyme, fennel and my prize-winning chives that always win at Lake County Fair. I shouldn't say that, now I've probably jinxed myself."

Everything is grown in raised beds. Are you an organic gardener?

"Oh, yeah. In the spring, I enjoy watching the goldfinches and indigo buntings eat the dandelion seeds. We also have a lot of flickers and woodpeckers here in the swamp."

When I called you last week, you were canning tomatoes.

"This afternoon, I'll put up some salsa. I also do pickles."

Do you grow all your own gourds for artwork?

"Not all of them."

I really like the design on this large gourd container.

"That's a Virginia creeper I burned into it; I just started coloring it in with dyes. I've been blessed with a vivid imagination. I'll look at the shape of a gourd and say, 'Now, this is a pepper.'"

Wow, a very large chili pepper painted red with a lid!

"I'll probably keep that one for myself."

When you have company and serve a bowl of your homemade salsa, you can fill that gourd with tortilla chips.

"I do birdhouses, baskets, watermelons – you name it."

What are your best sellers?

"Birdhouses."

I always see you and Bill reenacting as pioneers at Aukiki River Festival near Kouts and Baum's Bridge. What other festivals do you attend?

"We're getting ready to attend the Eastern Rendezvous which is located in Troy, Ohio. It's a four-hour drive, if that. There's like 2,000 camps; it's huge. They have one weekend that is open to the public."

How about the Feast of the Hunters' Moon in Lafayette?

"We used to go there, but it has gotten too overcrowded. But we do a wonderful event called Mississinewa. It's like 'The Feast,' but better. It's located near Marion and located right on the river."

How long have you been churning out your fine gourd art?

"Oh, gosh. I've always been interested in it; it's right up my alley with gardening and nature and everything else. Thirty years ago, I was making birdhouses and various odds and ends out of gourds for myself and friends, but never on this scale.

"Every year, I learn something new; it's a constant learning experience. I had a gourd that I would take to our re-enactments. I called it a goodie container; we'd put granola bars and stuff like that in it.

"People kept asking me, 'Do you have these gourd containers for sale?' I got to thinking, 'Maybe I could make a few bucks at this.'"

Anything else regarding gourds or gourd crafting?

"In October of 2013, the Indiana Gourd Society will hold its fall festival at the industrial building of the Lake County Fair Grounds. There will competitions and lots of other stuff. It's open to the public and has free admission. You can go there and buy things, look at things and ask questions."

* * *

What a pleasant autumn chat I had with the ever cheerful Kathy Voyles. Sipping sun tea while ruby-throated wonders hovered above glorious asters in full bloom.

You'd have to be out of your gourd not to enjoy that.

Loretta Barton *(Aug. 2007)*

"Hark, now hear the sailors cry
Smell the sea and feel the sky
Let your soul and spirit fly
into the mystic.
And when that foghorn blows
I will be coming home..."
-Van Morrison

I followed the railroad tracks until veering off Monon Road into a cluster of cottages nestled next to the Kankakee River. My destination? The home of Shelby's eldest resident, Loretta Barton.

* * *

Tell me about your roots, Loretta.

"My dad was originally from Kansas, but moved to Little Rock, Ark., where he ran a trap line. He married my mother and they eventually migrated to Momence, Ill., where I was born. We were always connected to the river.

"I've been in Shelby since the third or fourth grade. In between, we lived in Schneider, Hebron, Thayer, Roselawn and Lake Village. Back in those days farmers moved a lot. You didn't always have money to pay the farm rent. My maiden name was Ellis."

Did you have any brothers or sisters?

"I come from four boys and four girls. All of our names began with the letter L. We were one 'L' of a family. I started working outside the home in the summer after eighth grade. I went with the thrashing gang that worked on the Brown Ranch when they moved from one house to the other. Holton Brown owned the houses and the land. I helped the cooks.

"I started school that fall but also went to work for a couple uptown by the name of Naylor. She was not well. I put myself through high school – $3 a week in the summer, and a $1.25 a week in the wintertime by chopping wood and whatever else needed to be done.

"My mother died in '39. I started working at Youngstown Steel in Indiana Harbor that summer. Big wages. I found my pay stub about a year-and-a-half ago. I cleared $15 every two weeks flopping tin that was used for canning.

"All the workers who flopped tin were women. I eventually went into black plate because it paid more. Then I stenciled packaging for Youngstown. It was all done by hand back then. I worked in the mill until 1943. It was a 42-mile drive one way."

When did you get married?

"Dick and I were married in '41. I believe it was in 1945 that we got a chance to purchase the tavern that was uptown. We borrowed the money. The old people was wanting to get out. I did all the cooking.

"Neither one of us ever drank. It wasn't much fun serving people that did drink. We threw out a lot of customers who we never served a drink to – they'd come in pie-eyed. They never took it personal, and would come back another day. We eventually sold Barton's Bar and Grill. The tavern's gone now.

"In April of '49, Dick got the chance to get into conservation. He rose to become sergeant of the 1st district, which covered 21 counties back then. After eight years, he made lieutenant."

Your late husband was a game warden?

"For 24 years. He loved the job. Jack Parry from the Post-Tribune used to stop by here all the time. He was like a son to me."

Seashells.

"Let's go upstairs if you wanna talk shells! You first, it takes time for me to get up the stairs. This hip doesn't work like it should. It's just wore out.

"When I first started collecting, I carried this booklet, 'The Golden Guide to Seashells,' with me because I didn't know any of them. I got to where I could tell you the name of every shell I've got. I can't now; it's been 20 years since I worked with them. It's no fun to go up here alone. My husband did the biggest share of the shell cleaning..."

Oh, my. This is amazing, Loretta.

"We collected them for 40 years: Mexico, California, but mostly in Florida. Dick and I drove the coast to Florida. We shelled all the way."

Look at them all. Gallon jars and huge cardboard boxes loaded with seashells. And you have them all labeled and categorized... Conch shells, black jingle shells, snail shells, carrier shells, olive shells, worm shells, cockle shells... Murex, lacy murex, turkey wings, angel wings... Plus seahorses, starfish, puffer fish, shark teeth, sea mice, spiny oysters, sunray clams and sand dollars!

"Shells come in just about every color. Orange, lemon-colored... They call these tulips. This is the only red tulip we ever found. This is the way the sand dollar looks when you find them; they have hair on them. We used Linco to clean them. (*I have found that most old folks call any brand of bleach Linco*)

"We had to boil most of the shells we found to get the animals out of them. The body of this horse conch was bright orange. One time when Dick was manning the boat in Florida, I yelled out, 'Stop!' I netted two horse conchs at once – they were mating.

"Here are some of my precious shells. This white one with brown checkers is a junonia. Very rare. If I ever would've found a perfect one it would be worth a couple thousand dollars.

"This is my odds and ends box. Here's an old pipe that had washed ashore."

Cool. From some salty old seafarer, no doubt. The stories that briar could tell. This is really something. And the shellacked turtle shells mounted on the wall. Those snappers probably came out of the Kankakee.

"Yes, I love fried turtle. Back in those days you really lived off the land. Whatever you hunted or fished for, you ate. There was no refrigeration when I was a child. You had to cook it and eat it. I was swimming in this river when I was just barely walking. We camped and fished on the river. I used to love to fish, but I've not been in a boat since Dick died in '89."

Did you have children?

"No, just my husband and I."

"I get to thinking about it and can't hardly believe the change in the people. They can't hardly do without dishwashers. And they have to have everything when they first get married.

"My house is old here, and young here, and older there. The chair you're sitting in is re-upholstered. You couldn't afford to buy new ones. We redid several chairs in Naugahyde."

Naugahyde... I remember that stuff. Loretta, on a hot August night you could get up from the kitchen table and the chair would follow you into the living room – stuck to your backside like a barnacle clinging to a carrier shell.

"I've had cataract, knee, and hip surgery. I'm a cancer survivor. It's amazing what you can't do when you get old. But I'm fortunate that I can still take care of myself and remain here."

* * *

I watched a hummingbird hover just a few inches from her back window. A piece of driftwood floated by, making its way toward Momence... .

For 40 years, Loretta Barton and her best friend collected shells while combing faraway beaches. She has collected memories along the Kankakee River for nearly 90.

Willie Curtis *(Aug. 2009)*

"...Well, out of south Alabama come a country boy
He said, 'I'm looking for a man named Jim
I am a pool shootin' boy, my name is Willie McCoy
But down home they call me Slim..."
– Jim Croce

Several years ago, I interviewed a man named Jim for this column from Shelby. He was awarded a diploma while in his 70's because he quit Lowell High School to help stop the likes of Adolf Hitler.

No one called Jim Hall by his given name. Some folks probably thought Chub was Hall's real first name. Chub's brothers, Gabby and Sparky, also fought in World War II, as did Ham, Beans, Butter and Bugs Hammersley who grew up down the street in Shelby.

Beans and Butter were twins; so were Fat and Skinny Curtis also of Shelby. Because of health reasons, Fat couldn't serve in World War II. Skinny did; he was killed in Italy.

A portly towhead, Willie Curtis is the spittin' image of his Grandpa Fat, but was named after his Great-Uncle Skinny.

Willie's raven-haired brother could possibly be the only male child from Shelby who doesn't have a nickname; Tony Curtis is a detective who now resides in Lansing, Ill.

Willie, 34, is a lifelong Shelby resident who never has married. He is to competitive bean-spitting what Griffith's John Barenie is to growing giant squash or Cedar Lake's Ken Rasmussen is to cardboard boat racing.

I recently interviewed Willie at the Lake County Fair, soon after he'd finished competing in the annual bean-spitting contest.

* * *

What do you do for a living?

"Exterior construction," Curtis began. "I install vinyl siding, cedar siding, soffit, fascia, and gutters. We do roofs, windows, gutters, decks...."

Some of those roofs are probably a little on the steep side.

"I fell about three years ago; I was out of work for two years. I had to have a couple of surgeries on my shoulder because of it. Our planks slid off the ladder jack; I was lucky. It's a job."

Is your dad a roofer, too?

"No, he started working for Globe Industries in Lowell from the time he got out of Vietnam around 1970."

Hobbies?

"I like bass fishing and wild turkey hunting."

OK, enough small talk. You're the greatest "spitter" Northwest Indiana has ever known. How did it begin?

"My brother, Tony, and I were working maintenance here at the fair back in '91. Tony asked our supervisor, Ken Craft, if we could enter the contest. Ken told Tony he would keep us on the clock as long as one of us won the contest. Tony, told him, 'Don't worry, Kenny, I'll win.'"

Yeah?

"I won it all; I was only 15."

A star was born. Willie, other than in '93 and '94 – when you didn't compete – you've won it every year but twice.

"Yeah, the summer after I won the first one, there was this kid who worked maintenance here with me. He kept hounding me about technique. I had compassion for him because he was a fellow asthmatic. I taught him how to spit and he ended up beating me by like three inches. By the time it was my turn to spit, it was a downpour."

Are asthmatics at a disadvantage when it comes to spitting legumes?

"I believe we have an advantage; our lungs are probably stronger because of all the stress they've been through. Trying to breathe during an attack is quite a workout. Back when I wrestled for Lowell, you couldn't take an injury timeout for an asthma attack."

Willie, you're loaded with talent, but also quite a gamesman. Some even might consider you a hustler. Each year, you wait until the last second to sign up, so you can go last and know what it takes to win. Why, when you beat that guy from Sauk Village, Ill., today, it was classic Willie Curtis heroics – the crowd went wild.

"Yeah, I'll do whatever it takes to get an edge. But, today was too close for comfort. As you know, each contestant is allowed two successive spits. I prefer a walk-off; that didn't happen today. Richards had a best of 37 feet, 3 inches; my initial spit was 36 feet,-6 inches."

But you came back to win it with a clutch 38-4. Kid, do you have ice water in your veins?

"No, after last night, I'd say I have hops and grains in my veins."

Willie, from '95 to '05, you rattled off 11 consecutive championships. Then, in '06, came the return of your older sibling – Tony Curtis.

"Next question."

I don't know what's more impressive, the 11-straight victories or what you did in '05. Let's face it, a 35-foot effort will usually win it for you.

"I can't explain the 64-foot, 11-inch spit that year. I had had a couple of 50-footers practicing. Actually, I did have a spit of 70 feet in practice once, but I can't really count that one."

Wind-aided?

"Yeah, I ate beans the night before. The 65-footer was just the perfect spit; there was no extra air that escaped around my rolled-up tongue. It was just an absolute cannon-like projectile. It was pretty.

"I was thinking Guinness Book (of Records). I looked it up and the world's record is like 99-9, but that was on ice – counting the roll. Still, that's impressive. By the way, I kept the bean that soared nearly 65 feet; it's glued to the trophy."

Willie, is it technique or genetics? Was your father a great bean-spitter?

"No, but my mother was."

I noticed that you dip snuff. Maybe that has enhanced your ability to hurl soup beans.

"Not at all; I attempted to quit on New Year's Day and gained 18 pounds in 15 days. Then, I got into a see-who-could-lose-the-most-weight contest with my girlfriend. Like I said, I'll go to any length to win any contest. I started chewing again.

"I want to go on record saying that chewing tobacco is an addictive and dangerous habit. I don't want any young bean-spitters out there to ever use tobacco in any form, just because Willie Curtis currently does. As soon as I win my weight-loss bet, I'll bet my girlfriend that I can stay off the snuff longer than she can."

Well, Willie, like they say, "front teeth missin,' that's fine fer kissin." Do you have to get some height for a great spit?

"I like about a 38-degree angle. You can't go too high, but you can't go straight out, either. Dang. Now, people will read this in the newspaper and could possibly beat me next year."

Earlier you mentioned that you lodge the bean in your curled tongue. How do you do that?

"Do what?"

Curl your tongue.

"Simple, like this. It's the only method that's successful. What's the matter? Don't tell me you're in the 10 percent of the world's population that can't curl their tongues?"

Genetics.

* * *

I have found people living along the Kankakee River to be a hardy lot; most of them would gladly give you the shirts off their backs.

Once Curtis had won the contest and the crowd had dispersed, he raised his shirt. From just under his shoulder blades all the way down to the small of his back, Curtis' skin was the color of an eggplant. He said he went on a coughing jag about three weeks before, and that was the result.

It had to have hurt, to take long, deep breaths, then let those legumes fly with everything he had. He made no mention of the pain. I didn't ask.

I did ask him if he'd been to a doctor. He said he had not, but let Coyote Larson's wife take a look at it over on Bayou Road, along the river in Shelby. She tends to such things.

As a boy, Willie learned a lot about baiting limb lines for channel cat and running trap lines for muskrat from an old-timer who was a boyhood friend of Fat and Skinny.

He went by the nickname Chub.

Chub Hall *(July 2006)*

"...I was born in a small town
and I live in a small town
...and I can breathe in a small town
...gonna die in this small town –
and that's probably where they'll bury me."
- John Mellencamp

The Hall boys who hailed from Shelby went by nicknames: Gabby, Sparky and Chub. It's Chub, the baby boy, who I'd come to interview.

Hall, 79, has lived in Shelby all his life. He grew up two blocks from where he resides today.

Hall's first wife, Keturah, passed away in 1985. They had four children, Kris, Karol, Karen and Keith. He is now married to Lois; they were wed on her birthday, Feb.14, 1990.

* * *

"First thing I want to tell you is, I don't hear very good," Hall began.

Me either; I worked for Inland Steel in East Chicago most of my life. Let's get to shoutin', Chub.

"All three of us Halls worked right across the canal from Inland – for Youngstown."

Was your father a steel worker?

"No, he was a dredge operator."

What was his name?

"Millard Fillmore Hall. Went by Mid."

What year did you graduate from high school?

"In 2005."

Come again?

"After two years of high school, I joined the Navy. I would have graduated in 1945. They passed a law back in 2002 that permitted veterans from either World War to be awarded diplomas if we left school early to join the military."

Tell me more about your ancestors.

"My grandparents, nine of their children, several old hound dogs, a flock of chickens, and a few barrels of flour and apples floated down the Kankakee River from San Pierre to Shelby on an old 34-foot barge. Dad was a boy of 12 back then; that was the fall of 1900.

"Their journey came to a halt when they got to the 3-I (railroad bridge); they were puttin' in new pilings at the time. The barge couldn't get through until the work was finished which wasn't going to happen until springtime.

"They tried to survive on their 'houseboat' (nothing more than a canvas tarp covering part of the barge), but the winter got so cold, they had to hire a man with a team of horses to move them and their belongings to a house in Thayer.

"When spring came, they got through and eventually built a little shack here in Shelby right on the river. The river was still crooked in those days. I don't think it was dredged for another 10 or 15 years; my father helped dredge the Kankakee."

Shelby, before the dredging, that must have been something to see.

"Not too long after Grandpa Hall moved his family off the barge, another house or two popped up. He decided it was getting too crowded and abandoned the entire family. He went and lived the life of a hermit out on Shell Island in Florida. The Odd Fellows Society found him and buried him."

What was Shelby like for you during the '30s?

"We was all very poor. But we thought we was rich because everybody had the same amount. If we had somethin' to eat, we shared it with the neighbors. We ate beans a lot. We ate a lot of rabbit, raccoon and muskrat, too."

I've eaten muskrat hams; they're a clean animal – vegetarian.

"I used to work for Dean White's parents here in Shelby; I made $25 per week. I helped Dean get started. Today, he's made billions of dollars. I'm still workin' on my first billion.

"What did you think about our Shelby Grade School reunion we had the other night? My kids came back home for it. They weren't here very long, but it seemed like a dream having them all home.

"Did you see our memorial in the park? Wilma McLean did all the artwork for it. There's over 300 names of men and women from Shelby who served their country in the armed forces. I've got to add about 12 names to it."

It's really a nice tribute, Chub. Shelby suffered losses just the same as Chicago or Indianapolis. Reading the names, it looked as though there were a number of siblings from town who served.

"Oh, yeah. Butter, Beans, Bugs, and Ham Hammersley all fought in World War II; Butter and Beans were twins. Fat and Skinny Curtis also were twins. Fat didn't have to serve; Skinny was killed in France or Italy. We can thank our trustee, Alice Dahl, for that memorial; she's been so good to us.

"After I retired, I done a lot of limb lining. I was called 'The Catfish King.' For 13 years, me and another guy would catch catfish all year long, then, we'd have a big fish fry at the Lion's Club. We'd have people bring in side dishes. Catfishin' is like dairy farmin'; you have to run them lines twice a day."

What did you use for bait, crawdads or crawlers?

"Catalpa worms, mostly. Stink bait, too. My dad and his dad were the real outdoorsmen. They ordered 126 dozen traps one year – the largest order ever received up in Chicago. Dad and Uncle Frank caught 40,000 muskrats back in 1912. They'd ice skate while pulling a tent full of pelts behind them throughout the marsh.

"Hunters would come from all over the world to hunt ducks in Shelby; they'd stay in hunting lodges and hotels here. My dad and grandpa served as guides."

Were there ill feelings because of your grandpa's sudden exodus?

"My dad was an easygoing fella; he took me, Gabby, Spark and my sister down to the Fort Myers Town Hall to look for grandfather's grave.

"They said at the time Grandpa was buried, it would've had to been out at the old cemetery. They had a special section of people who was buried by the Oddfellows.

"There were three unmarked graves. His had to have been one of those three. That's all we ever found out about his demise. Here's a picture of my mother when she was young.

"Our little town... . We don't have much, but it's a great place to live. The Stowells, Lattas, Carlsons, Estills, Hammersleys, Ellis'... . We've all been like family."

* * *

Chub has been known to say, "Do today, what you can get done today. You might not be here tomorrow." For 30 years while serving in the Lion's Club, he did just that. He also was a charter member of the Shelby

Fire Department back in '48. He's a veteran who has been known to do whatever he can for his fellow vets. Chub Hall's real name is Jim. He was named after "The Hermit of Shell Island." Old Jim Hall was a loner filled with wanderlust; he was buried in a pauper's grave.

And yes, Jim "Chub" Hall might still be working on his first billion, but when his time comes, he will have amassed much wealth, a wealth of family from a small town – Shelby, Indiana, USA.

Up to the Challenge

Daniel Lang *(May 2005)*

"...God it looks like Daniel,
must be the clouds in my eyes..."
-Bernie Taupin, Elton John

Daniel Lang loves to sing. His friends call him D. Lang and he has lots of friends. He also has an incredible memory for names and faces.

Lang, 24, lives with his mother, Jane, a music teacher in the Crown Point school district.

He is the son of Mark Lang and the older brother of David, who was quite a field goal kicker for the Lowell Red Devils and is currently kicking them through the uprights for Butler University where he's studying to become a lawyer.

Lang attended Lowell High School about the same time as my twin daughters; he was chosen as prom king his senior year at Lowell High School.

Lang possesses a huge CD collection and a great laugh; he works at Jewel-Osco in Crown Point.

* * *

You've always liked to sing, Daniel.

"Yes, I've been singing since the fourth grade when I joined the Nifty Notes choir," he said. "I've loved singing ever since."

Nifty Notes, my twins were in that.

"Yes."

Who are some of your favorite singers?

"My mother, of course, and Celene Dion, Shania Twain, Reba McIntyre, LeAnn Rimes. I also like Ray Charles, Charlotte Church, Luciano Pavarotti, Andrea Bocelli and Sarah Brightman."

That's a beautiful picture of you and your brother with all the different colored leaves in the background. It must have been taken in the fall.

"Yes, it was. We took that at Evergreen Park in 2003. Are Natale and Nicole doing well in college?"

Oh yeah, they've both graduated from Indiana University.

"Yes; what else did you want to ask me?"

Besides singing, what are some other things you like to do?

"I like to hang out with my friends, of course. I'm just enjoying my life as much as I can."

You go to church almost every Sunday.

"Yes."

I interviewed Erin Aquino for this column a few years ago, I bet you remember her.

"Erin Aquino is one of my best friends. We were in Drama Club together."

That's right, you've been known to tread the boards.

"In high school, I also was in Letterman's Club, Fellowship of Christian Athletes, Student Council, and Choir, of course. Have you heard of the International Thespian Society?"

No, does it have something to do with acting?

"Yes, I was in 'Androcles and the Lion' and 'The Wizard of Oz.' I also was a guard in 'Joseph and the Amazing Technicolor Dreamcoat' and portrayed Mr. Brownlow, the rich man, in 'Oliver.' Erin was the Artful Dodger. She is really a nice person."

With that memory of yours, you must do OK memorizing your lines.

"If there's a deadline, I meet the deadline."

What's on the horizon?

"I would like to perform in my own concert. Like have it at a certain school here in town, but I would need a lot of help in putting that together."

Like your own solo deal where you sing six or eight songs?

"Or maybe even like 10 or 20. The whole ordeal. Yes. That would be really nice if I could do that. I would love to do that some day."

Favorite sport?

"Basketball. I go to all of the Lowell football games. David is a great football player. He does a very good job for Butler University in Indianapolis."

Who were some of your favorite teachers when you were in

school?

"Definitely Mrs. Rollins. Mrs. Sarkey and Mrs. Runyon, too."

Well, kid, I've got to hit the road, I might have to cover The Purduettes; they're performing at the Lowell Middle School this afternoon.

"I'll be there, too. The Lowell High School and Middle School choirs are performing as well."

See you there, D. Lang.

* * *

While walking toward the middle school and The Purduettes traveling bus, I realized I'd left my reporter's pad on the dashboard of my car. As I headed back to my Ford, I glanced toward the top of the hill where the old football field and track are situated.

Dreamlike, I drifted back eight or nine years to a time when I volunteered to help with the Special Olympics in Valparaiso. I really didn't know what to expect. I certainly didn't expect to see anyone I knew. I remember how those wonderful people in charge told me my job was simply to dispense ribbons, times and hugs.

As with most sporting events, the National Anthem was sung. I remember the hair on my arms standing up and my eyes getting a little watery, too. It really wasn't windy or cold. But you see, that's what happened to me. The day D. Lang stood up to the microphone in the middle of Valparaiso High School's football field and sang the "Star-Spangled Banner" so beautifully.

And then Daniel ran.

Raymond Montgomery *(Jan. 2008)*

"... When will it stop?
Til God return me to my essence;
Cuz even as a adolescents; I refuse to be a convalescent;
So many questions, and they ask me if I'm still down;
I moved up out of the ghetto, so I ain't real now? ..."
– Etterlene Jordan, Drew Delmar, Tupac Shakur

Raymond Montgomery, 28, graduated from Merrillville High School and Purdue University Calumet in Hammond.

He is a handsome young man who dresses impeccably. He also wears a genuine smile.

I interviewed Ray at his workplace – the studios of radio station WGVE- located within the Gary Career Center. Ray will never see his interview in print; he is blind.

* * *

So, Ray, you're a DJ.

"I would say I'm an on-air personality," he said. "I'm kind of a shy person; that's what they tell me. I never would have thought this was for me, but I guess I grew. I just put two and two together because I liked music a lot. So I do the music thing. It happened like that.

"I'm usually on the air from 3 to 7 p.m. Wednesdays and Thursdays. I've been working here since 2005. I call my show, 'The Best of Both Worlds.' I'll give you the best of hip hop and R&B at WGVE, 88.7 FM. I play a lot of people from Chicago and Gary that are underground artists – ones that don't have record deals."

Your parents are probably about my age. What did they listen to when you were a kid?

"Motown; Earth, Wind & Fire; Luther Vandross; Teddy Pendergrass... I listen to a lot of that when I get home. I grew up to appreciate that kind of music. It's like everlasting – it don't go anywhere.

"The stuff I play here, sometimes I don't want to hear it. I don't like everything I play. I hear it so many times I just get tired of it."

Were you taught braille?

"Yes, but I only use it for certain things. I usually get my books on tape. I like to read short stories."

Ray, how did you lose your eyesight?

"I'll tell you, everybody asks me. It's not like it's anything sacred. I got stopped by a train one night in Glen Park; it was the summer of '97. A guy approached me and said to get out the car. He didn't even get any money – I was broke. They never caught him. I got shot in the head, neck, wrist, and in the back."

Raymond, I'm not downplaying your situation whatsoever, but I would think it's better to have seen as opposed to someone who was blind from birth.

"Yes, I can imagine things. I can visualize certain things in my head when I walk. I know colors because I've seen all that stuff."

I've been watching you work with all these buttons and switches. Ray, you're amazing.

"It's just practice, diligence. When I went to college, I took a radio course. The board was very similar to the one that's in here."

What are some of the toughest challenges you face?

"Transportation; I'm fortunate because I got people who look after me. Sometimes you want to go somewhere that instant and you don't want to wait on nobody. That can be a challenge right there. Sometimes reading your mail can be tough.

"But there's other things out there blind people can do. There's other things that we can contribute. You can't let things get you down just because you're blind – you still got all your other senses. Sometimes, it's hard, but you have to overcome those adversities. You just got to keep on pushin'. That's really all I can say."

You just said whole bunch, Ray. Are you married?

"No, but Candice stays with me. She just had my son December 18.We live right around the corner from where I grew up. Raymond Montgomery Jr. was born healthy."

Do you listen to sports?

"I enjoy somebody who gives you the play-by-play. They really do it well on the radio. It's better to listen to sports on the radio than to watch it on TV."

Ray, an entertainer and former talk show host by the name of Steve Allen once said, "Radio is the theater of the mind. Television is the theater of the mindless."

"Ha! That's deep right there."

Are there radio personalities you admire or from whom you've learned from?

"Michael Basting has a syndicated radio show more for grown folks. He does a lot of real good topics for older adults. I like Tom Joyner, too. I really don't have too many heroes. My parents are my heroes."

All-time favorite singer?

"2Pac. He was inspirational, real deep."

Like you, he took four slugs. Unlike you, he didn't make it.

"We need to walk over to the other studio across the hall, that's where I'm doing the show this afternoon."

(With a flick of his wrist Ray unfurls his red-tipped walking stick.)

If you need any help just say something to me, Ray.

"I'll let you know. If you could help me find a garbage can. I need to get rid of this gum before I go on the air. Somebody moved the waste basket.

"...I always start the show off crunk."

Crunk?

"Crunk means hype. I like to start a show off on a high note with a song that has a lot of energy. Like we say in the hip hop world – poppin'."

Ray, the clock says 2:57. You tell me when to shut up – everybody else does. Do you talk exactly like you're speaking to me when you're on the air?

"I got my radio voice."

Like Wolfman Jack?

"I got my own style."

"...This is your boy, Ray Geezy (Raymond's stage name) back in the building on December 27. Man, I'm about to hold it down for the next couple hours right here on 88.7 – a hip hop education and smoke-free nation. I hope everybody had a happy Christmas, Kwanza and all that good stuff. We gonna work it out right here at 88.7; give me a line at 963-0168. Let's get to it with Kanye West... ."

(While Ray does his thing, hip-hop artist K-Gib of Gary arrives on the set toting his latest CD. Ray asks K if his art is clean before he plays the music. Ray also promotes an upcoming event at the Glen Theatre that K-Gib & M.C. are hosting and performing in called The Midwest Movement Tour.

"...We also got Jeff Manes from the Post-Tribune here with us today. He's interviewing your boy right now. Do you meet a lot of interesting people, Jeff?"

Everybody got a story to tell, Ray Geezy. Are you taking requests? Play me something political, powerful and poetic. Something by Tupac Shakur.

"Okay, we got a little 2Pac for Jeff at 88.7 called, 'I Ain't Mad At Cha...'"

...Thanks, Ray.

And keep smilin', my brother.

Travis Seibt *(Nov. 2010)*

Pud: *"...Where we goin', Gramps?"*
Gramps: *"Oh, yeah, by golly, that's important."*
Mr. Brink: *"You'll find out."*
Pud: *"How long will we be there?"*
Mr. Brink: *"For eternity."*
Pud: *"How long is eternity, Gramps?"*
Gramps: *"A right smart piece of time, boy."*
– From the stage play and 1939 film "On Borrowed Time"

I first met Travis Seibt on the set of "On Borrowed Time" in 2005. My character, Mr. Brink, personified death. Travis portrayed a young boy named Pud whose time had come. Brink visited Pud's grandfather, too.

Today, Seibt is 14 and a freshman at Kankakee Valley High School in Wheatfield. He is the youngest son of Jeff and Debbie Seibt (pronounced Sipe). Travis' older brother, Cole, was the fiddler in L'arc en Ciel Theatre Group's production of "Fiddler on the Roof" about two years ago. Travis also has played the violin since he was 3.

The Seibt family lived in the Miller neighborhood of Gary before moving to DeMotte almost four years ago. Travis was home-schooled until eighth grade.

"Pud" died in "On Borrowed Time," but that was make-believe. Three years later, Travis Seibt was supposed to die in real life. B-cell lymphoma is the real deal, too.

* * *

Hey, "Pud," you're sure sprouting up, but you still have that all-American boyish grin.

"Come on in, 'Mr. Brink,'" Travis said.

Interests?

"I'm in a group called Civil Air Patrol."

Tell me about that.

"I'm a chief master sergeant. So far, it's a small squadron of seven cadets. There also are five senior members, including my parents. It's an auxiliary of the Air Force; it's like Boy Scouts for the Air Force. We dress up in camouflage uniforms, we call BDUs."

BDUs?

"Battle dress uniforms. We go through drills and do all kinds of different things. We study aeronautics, rocketry and do search and rescue missions."

Is Civil Air Patrol similar to Reserve Officers Training Corps?

"Sort of; we go through all the Air Force ranks, not just officers. We can start as young as 12 and we can go until we're 21. Then, we can become a senior member and continue to go up in rank."

Your ultimate goal?

"To go to the Air Force Academy in Colorado and become a fighter pilot."

You probably read up on all the combat jets.

"Yeah, the F-35 Lightning, F-22 Raptor, F-18 Hornet, F-15 Eagle, F-16 Falcon... ."

Do you like movies that pertain to flying?

"Yes, I like 'Top Gun' and 'Behind Enemy Lines;' I'm also interested in the history of the Tuskegee Airmen. When we lived in Gary, I first read about them at the Aquatorium by Miller Beach."

Do you want to talk about when you got sick?

"They found out I had a tumor in my chest on May 28, 2008; it was the size of a grapefruit. I started showing symptoms six months earlier; I was treated for asthma because I was having a hard time breathing. On Memorial Day weekend, I came down with a real bad cold; the doctor thought I had pneumonia. They did a chest X-ray on me and that's when they saw a big white mass in my chest."

Then what?

"I was sent straight to Comer Children's Hospital at the University of Chicago. I was in intensive care for two weeks."

Was the tumor inside one of your lungs?

"On top of my lung; a lymph node in my sternum got big enough that it compressed down on my lung and heart; it also compressed my trachea to under a centimeter."

Did you think you were going to die, Travis?

"I was thinking that a little bit; I got real skinny and lost all my hair because of three months of chemotherapy. But I also thought everything would eventually go well."

Your thoughts, Dad?

"Every day we're grateful," Jeff Seibt said. "The first day in Chicago, the doctor said Travis wasn't going to make it. He said, 'From my experience, looking at the X-ray, and the size of the tumor, there usually isn't anything we can do.' That was the first thing we heard.

"But they asked our permission to perform a very aggressive treatment they never had attempted on children before; there were no surgeries after the biopsy – strictly chemo. Because the tumor was so big and pressing on his trachea, it was basically strangling him."

Those adult-sized treatments of chemotherapy had to be tough on the little fella.

"It hit him hard, but it also shrunk the tumor to half its original size the first week," Jeff said. "Travis was in the hospital for 75 days that summer, from Memorial Day to Labor Day. And then, because his immune system was down, when he finally got to go home, he got shingles and ended up right back in the hospital for another week."

Mom?

"Jeff and I decided that as long as Travis was not crying and not upset, we wouldn't be either," Debbie said. "So, we played tag team parents."

Tag team parents?

"We took turns walking out of the room every so often when it was getting too hard," she said.

* * *

Jeff and Debbie Seibt invited me to read the blog they maintained on carepages.com while Travis was being treated. I've included a small portion of their posts...

June 17, 2008: (Jeff) "I am sorry that I have not updated lately... I was let go from my job. I was told it was because of economic cutbacks and I guess I was one of the cutbacks. Please pray that Jesus leads me to the right thing to do. That's enough about me. Travis took his treatments... He threw up his dinner when he tried to take his medicine."

June 17, 2008: (Jeff) "Please keep praying! Thank you, Jesus, for such careful doctors. I know Travis is in good hands."

June 19, 2008: (Jeff) "Travis is amazing! He is so strong. God is giving him so much strength. He has a smile almost all the time. ...They started a morphine drip to help his pain. Travis did not like the Tylenol 3."

June 20, 2008: (Jeff) "One big change is that Travis' hair is falling out in clumps."

June 30, 2008: (Jeff) "I got a new job today! It is much better than the one I had."

July 8, 2008: (Jeff) "Travis has real bad sores in his mouth and throat. He has a tube in his mouth to suck out saliva. It's hard to see him in pain. Everyone please continue to pray for Travis."

July 8, 2008: (Debbie) "Travis had a rough night. He is trying hard to eat, but he is still losing weight. His favorite food right now is cherry Popsicles."

Aug. 12, 2008: (Debbie) "Travis had a lumbar puncture to put chemo into his spinal fluid today. He doesn't mind them because they give him medication to make him go to sleep. Generally, when he wakes up, the first words out of his mouth are, 'I need more knockout drugs.'"

Aug. 12, 2008: (Debbie) "All and all, Travis had a good day. I think the highlight was when Mark Buehrle, the White Sox pitcher, came to Travis' room to say, 'Hi' to him."

Aug. 16, 2008: (Debbie) "Well, the chemo has taken its toll on Travis...

* * *

Miraculously, Travis made it through all that. Mr Brink was denied the second time around.

Each summer, Travis attends Camp Catch-A-Rainbow in Jackson, Mich. The camp is sponsored by the American Cancer Society. Next year, Travis wants to be a counselor there.

The folks from the ACS and Relay For Life always treat Travis like a king during their event at the Gary Air Show.

The Leukemia and Lymphoma Society does research for the type of cancer Travis has. The LLS also helps families financially.

Once his treatment was completed in December of 2008, Travis attended Disney World thanks to the Make A Wish Foundation. He attended Ronald McDonald House while at Comer Children's Hospital.

Jeff and Debbie told me all those organizations have had a great impact on Travis.

And the Seibts have not taken their miracle lightly; they remain filled with gratitude. That is why they raise money for Relay For Life and the Light the Night walk. The Seibts also collect pop-can tabs for Ronald McDonald House and Make A Wish.

As for Travis, well, he doesn't like to climb trees or find himself on the top rung of a ladder. Ironically, in our play, he had to climb a ladder and reach out to Mr. Brink who was perched high in an apple tree.

Yet, this young man from DeMotte, who has a fear of heights, plans on having his pilot's license before he graduates from KV.

Courage.

As a matter of fact, Travis accumulated what the folks at Comer Children's Hospital call the Beads of Courage. More than 200 beads make up the unique piece of jewelry.

There are beads representing the days Travis spent in the hospital, clinic days, IV pokes, CT scans, chemo and biopsy beads.

Red beads denote blood transfusions; silver beads signify days when his dressings were changed. There is a bead with a bald head recalling the day Travis' hair started falling out, and beads for days he had to have high doses of pain killers, too.

Bumpy beads were earned when he had really bad days. But the Seibt family agrees the most precious piece among Travis' Beads of Courage is that of a purple heart. That one is for the day "Lil' Pud" was deemed cancer-free.

Maybe Debbie Seibt summed it up best: "Thanksgiving shouldn't be celebrated once a year. Oh, no; there are too many things to be thankful for, whether it be remission from cancer or feeling the warm sun on a cool autumn day – Thanksgiving can be celebrated every moment."

Travis Seibt and Jeff Manes in the play "On Borrowed Time"

Barbara Weaver

"Character cannot be developed in ease and quiet. Only through experience of trial and suffering can the soul be strengthened, ambition inspired, and success achieved."
– Helen Keller

I trimmed my mustache just prior to interviewing Barbara Weaver. She has 90 percent hearing loss and relies heavily on reading lips.

Weaver, 61, is regional library director at Ivy Tech Community College, Northwest. Our interview took place at the Gary campus.

* * *

"I grew up in Carroll County," Weaver began. "I'm a farmer's daughter; my maiden name is Minich. My parents are deceased, but they were very influential in my life.

"Dad met my mom after World War II at Grissom Air Force Base near Logansport. My mother's dad was a farmer; that's how dad got into farming.

"Basically we were just tenant farmers. Since my brother David has taken over the operation, we farm thousands of acres. Three or four years ago, he was named top producer in the United States."

Did you attend public school?

"Yes, Carroll High School in Flora. I had meningitis when I was 3; it was a very precarious situation. My hearing loss was the only side effect; it could have been worse. I was fitted with hearing aids, by the time I was 5."

Was your education affected?

"By the time I was 6, I was put in the mainstream school system. I worked closely with the teachers.

"Classes back then were very small. My teachers were very

understanding; they made sure I had speech therapy in Chicago or Purdue University in West Lafayette. Those early days of them doing that, is why I didn't have to go to a special school."

College?

"I went to Ball State University and earned my undergraduate degree in social work and a minor in history. I earned my master's at Indiana University in library science."

Remarkable.

"At the age of 7, I decided I wanted to play piano because my friend was taking lessons. Dad said: 'My little girl wants to play piano, we'll buy her a piano.'

"I took piano lessons for eight years. I've played piano for churches, organizations, worship bands.... I can feel the music through my hands. My heart, my soul, sings."

Reading?

"My parents made sure I learned how to read at an early age. We didn't have a public library where we lived; we were really out in the boonies. Mom would get books for me at the library in Kokomo.

"Reading enhances your writing abilities as well. I tend to look for the beauty in things rather than deal with concrete things like numbers."

What were some of your favorite books as a kid?

"I loved reading Nancy Drew mystery stories. Every week, I 'd get an allowance for doing chores around the house. Every Saturday, I'd buy another Nancy Drew story for a $1.25. I have quite a collection of them."

What attracted you to the series?

"I loved how Nancy solved the mysteries. That must have carried over in later years, because I decided to become a reference librarian."

You could solve other people's questions through research.

"Exactly. My first two jobs were that of a reference librarian."

Where?

"In 1976, I was hired at Lake County Public Library. They were very supportive of my hearing loss. One of the ladies who hired me said that was one of the reasons they hired me."

Explain, please.

"Because she felt I'd have a sensitivity to people with disabilities. I worked there for about seven years. Then, there was an opening at the library in Crown Point and I was hired as their very first head of reference.

I worked there 11 years; it was a wonderful experience."

How long have you worked for Ivy Tech?

"Eighteen years; I love the freedom it gives me to organize, provide services, and work with staff. It's really a family environment here. If we can make our students feel at home and comfortable here, that supports their future careers. We're trying to make a difference in their lives."

You're a big Indianapolis 500 fan.

"Yes, our landlord would treat my parents, brother and me to a trip to the Indy 500 every year. We had great seats right by the finish line. I really got into it.

"That was about the time Mario Andretti made a name for himself. He was just phenomenal. Instead of following Elvis Presley or The Beatles, I followed Mario; he was dominant. I have a huge scrapbook of newspaper clippings and program guides about him."

Did you get his autograph?

"Yes, back in those days, you could get back in Gasoline Alley. I slipped underneath the tunnel and there was Mario. He signed a life-sized poster I had purchased."

Hero worship rewarded.

"When I graduated high school, my dream was to be a journalist and cover the Indianapolis 500. I wanted to be a female sports reporter. I majored in journalism my first year at Ball State, but, I guess reality set in. With my hearing loss, I realized I probably couldn't catch everything."

You recently won a very prestigious award.

"Yes, the Carnegie Corp. of New York-New York Times I Love My Librarian Award in New York City; about three blocks from Times Square.

"I give the person who nominated me, Becky Sacopulos, a lot of credit for believing I was worthy of it and taking the time to fill out all the paperwork.

"I didn't think there was a chance I'd win nationally; it was beyond my wildest imagination. There were 1,700 nominations. Caroline Kennedy was there."

Well done.

"I had to give a two-minute speech in front of more than 300 people. I'm not a very good speaker, but I told the audience that when I received the phone call telling me I'd won, I felt like I was being crowned Miss Indiana. The crowd burst out laughing and that certainly broke the ice."

You're an amazing person. I know it hasn't always been easy. Over the phone, you told me there's been more than one occasion when people tried to deter you. Would you care to talk about that?

"After I had filled out an application, a lady from admissions questioned me. She said, 'Do you really think you'll be able to handle it in this profession? Not being able to hear?'

"Jeff, I'm sorry ... (she starts crying) . That's not a pleasant memory."

It's OK; take your time.

"I told her: 'Yes, I do. I've done well in school. I'm an avid reader who graduated sixth of 123 and was on the National Honor Society in high school. I had great role models. My parents loved me and I have a brother I look up to. I don't see why I cannot achieve my dream of becoming a librarian.'"

Barb, read my lips: I'm speechless.

* * *

Weaver believes her involvement in Books to Bridge the Region, a reading initiative for all ages from Jasper, Lake, LaPorte, Newton, Porter, Pulaski and Starke counties was instrumental in her being chosen for the I Love My Librarian Award.

It's been quite a journey from the cornfields of Carroll County to Times Square.

In my eyes, Barbara Weaver *is* Miss Indiana.

Jigger Sirois *(Sept. 2009)*

"'...O my Lord, I am not eloquent. ...I am slow of speech and of a slow tongue. ...'"

"...Is not Aaron the Levite thy brother? I know that he can speak well. ...Thou shalt speak unto him."

– Moses and God

Leon Duray Sirois was named after a race-car driver. He was nicknamed after a race-car mechanic. From 1957-77, Jigger Sirois drove midget, sprint and stock cars.

Sirois, 74, lived in Shelby for the first 29 years of his life, then resided in Hammond for more than 20 years. He and his wife, Juanita, currently live in Williamsburg, Va. But he comes back home to Indiana every year to watch the Indianapolis 500.

Sirois recently returned to Northwest Indiana. He stopped by my apartment for a chat the day before his Lowell High School reunion. Sirois had something to tell the Class of '54. No small feat, he has been a stutterer most of his life.

* * *

The 1969 Indianapolis 500 time trials?

"We went out first to qualify," Sirois began. "You get four laps. During the four laps, the owner has the option of waving off the run at any time. I was so excited; I got my three laps in. I remember coming off the fourth corner like it was yesterday. I was thinking, 'I'm going to get qualified.' But out of the corner of my eye, I saw the owner waving the yellow flag.

"As I slowed down on the back straightaway, it started raining. That was it for the day."

And the rule at the time was the fastest car on the first day received the pole position for "The Greatest Spectacle in Racing."

"Correct. It would have been a fluke, but I would have had the pole position as long as their weren't 33 faster cars. It ended up that we would've been the 31st fastest."

But drivers get three stabs at it; what happened?

"Our second attempt, the next weekend, I was running even faster than the first day. The owner waved it off again on the final lap."

Why?

"He was wanting to go faster. He admitted after the first day, that he was confused and didn't use good judgement. The second weekend would have made me 26th fastest.

"But I was still sticking with my crew because they took me there. Maybe someone else could have driven it faster, but I was on the edge with the car. I was hanging it out, so to speak."

Your third and final chance for fame and glory?

"The engine blew."

Jigger, a good horse can be run to death. Sounds like Mr. Offenhauser's turbo was all tuckered out.

"I did qualify for Indy in 1970 and '74, but ended up getting bumped out by faster cars. Both years I was 35th.

Worst crash?

"Springfield, Ill., 1962. It was a wicked little quarter-mile track with high banks, good for the fans, but the cars slid around a lot. I got bumped by another car. There were no cages on those cars."

What happened?

"I was told the car went end over end eight or nine times – really high. I was unconscious when it came to a stop. The exhaust pipe ran down the right side of an Offy four-cylinder engine."

Jigger, while we've been talking, I noticed that long scar on the inside of your right arm. It's the shape of an exhaust pipe.

"Yes, it is. I came to a week later. There was another time when I was on fire from alcohol when a fuel tank split open.

"Jeff, there is fear that goes along with automobile racing, but it doesn't compare to the fear a youngster who stutters feels when asked to talk in school."

Would you like to talk about it?

"I would like nothing better than to talk about it."

You speak perfectly; how did you overcome stuttering?

"My first class therapy wasn't until age 65 at the Hollins Communications Research Institute in Roanoke, Va. It's a 19-day, 100-hour program. I was part of a class of 14 which was comprised mostly of youngsters ages 13 through 19.

"Everybody makes a final three-minute speech there. Some of those kids, on the first day, could hardly say their names. By the conclusion of the program, some of them spoke almost perfectly. I was so inspired, I decided to become involved with helping stutterers."

Why did you wait so long to get help?

"I tried professional therapy after high school for an extensive period of time; it was quite costly and didn't help me. That's how it was 50 years ago. There wasn't a lot of proven therapy in this area."

Some researchers believe stuttering is a physical thing, resulting from a distorted pattern of muscle movements by the speech mechanisms. Can emotional disorders attributed to, say, an abusive childhood or maybe a single traumatic event cause stuttering?

"Jeff, when I was 3 years old, I was in a car with my mother, sister and a neighbor lady. We were going to Albert Larson's farm between Shelby and Lowell to get eggs and butter like people did in 1938."

And?

"A tornado hit. I remember our old Chevy bouncing up and down; the car ended up stuck on top of a fallen tree. They made me get down on the floorboard. What was worse than the tornado, was those ladies screaming.

"We went inside the farmer's house. I looked upward; rain was hitting me in the face – the roof was gone. There was a piano with a washtub on top of it. I was perplexed by that.

"They said I lay in bed for three days and didn't utter a word. After the third day, I started to talk.

Yeah?

"I stuttered. It didn't bother me until third grade. You become more self-conscious by third grade. Well, that exacerbates the condition.

"The doctors in that era told parents if you discuss it with the child it could increase the problem; they didn't know what to do about it. My stuttering was never talked about at home.

"I dropped out of Sunday school; we had a wonderful Sunday school teacher, Red Luchene. I was never made fun of in Sunday school, but I was ashamed of the way I talked. Jeff, I wanted to become a Boy Scout so bad."

Scouts recite oaths.

"Yes; I remember trying to read from a book in the seventh grade. They always had you stand back then. I was really struggling with speech blocks and repetitions. The teacher, God bless him, always placed strong emphasis on certain syllables when he spoke. He also used long dramatic pauses between each word.

"Jeff, it's indelibly etched in my psyche, he said, 'Leon, I cannot understand why you have such difficulty talking and reading. Your brother and your sisters were good talkers and readers.'"

You know, Jigger, God can get away with mentioning to Moses that his no-account golden calf-idolizing sibling was a better orator. But that teacher needed a good punch in the chops.

"I wasn't angry at him, but I was crying. I felt ashamed."

Were words beginning with the letter "s" the toughest?

"I would have given anything to change my surname to Brown or Jones. I became very accomplished at two things that are self-defeating. I used substitution words and starter sounds."

Example of a starter sound?

"'Uh-Sirois.' It is imperative for boys to start therapy before the age of 5, age 7 for girls. Four times as many boys stutter as girls."

You mentioned helping those afflicted.

"Yes, I became involved with The Stuttering Foundation, a not-for-profit organization based out of Memphis that provides self-therapy resources in the form of books and DVDs. There are 8,000 public libraries across the country that have the resources available.

"The big difference between self-therapy and professional therapy is economical. My therapy cost in excess of $3,000 for 19 days, 10 years ago. For some families, that is cost-prohibitive."

Are you paid a salary for spreading the word and distributing the resources?

"Not a penny. I just want to help people. Jeff?

Jigger?

"Have a 'green-flag' day."

* * *

Many years have passed since that day Sirois stood stammering and trembling with a book in his hand. He told me that never once in four years at Lowell High School did his classmates make fun of him.

Sirois said he wanted to stand in front of the class one more time and do something he couldn't do back then.

Leon "Jigger" Sirois wanted to say, "Thank you."

Tim Ispas *(Nov. 2011)*

"We often take for granted the very things that most deserve our gratitude."
– Cynthia Ozick

Today is a day when we give thanks for our blessings. It also is Tim Ispas' 41st birthday.

Ispas lives in Highland; he is the youngest of eight children and the son of a steel worker.

Our interview took place at Blythe's Sporting Goods in Griffith. Rodger Blythe and Ispas are close friends.

Ispas played football, basketball and baseball for Highland High School. He has been hunting since grade school. He doesn't kick a football, shoot a free throw or steal a base anymore, but he still deer hunts.

When Ispas puts his sights on a buck while using a crossbow, he pulls the trigger with his teeth.

Tim Ispas is a quadriplegic.

* * *

College?

"I have a bachelor's degree in human resources management from Purdue University Calumet and a master's degree in the School of Education, also from Purdue Cal."

You recently harvested a nine-point buck.

"Yes, I grew up as a hunter. My brother, Jeff, got me into deer hunting. I started at age 12. I just love the outdoors – hunting and fishing. But deer hunting was my passion; I started with bow hunting, using a recurve. I've harvested most of my deer with the bow; anyone can shoot a deer with a shotgun."

Can you explain how you're able to hunt?

"My hunting device is completely electronic; it's almost like a video game. It's powered by my wheelchair batteries. There's a joystick that controls the apparatus which is mounted to my wheelchair.

"Basically, there's a turret that holds my gun or crossbow. To go left, I push the joystick to the left; if I want the gun or crossbow to go right, I push the joystick to the right. I also can push the joystick up and down."

You can move your hands somewhat, but can't use your fingers.

"Correct. To fire my weapon, my brother devised a system where I bite down on a strap that's attached to the trigger. Jeff is a millwright in the steel mill. Without Jeff, I wouldn't have been able to utilize my gun or bow."

Tim, let's switch gears. Are you Catholic?

"Yes, we were raised Catholic. I went to Our Lady of Grace for seven years."

The only reason I ask is, I was wondering about your views on stem cell research. It can be a controversial subject.

"My beliefs on stem cell research are that it's a good idea. Morally, I have no issues with it. It would be great if there was a cure. I've always been told we're five years away from finding a cure."

How long have you been paralyzed?

"It's been 16 years; I was 24 when it happened. I've talked to the leading researchers, leading neurologists and the top neurosurgeon. When (actor) Christopher Reeve was injured, he was called in. That neurosurgeon told me we're just chipping away at the bottom of a mountain with a pickaxe as far as curing spinal paralysis."

Do your buddies still come around?

"Most of my friends have disappeared because I can't do the things that I used to do. The guy who was with me when I was injured, Rob Sabol, is a true friend who has stuck by me. He's my hunting buddy."

I can only imagine what you go through every day. I mean, if your nose itches, you can't scratch it. If you're in the woods and a mosquito is biting your cheek, you can't swat it.

"It's difficult. Every morning, I heavily rely on a nurse; she's been with me for 13 years. She's been very faithful. I can't put into words how grateful I am toward her. Her name is Jean Marie. I'm so thankful for her. She comes seven days a week. Without her and a loyal aide, Melissa Thompson, I wouldn't be able to get up.

"Every day, there's this routine I dread when Jean Marie and or Melissa are working on me. As soon as I get in this wheelchair, my day begins.

"Sometimes, I don't sleep at night. It's like a nightmare – the demons come out. I have a lot of back pain and issues like that."

Jean Marie or Melissa has to feed you.

"Yes. Basically, I have to be taken care of like a child."

Tim, how did the accident occur?

"Jeff, it wasn't an accident. On Oct. 24, 1994, I was duck hunting with my cousin (on Hawthorne Lake in Linton). We had a spread of decoys out. While we were hunting, we heard someone randomly shooting a .22-caliber rifle. A car pulled around a corner and started taking pot shots that were coming very close to us.

"My cousin stood up in the boat and shouted, 'Hey, don't you see us? Your bullets are just missing us.'"

Then what happened?

"The car sped off. That was about 4 p.m. Around 5:30 p.m., a flock of ducks came over and I shot one and my cousin shot one. We rowed the boat over to retrieve the ducks.

"I was standing in the boat, and my cousin was sitting. We got my cousin's duck first, and we were rowing to get my duck when the vehicle came back."

And?

"This individual, we don't know why, intentionally shot me with his .22 caliber rifle; it had a scope on it."

Did you know this guy?

"No. The story was that he didn't know he hit me. There was a 16-year-old kid with him.

"After he shot me, he went down the road and shot a cow. Then, he started slaughtering the cow for its back legs – for the meat. The farmer saw him doing that and got his license plate. It was his mother's car."

Then what?

"His mother got hold of him and told him, 'You did something wrong; you better hide.'

"In the meantime, he threw the gun in a local river and threw the scope in a different part of the river. The police could only find the rifle."

Was he convicted in a court of law?

"He received 8 1/2 years for shooting me and three years for shooting the cow. The weekend before the trial, he got caught drinking and driving while spotlighting deer; he had a rifle in the front seat. Three more years were tacked onto his sentence for that. So, he got a total of 14 1/2 years; he only served 8 1/2 years.

"But, he's been in and out jail for DUIs; he was released (recently) for a another DUI. So, in total, because of his DUIs, he's served his 14 1/2 years.

"I'm the one serving a life sentence."

* * *

Ispas told me that hunting almost took his life, but he looks forward to Oct. 1 every year – opening day of deer season when the leaves are starting to fall and he can hear when a deer is walking through the woods.

Personally, I don't hunt anymore, but to see Tim's smiling face with his chin up in a photo with his buck made me think a little bit.

And you know what? I have it pretty damn good, and I don't think I'll carp or complain about anything for quite a while, thanks to Tim Ispas.

Dan and Jenny Luce *(July 2011)*

"...Well we're on this earth together and we're all gonna die
So let's forgive a little more and let others live their lives...
...And I don't need no rich man tellin' me how I'm supposed to think
Because he owns some TV stations and some newspaper ink
'Cause it's the common ones, like you and me
That keep the country running, keep the flag flying free...
...So I wanna see them dues, yes I wanna see that respect
For that blue collared shirt and that weekly paycheck..."
– American Graveyard

Jenny Luce told me the lyrics of American Graveyard's "Common Ones" reminded her of the folks I interview for this column.

Jenny is the wife of Dan Luce; they've been married nine years and live in St. John.

Dan has an adult daughter, Amie, from a previous marriage. Together, Dan and Jenny have two sons, Danny, 8, and Donovan, 3. Dan is 53; Jenny is 37.

I've known Jenny since she was a little girl; her maiden name is Rosinko. The Rosinkos moved from Griffith to Lowell in the mid-'80s when she was in the third grade. She is the daughter of an ironworker and the seventh of seven children.

I've known Dan longer than I've known Jenny. In 1979, we began our welding apprenticeship at East Chicago Roosevelt High School while working for Inland Steel Co. A couple decades later, we ended up in the same department when we became overhead crane repairmen.

Dan was a state qualifier in wrestling for Highland High School as a sophomore and hardly was sick a day in his life. But, he has had some major health issues since 2008.

Jenny did all the talking during our interview; Dan had his larynx removed a while back. He used an erasable board to "converse."

* * *

Dan, are you officially retired?

"Yes, the guys at work chipped in and gave me this clock," Dan wrote.

Let me read what it says. "To our union steward, co-worker and great friend. Enjoy your retirement. The Crane Crew, October, 2010."

"I worked in the weld shop for 20 years and the crane crew for 13," Dan wrote.

Added Jenny: "He would've stayed longer if he hadn't gotten sick. On June 30, 2008, his birthday, Dan found out he had larynx cancer. From there, he had radiation and kept working at the mill. His dad died right after that.

"Eventually, Dan got a clean bill of health. But when they did the scan to see if the cancer was gone, they found a very large brain aneurism; he'd had it for a long time and could have died at any moment."

What happened?

"In January of '09, Dan went in for brain surgery," Jenny said. "When they were clipping the aneurism, Dan had a stroke; it paralyzed the entire left side of his body."

You have quite a scar, Dan.

"It took 144 stitches and staples to patch my head back," Dan wrote. "Donovan told me the other day, 'Daddy your zipper head is looking pretty good.' He thinks I had a zipper inserted into my skull."

Added Jenny: "Dan was at the University of Chicago for three months after the stroke. And then he was in a nursing home for three months. They didn't say he could come home, I just brought him home. I figured I could take care of him as well as they could; I'm a (licensed practical nurse)."

Continue, please.

"On Thanksgiving weekend of '09, Dan got pneumonia and ended up back at the University of Chicago. When they were putting in the feeding tube is when they found the cancer had aggressively come back."

Dan, you've been knocked through the ropes, but you're still standing.

"In January of 2011, Dan had a 20-hour surgery," Jenny said. "They took out his larynx and esophagus and then took muscle from one leg and skin and flesh from his other leg and rebuilt his entire throat and sewed it back in."

Amazing.

"That's why we went to the University of Chicago; they were the only ones who could do it," Jenny said. "In early March, they started the chemo and radiation. You should have seen him not that long ago; he was naked looking like a baby bird – no beard, hair, eyebrows... ."

Is he done with chemotherapy?

"Yes, but he started having seizures and has to take medication for that," Jenny said.

This has had to been hard on you and the boys, too.

"Donovan has only seen his father as he looks now. It's been hard on Danny because he remembers when his dad was healthy."

Dan wrote, "I'm going to have to sell my Harley because of the seizures." .

Added Jenny, "But he can still ride his lawn tractor; he mows almost everyday.".

Dan, what are some of your hobbies?

"Woodcarving, gardening, antiquing, hiking and fishing," he wrote.

Remember when we had the booth together at Uncle John's Flea Market?

"Good times," he wrote.

Jenny, do Dan's friends stop by and see him on occasion?

"It's funny, when stuff like this happens, you're always surprised at who comes around and who doesn't. At Christmastime, the guys from the mill brought us $300 cash and $500 worth of Christmas presents all wrapped... . We were really broke at the time."

Some good people in that mill.

"Previously, they collected $800 for Dan. Those guys are amazing."

What are you writing, Dan?

"Jillson and Hamilton."

Doesn't surprise me that Al and Jeff were two of the guys passing the hat.

* * *

For now, Dan can't do all the things he'd like to do with his young sons. But Jenny can.

The Rosinkos were our neighbors when my family lived outside the city limits of Lowell. Jenny was a tomboy and she is the perfect mom for the boys.

They went for a nature walk the other day and collected a small container of tadpoles, some of which are starting to sprout legs. They also witnessed a huge snapping turtle lay her eggs.

As I pulled out of the Luce driveway, I took a good look at those folks as they stood on the porch of the house Jenny's grandfather built just before the Great Depression: American flag, rocking chair, a mother with her arms around two boys – fallen catalpa blossoms at their bare feet.

And the son of a steelworker who became a steelworker, standing proud with the aid of a cane – still standin'.

The common ones.

Miri Silvert *(July 2009)*

"The baby girl without a chance
a victim of the circumstance."
–Reba McEntire

Living in the woods near Boone Grove High School makes it very difficult for Dr. Michael Silvert and his wife, Debra, to attend temple. Being Sabbath-observant, they don't drive cars on Saturdays; the Silverts pray at home.

Michael and Debra have four children: Jared, 18; Mirjana (Miri),16; Rani 15; and Kaile 13. All of them have been home-schooled.

It was their second-born I came to interview.

The harmonica player Samuel Lozada of Portage tipped me off about Silvert. Lozada was a judge at an Indiana Idol contest last fall in Valparaiso; she was a contestant.

Miri was receiving occupational, physical and speech therapies in Chesterton when I knocked on the Silverts' door. It gave me a chance to talk to the girl's mother before she got home. I knew coming in that Miri was blind, but Debra felt the need to prepare me regarding the extent of Miri's autism.

Miri receives residential habilitation services from professionals who help her get through her life on a daily basis. Her condition is called Septo-optic dysplasia. Part of her brain and optic nerve did not develop properly. Nor did her pituitary gland. Miri is 5 feet, 6 inches tall, but if not for growth hormone replacement therapy, she would have been a little person.

* * *

"What is your favorite music?" Miri asked.

Well, Miri, I like classic rock 'n' roll and I'm a fan of the blues – older stuff like Robert Johnson's "Crossroad Blues" or tunes like "The Sky is Crying," which was covered by the late Stevie Ray Vaughn.

"Are you a singer?"

You tell me; check out my Leon Redbone imitation.

"Fare thee well, fare thee well,
Fare thee well my fairy fay;
For I'm goin' to Lou'siana for to see my Susy Anna.

Singin' Polly Wolly Doodle all the day."

Miri, what's so funny? That wasn't shtik; I was singing my heart out for you. Besides, who's interviewing whom here? What's your favorite type of music?

"Country; Reba McEntire is my favorite singer."

Favorite TV Show?

"American Idol."

Hobbies?

"I have my own horse."

What is your horse's name?

"Sam."

That's a fancy cowgirl blouse with matching scarf you're wearing. Your mom told me you received a very special Hanukkah gift last year.

"Yes, a professional karaoke machine."

Have you always enjoyed singing?

"Yes."

Do you like singing in front of crowds or do you have a little bit of stage fright?

"I get scared."

You're very brave. I heard you've been working on the "Star Spangled Banner" and you also sang for some kids with disabilities who play on the Chesterton Challengers Little League team.

"I'd like to sing at a RailCats game. It's hard to sing in B Flat."

Your mom told me you have a huge CD collection and you're into all kinds of music.

"I love (singing) 'doo wop doo be doo doo wop wah doo...'"

Oh, my. Miri, my dear, from what incredible finger-snapping place did that sound come?

Mrs. Silvert, ahem, you didn't prepare me regarding the extent of your daughter's talent.

"Miri, do you want to show Jeff the first-place trophy you won at the Porter County Fair last year and the CD you did with Sam Lozada?"

"No."

"Do you want to show Jeff your karaoke machine?"

"No."

"Will you sing a song for Jeff?"

"No."

Miri, please? I sang for you.

"O.K...

'Crazy, I'm crazy for feeling so lonely,

I'm crazy, crazy for feelin' so blue...

...I'm crazy for tryin' and crazy for cryin'
And I'm crazy for lovin' you.'"
Beautiful. Thank you, Mirjana.

* * *

Debra Silvert told me you never know what you're going to get with Miri; her autism changes from day to day. But there is more going on inside Miri than meets the eye.

At last fall's aforementioned Indiana Idol contest she competed against mostly adults. She was the only person in the contest who had a disability. She auditioned with "Crazy"and advanced several weeks by singing the Reba McEntire hits "How Blue" and "I'm A Survivor," plus Olivia Newton John's "Hopelessly Devoted To You." She attempted to sing "Somewhere Over the Rainbow" in the semifinal round, but was eliminated. She was ill, and, later that week, ended up in an intensive care unit.

Miri really doesn't have anything going as far as reading, writing or arithmetic. Mrs. Silvert told me that when you have a child who is severely challenged like Miri, it's important to focus on what *isn't* broken.

Miri has the music in her. She can do things by ear that college music majors cannot do. She's a soprano who has perfect pitch and is terrific at memorizing lyrics.

Miri has the ability to identify all kinds of composers: Bach, Beethoven; she recognizes their styles. If she isn't familiar with a particular composer, she will still know what period it is and say, "That's Baroque." She knows Classical, Romantic, Renaissance... .

Not unlike several other singers, musicians, artists, actors and writers I've encountered, Miri can be somewhat temperamental or moody. She gave up her Braille several years ago because she was at odds with her teacher. There is a set of anger rules posted in her bedroom.

Around me, she was all smiles. While I stood talking with her mother, Miri reached out and squeezed my hand.

But music pitches are Miri's best friends; she knows them by name. It doesn't matter what instrument is playing; she knows how high or low her friends are.

I'm glad I made Miri laugh when I tried to carry a tune for her. But that's not when she put her fingers in her ears. She did that as she reached the last verse of her hauntingly beautiful rendition of "Crazy." She always does; applause scares her.

And I do believe Patsy Cline must've been listening to Miri from the sky above. Obviously, Cline was crying.

How else could I explain the tears rollin' down my nose?

Koko Works *(Aug. 2010)*

"...When you refused to help the least of these, my brothers and sisters, you were refusing to help me."
– Jesus Christ

My friend Red Feather Remesnik rode with me to meet her friend, Koko Works. It was the week of the Lake County Fair and the temperature that day approached 100 degrees. My car's air conditioner barely kept us comfortable.

Red Feather and Koko are artistic types. They also have survived numerous surgeries; both are on disability.

In high heels, Red Feather, 40, might max out at about 5 feet. She was diagnosed with endometriosis when she was 19 which turned into full-blown cancer by the time she was 29. She battled and beat it.

Red Feather is small, but mighty.

Barefooted, Koko is 7 feet, 5 inches tall. She has never married or had children.

Koko, 32, is a native of South Bend who has lived in North Hammond about five years. She lives in a one-room, second-story apartment.

Red Feather and I sat on each side of Koko at the foot of her bed for this interview. She doesn't own a couch or chairs. Koko's two dogs were sprawled out and panting at the head of her bed.

Heat rises to the top.

* * *

High school?

"South Bend Clay, Class of '97," she said.

Koko, I realize all tall people get asked this question, so *forgive me for being common: Did you play basketball?*

"No, I didn't play any sports, but at 6 feet 8 inches, I was the tallest person in my graduating class. I liked to read; reading is still my 'sport.' I had issues in high school. Because of my ethnicity, morals, height and because I was pretty and they were jealous of my looks, I got picked on a lot.

"I'm of Irish, Polish, Swedish and African-American descent. I look white on the outside, but I have brown eyes and curly hair. The natural color of my hair is called beaver, which is medium brown-auburn with bright red highlights. As soon as summer comes, I start getting strawberry patches; that's the Irish in me."

Are either of your parents unusually tall?

"No, they're still trying to figure out where I got the height. The growth plates in my knees haven't closed. I have the bone density of a 16-year-old. I'll be 33 in November and I'm still growing."

Has your growth caused other physical problems?

"I have pulled muscles in my upper back; scoliosis in my lower back, fibromyalgia and severe degenerative disc disease. All I can say is, gravity is a biznitch."

Biznitch?

"I try to respect myself by not using profanity."

Siblings?

"I have an older half-sister and a younger half-brother by my dad; he wasn't very much a part of my life. I'm the only child my mother ever had.

"I'm also a firm believer in karma – what goes around, comes around – but also practice do unto others as you would have them do unto you. My maternal grandfather, who was a fireman while I was growing up, always told me, 'Don't start nothin', won't be nothin'.' That is what I live by."

You have a nice collection of Notre Dame memorabilia on display.

"I'm a huge Notre Dame fan. We have our first home (football) game coming up on September 4 (against Purdue)."

Tell me a little more about your love of reading.

"I read anything I can get my hands on; I don't have a computer. I just read 'Seven Habits of Highly Effective People' by Stephen R. Covey. I also read children's books to my dogs."

Really?

"My little white dog has about a 175-word vocabulary when she chooses to use it. She also sings and dances."

What kind of dogs are they?

"Momo is an American-Eskimo Spitz and Joe Mo is a German shepherd-chow mix."

College?

"I did almost two years at Davenport University in Granger. I taught as a substitute teacher for seven years. I've done everything from kindergarten to seniors. I'm only about three semesters from being able to teach in Hammond. I just can't afford it right now."

Do you have a job?

"Yes, at Little Caesar's in Whiting. I walk to work because I don't own a car. I'm also a starving artist who makes jewelry by braiding shoelaces."

What do you do at Little Caesar's?

"I'm a shakerboarder; that's the person who stands outside with a sign advertising the $5 pizza. I use my dance moves to attract attention. I only work a couple of days a week."

Do you qualify for food stamps?

"Yes, $25 worth for a month. Last month, I used my Nipsco money to buy food. Is that wrong? Maybe. But I feel my Nipsco can wait because I'll get a check between here and there. It's not going to be a big check, but it will take care of my bill. I once went 16 consecutive months without Nipsco. As long as my rent is paid and I have a roof over my head, I will survive. I read "Genghis Khan" under blankets with a flashlight and no heat and no food for three days last winter."

I read "Moby Dick" in about three years. Koko, that was a dumb response. I just don't know what to say.

"I've read 'Moby Dick.' And I've also read encyclopedias from cover to cover to keep my brain stimulated for knowledge. Nobody can take my knowledge from me."

What worries you?

"Our reliance upon oil. One day, Mother Earth, she's just gonna stop. What happens to a car engine when it runs out of oil? It comes to a stop and catches on fire.

"Jeff, I believe our government wants people like me to die as soon as possible. But there's something the government might not realize."

What's that, kid?

"What doesn't kill me, only makes me stronger."

* * *

After our interview, I treated Red Feather and Koko to lunch at the Cavalier Inn, a few blocks from Koko's apartment. Being a little short, I put it on my Mastercard. It was nice to see restauranteur Mary Kasprzycki again.

I polished off five potato pierogi and a Polish sausage at "The Cav"– when in Rome, right?

Koko had a couple iced teas, fried chicken, mashed potatoes, green beans and cottage cheese. She only ate part of it, but asked for a doggie bag. The remaining slices of rye bread on our table also fit nicely in her Styrofoam container.

Red Feather occasionally brings me an assortment of frozen leftovers. She's a great cook who drives from Lake Village to my modest apartment in Lowell to do her laundry. Red Feather doesn't own a washer and dryer. They don't have Laundromats in Lake Village.

Koko claims to be a self-taught gourmet chef, but says $25 can buy a month's worth of peanut butter, jelly and bread, if she catches those items on sale.

Koko Works hand-washes all her clothes in her one-room, second-story apartment. They have Laundromats in Hammond.

The least of these.

Denny Bruckman *(May 2009)*

"If I had a single flower for every time I think about you, I could walk forever in my garden."
– *Claudia Gandhi*

Denny Bruckman's last day of work was April 24. There's something poetic about a guy who loves to garden retiring on Arbor Day.

Bruckman was the head bagger at the Strack & Van Til supermarket in Crown Point. He was with the company for 25 years, but has sacked groceries for 41.

Bruckman will turn 62, May16. He lives in Crown Point with his sister, Susie, who was present for our interview.

He was born the eldest of six children. Denny also was born with a harelip, cleft palate and no cheek bones. To say his permanent teeth came in crooked would be an understatement. Bruckman lived that way for nearly three decades, but eventually saved enough money to get his teeth fixed.

Denny Bruckman hasn't stopped smiling since.

* * *

"Because of my harelip, the doctor wouldn't let Mama see me until I was 1 month old," Bruckman began. "We lived in Lowell when I was real little; I didn't have much schooling when I was younger.

"When we moved to Crown Point, there was an older lady who lived behind us; she was a retired principal for a boys school in Chicago. She taught me how to read and write. Everyday we would start off by saying the Lord's Prayer together.

"She had severe arthritis. In return for my lessons, I would run errands for her. Mama would clean her house and Susie would mow her yard. Her name was Elizabeth Hughes; she used to own the Lake County Star. I read four newspapers every day now."

Susie told me you were blessed with an incredible memory and whenever she wants to know a fact or figure she asks you. Any other childhood memories you'd like to share?

"I remember Mama would wash and iron for other people and Daddy trapped muskrats down in Schneider for extra money. They never did know that I was eligible for Social Security at birth.

"My great-grandfather was in the Civil War; his name is on a monument in Lowell. My great-grandmother had three or four sets of blue willow dishes. I can spend three or four hours at the Antique Mall here in Crown Point."

Denny, sometimes kids can be cruel. Any unpleasant childhood memories?

"I had a few neighborhood kids make fun of me, but it never bothered me. Sometimes adults would point and tell their children to look at me. That bothered me a little bit.

"I also can remember buying candy for my brother Randy every day. I was the one who found him."

Found him?

"He bit his tongue off. Randy also had a learning disability. I remember he was face down on the floor; one leg was on the bed and one wasn't. But I knew my little brother went to a better place. I was more worried about Mama's heart."

Are your parents deceased?

"Yes; Daddy died in'82 and Mama died in '98."

Added Susie Bruckman: "I promised Mom, I'd take care of Denny. My brother, David, lives here, too. Denny was worried about what would happen to him after Mom passed away. Forty years ago, our mother went to the manager of the National Tea Grocery Store on Main Street and asked him if he'd take a chance on her son.

"A lot of people love Denny in this town," she said. "When Key Market bought out Thrifty Mart, they were going to make the employees rehire and start back at the bottom of the pay scale. Of course, there was a chance they might not rehire Denny at all. Mayor (Richard) Collins assured the new owner that the citizens of Crown Point would boycott the store if Denny had to start over."

Denny, when I came to visit you on your last day of work yesterday, it was heartwarming to see the bond between you and your colleagues, and especially between you and the customers.

"It says in the employee handbook that we are supposed to be friendly to the customer, but I would be that way anyway. At Strack & Van Til's, I was a member of Local 881. Daddy was a Teamster."

When did you get your teeth fixed?

"In the late '70s, my insurance paid half and I paid half. Dr. Redding worked on my teeth for nine straight hours; I got my glasses from the Lions' Club."

Added Susie: "When Denny was in his 50s, we found out he was a diabetic. He also has severe asthma and allergies."

Denny, did you miss much work because of health issues?

"Except for being off for two weeks when I was hospitalized because of congestive heart failure, I never called off work in over 40 years."

That's incredible. You mentioned your love of antiques; I hear you also enjoy old movies.

"Yeah; I like Shirley Temple, Abbott and Costello and those other two guys who were always together..."

Laurel and Hardy?

"Yeah! Daddy used to laugh so hard when he was watching The Three Stooges."

I see you have a Dean Martin album; I was a big fan of Dino, myself.

"I like Jerry Lewis, too."

Well, Denny, we can't agree on everything.

"I enjoy all kinds of music: Folk, opera, a little bit of country. I like Elvis Presley. My brother David and I made $500 from our garage sale and used the money to pay for a vacation. We saw where Elvis lived. I don't drive, but I want to do more traveling. I've been to Memphis, Disney World and Michigan City."

What's your favorite Elvis song?

"That Hawaiian wedding song."

Denny, you seem to be really interested in the past. What about current forms of entertainment; are you a sports fan?

"Not really. During the Olympics I enjoyed figure skating. I never miss 'Dancing With The Stars.'

"We're in the process of moving; I want to grow a big garden.

Every Mother's Day, I always planted flowers in the yard for Mama. Now, every Mother's Day, I plant them for Susie. Then, on her birthday, I pick a bouquet for her. Susie has done a lot of nice things for me down through the years."

* * *

I like to imagine Denny Bruckman years from now when he's in a more celestial place. I see him wearing a top hat, tux and tails, lookin' suave, like Fred Astaire. He's flashing that beautiful smile. His angel mother and little brother are in the audience.

Mama, look at Denny, he's dancing with the stars.

Characters

Omar Farag *(Jan. 2008)*

"The colored folks been singing it and playing just like I am now, man, for more years than I know. They played it like that in the shanties and juke joints and nobody ever paid it no mind 'til I goose it up. I got it from them. Down in Tupelo, Mississippi, I used to hear old Arthur Crudup bang his box the way I do now, and I said if I ever get to that place I could feel all old Arthur felt, I'd be a music man like nobody ever saw."

– Elvis Presley, June 26, 1956

Omar Farag was born and raised on Gary's west side. Today his home is situated along the Big Lake in Miller.

Omar's parents came from Paris and Cairo – not Illinois. His mom emigrated from France when she was a little girl. His dad came to America from Egypt when he was 18.

Omar, 57, is one of 11 children and is a lifelong bachelor.

The first 20 minutes of our interview were spent discussing the Chicago White Sox; Omar is a diehard fan.

I like him already.

* * *

"We got (Paul) Konerko, we got (Jermaine) Dye," Farag began. "Hopefully, we'll have (Joe) Crede for the whole year. And now, we actually have a shortstop who can hit – and steal bases (Orlando Cabrera)!

"Jeff, what was Turk Lown's real first name?"

Mr. Farag, please. It was Omar. Walt William's nickname?

"No Neck."

"I was raised Catholic; I went to Sacred Heart right across from Tolleston, but my father helped get the mosque built on 11th Avenue. He worked as a machinist for 35 years at U.S. Steel in Gary. My parents met at the 1933 World's Fair.

"I have five brothers – Henry, Bob, Joe, Ray and Anthony. It was like my dad said to my mom, 'Hey, I get to name one of them, OK?'

"I worked in the mill for about five years. All of us worked in the mill at some point in our lives. But my mother preached from the day we were born, 'Do not work in the mill!'"

You produce concerts. When did you get interested?

"Let me tell you a story about my brother, Henry; he was always in a band. Around the time we were in grade school Henry's band was called PJ and the Gents. He wrote a song called 'The Wounded Camel.'

"It was all AM radio back then, 1961-'62. We'd call in to WLTH and request Henry's song. Then, we didn't have to because other listeners started requesting 'The Wounded Camel.' It rose to the top of the charts at WLTH. We didn't know what to do! The song should have been a national hit. That experience is sort of where I got an interest."

You mentioned the mosque. There couldn't have been that many Egyptian-Americans in the neighborhood back then.

"It was mostly Greeks and Slovaks in Gary Heights, which was between Tolleston and Brunswick. My dad read Egyptian newspapers, but he was all about being an American. He would shout in English at the TV whenever he'd hear Maurice Chavelier speaking with his French accent. 'Learn the language!'

"I went to Andrean High School as a freshman. I paid for it by delivering Post-Tribunes. My second year, they doubled the tuition. Here I am a kid with a paper route.

"So, I went to Edison my sophomore and junior years – Michael Jackson and his brothers played at the prom. My senior year, I was part of the first graduating class of Gary West Side. Three different high schools; I like to call myself a 'Roads Scholar' because I traveled around so much.

"I started and finished college at Indiana University Northwest. In '72, '73 and '74, I went to IU in Bloomington. After getting my degree in political science, I taught the children of American oil riggers for a year in Egypt. Egypt is a cool country; I had a lot of fun.

"I was a disc jockey in Bloomington. I also put on live gigs down there during the Little 500 week – our 'Annual Boogie.' They'd have cornball performers at the Little 500, but I'd rent Diamond Shoes Stables and get four or five good local rock-'n'-roll bands to perform. We'd have 6,000 or 7,000 thousand people in attendance on Saturday – the day of the Little 500. We were the alternative party; it was Woodstock. I'd spent my time in the war from '69 to '71; Bloomington was nirvana.

"My parents died while I was in the service. My dad passed when I first went overseas. I only had three months left to serve when my mom died. They didn't make me go back to 'Nam after her funeral."

You were a private dick.

"Ahem, yes. My brother, Henry, owned the private investigation company; I worked for him during the mid-'70s. Insurance fraud is what he specialized in. I had to go undercover. I was made once; the guy threatened me. I told Henry: 'I'm done. Look, I lived through Vietnam. I don't need this shit. What else do you want to talk about?"

"The King."

"We were doing a lot of shows at The Holiday Star Theatre in Merrilliville. They needed shows in January. A lot of these guys who impersonated Elvis would come to my oldies show. They kept sayin, 'Omar, you should do an Elvis show.' I've been doing Elvis shows for 21 years now. Twelve cities a year: Skokie (Ill.), Aurora (Ill.), Cleveland, Cincinnati, Indy, Louisville, New York... . We've done Elvis shows in Switzerland.

"For the Merrillville show, we use three 'Elvi.' We do it era by era. The 'Love Me Tender' years, the military uniform, and the black-leather comeback thing when hippie was really big.

"In 1968, Elvis came back in true Elvis style – in full black, sexy leather, looking as good as a dude could look. He re-establishes what cool is. You see, Marlon Brando was the original guy-cool. OK? On the motorcycle...."

"The Wild One."

"Right; if you see 'cool' in the dictionary, you see Marlon Brando in 'The Wild One'. After 1968, you see Elvis in the dictionary. He was just the ultimate.

"When Elvis started making movies – thumbs down. To this day, we have a movie segment in our show; I'd like to get rid of it. I hate any of that shit. Once he started making movies, it was disgusting. When the Colonel took over, he made this big movie deal – Elvis had to do it. He was bored. It killed him. With the exception of 'King Creole' maybe, they never gave him a movie worth his talent."

Have there been some pretty bad impersonators audition down through the years? I mean, when you could hardly keep a straight face?

You know, like maybe a 4' 11", 300-pound, blond-haired guy from Connecticut?

"Oh, yeah; I've used a lot of different guys. This Shawn Klush I've got now is incredible. The guy sounds, looks, walks, talks – he's himself though. No surgeries, no nothing. Ryan Pelton, he puts that black leather on and walks out there, and I always say – and this is blasphemy – that he looks better than Elvis!

"I'm an extremely lucky guy that I get to do what I do – it's like being a professional baseball player."

* * *

The loquacious and indefatigable Omar Farag. A man who has many stories to tell, albeit some of them unsuitable for this publication.

Mr. & Mrs. B *(Feb. 2006)*

"Let the wife make the husband glad to come home. Let the husband make the wife sorry to see him leave."
-- Martin Luther

For Valentine's week, I traveled to Shelby to interview a couple, rather than an individual: Waldo and Eleanor Bartz.

Waldo "Babe" Bartz is a rugged old codger with a voice as coarse as No. 4 sandpaper. Mrs. B is a sweetheart of a lady with one of those charming voices reminiscent Aunt Bee of the Andy Griffith Show. Mr. and Mrs. B have been wed for 66 years.

The B's don't drive anymore. They are both 85 years old. Waldo has emphysema, and is legally blind. He worked in the construction trades. Eleanor was Shelby's librarian for many years.

The B's raised four children, Kathy, Steve, Karen, and Mark who have given Mr. and Mrs. B 10 grandchildren, 18 great-grandchildren, and two great-great-grandchildren. Like many couples who have lived together for a long time, they sometimes speak as one, finishing each other's sentences. They call each other Mom and Dad.

* * *

Crockett's Victory Garden! I've got that book at home. Do the two of you enjoy horticulture?

"Oh, yes. Nothing like gardening," Eleanor began. "I don't wear gloves, I like my hands in the dirt! Mr. B was quite the gardener, too. He grew enough vegetables to feed all of Lake County. And gladiolas, I love gladiolas. He had more than 300 of them growing in the garden at one time. I'd liven the library with them. Dad's glads graced the altar of several area churches as well."

"Well, I always figured my garden was part of my income," Waldo said.

"You sold some vegetables, yes, but you *gave* most of them away, Dad."

"Now, Mom, I was talkin' about you – the tomatoes you put up, your green beans."

"Oh, yes, I always canned. Even made my own ketchup and sauerkraut."

What was your maiden name, Eleanor?

"Sirois. I was the oldest Sirois girl. Frenchie Sirois was my father. He was the son of old Sam Sirois, who was quite a character here in town – Grandpa came from Canada."

I knew a Jack Sirois; he ran the lumberyard in Lake Village. I bought my first pocketknife from him when I was a boy. While making the purchase, I remember a man coming into the lumberyard with his son and asking Mr. Sirois if he sold Daisy BB guns. Ol' poker-faced Jack looked the guy straight in the eye, chomped down on his stogie and muttered, "Yep, sell window panes, too."

"Jack was my first-cousin."

Have you two always lived in Shelby?

"I was born right down the street," Eleanor said. "Lived here in Shelby all my life except for the six years when I was following you-know-who during the war. Mr. B was born in Black Oak (neighborhood of Gary), but his family moved down to this area when he was 2."

"Come from Sumava and Lake Village, huh?" Waldo asked.

Yes, sir.

"My father was asked to go down there one time to cut meat for some European fellas who couldn't speak English. Somebody had peddled a bunch of goats to them during the Depression; they were selling goat milk to the TB sanitarium. Although my dad only went to the third-grade, he could speak nine languages – he went to sea when he was 9. "

Waldo, Mrs. B tells me you built this house by yourself, 49 years ago. What did you do for a living?

"Carpenter, bridge builder, pipe fitter... ."

"He wasn't home much, Jeff. Dad worked at power stations a lot. He was out in Wyoming once for three months. We had a boy in high school back then. I didn't think it was right to move him all around. I stayed here with Mark while Dad was on the road."

Heard tell you played on some pretty good football teams at Lowell High, Waldo.

"We were undefeated two years in a row."

"Dad was pretty good at quarterback."

"I think Ralph Combs had us pegged at 34 wins, 2 losses, and 1 tie during the three years we played together."

"Ralph's brother played with Waldo; Bill Combs was a pretty good player too, wasn't he Dad?"

"Well, he played end at Purdue, Mom. I guess he was 'pretty good.' Thirty-seven one – I bet John Keithley would remember that. Thirty-seven one was a short pass play behind the line of scrimmage where the end would go out into the flat zone. John was fast. Yeah, Keithley was quite a long distance runner, too."

What year did the two of you graduate from Lowell High School?

"1939. Dad was the class president. Jeff, 10 or 15 years ago he got up to speak at our class reunion. He started off by saying, 'I married the sexiest girl in high school, and then she turned into a Sunday School teacher and a librarian!' Why, I thought I'd kill him! Everyone thought he was hilarious."

Hah! That was a....good... one... (awkward silence). *You told me you enjoy watching Jeopardy! and doing the New York Times crossword puzzles, but you love books most of all, don't you, Eleanor?*

"Oh my, yes. I'm a big John Grisham fan, but I read all sorts of things – seven to nine books a week to this day."

Waldo ever watch Jeopardy with you?

"I can't hear it and I can't see it!"

The Shelby branch of the Lowell library started out at the Catholic Church here in town, correct?

"Yes. And Jeff, I'm so sad that St. Theresa closed down. Forty-seven families... I was in their basement for 13 years. Those people were so good to me. I left when the Lowell Library bought the new building for me. They rent half of it to the post office. The building has become sort of a social center for Shelby, which is nice. I'd have basket classes and gingerbread house classes at the library as well.

"When I was still working, people would come to the post office and then stop in to chat with me. Eventually, I'd get them hooked on a book. I loved the job. Dad was my courier; he'd go into Lowell twice per week with supplies and then have breakfast at George's Restaurant."

You mentioned moving around during the war years.

"Yes, when Waldo was in the Coast Guard we lived in Staten Island, Chicago, Milwaukee, and Kilgore, Texas. We ended up in San Pedro, Calif. just before the war was over. I loved it there, swimming in the ocean."

Coast Guard during WW II. That must have been quite an experience, Waldo.

"I was on a subchaser. It was a 125-foot, 44-man ship; we were manning it with 16 sailors. One of my pastimes is counting the American flags that appear in the obituaries of the Chicago Tribune. I check 'em to see how I'm runnin' – whether I'm younger or older than the deceased. You'd be surprised at how many 90-year-olds are still poppin' up in there."

"Dad could have gone to college, but his father talked him into joining the Coast Guard. I went to college, but came home at

Christmastime. That's when we eloped. And that was it for my college. We went steady all through high school. I tell you, Jeff, you wonder where the years have gone.

"I enjoyed your Salt column on Jack Eskridge. Our daughter, Kathy, graduated with Jack. His father was a great guy. I'd see him in the grocery store; he always was shopping for a beef tenderloin. When I think of beef tenderloins to this day, I think of him. What was Jack's grandfather's name again?"

I've got it on the tip of my tongue, Eleanor. I mentioned it in the story.

"They called him Ornery," Waldo croaked.

"What was his real name, Dad?"

"Eskridge."

"Oh, fiddle faddle! Come on, help me think of that man's first name! And why did they call him Ornery anyway?"

"Because he was."

What's the secret to staying married for 66 years, Eleanor?

"Patience is virtue," Eleanor said while staring a hole through Waldo.

"Marriage is more legal," Waldo said.

Thanks for your input, Mr. B. Your father was quite the businessman around these parts they tell me.

"Yeah, he ran several stores in Lowell. One on Mill Street, one on Commercial across the tracks up by Zuni's, and he had one right in town by the funeral home. The rationings during the war got the better of him so he went to farming about 20 acres in Thayer; he eventually opened a saloon on his farm. They'd have barn dances on Saturday night. Purty nice.

"At one time my dad and Dick Schmal's dad had businesses right next to each other. Me and Dick are old friends. We used to swim naked when we was boys in the old north and south swimmin' holes."

"Well, I hope there weren't any girls near by, for goodness sakes!"

"Down through the years, I was a supervisor on a lot of jobs," Waldo said. "I was the kind of boss that if someone didn't know how to do a certain job, I'd try to teach him. I treated all my men like that. Figured you ought to be able to teach a guy something instead of always layin' him off. It's easy to fire a man just to guard your own ass."

"Jeff, it's been so nice to meet you," Eleanor said. "Come here, I think you need a hug. You come back and visit us."

* * *

Mr. and Mrs. B...
Gotta love 'em.

Dr. Quackenbush *(Oct. 2007)*
(Merle Miller)

"I was born in the wagon of a travelin' show
Mama used to dance for the money they'd throw
Papa would do what ever he could
preach a little gospel,
sell a couple bottles of Dr. Good"
– From the song "Gypsies, Tramps & Thieves" by Cher

Merle Miller and his wife, Suzanne, live in a 13,312 square-foot schoolhouse built in 1923 in LaPorte.

We first met a few autumns past at the Buckley Homestead Fall Festival in Lowell. He was hustling snake oil and performing rope tricks.

Miller was plying his schtik in the guise of a self-created alter ego, Dr. Quackenbush. Think Strother Martin *and* Henny Youngman.

Some might consider Miller eccentric.

Me, I like eccentric.

* * *

"Come on in, Jeff," Miller began. "Let me give you a tour. The kitchen was the teachers' lounge. The living room was a full classroom. There are six classrooms altogether. Here's my daughter's former bedroom, which was half of a former class room. This was the secretary's office. Note the old toilet with the tank and flusher up above."

Nice claw-foot bathtub – and brilliant red, too. And the restrooms still have antique "Boys" and "Girls" signs above the entrances. Old wooden school desks. A restored icebox. Are these benches from a bowling alley?

"Yes. Here's our stage – it's 20 feet deep. Right now we're about to put on an 'America's Got Talent' spoof . It's half-play and half-talent show. We'll incorporate magicians, jugglers, ventriloquists – a little bit of everything. Some people will get gonged. We also put on a tongue-in-cheek 'Midwest Annual Country Music Awards Show.'

"Suzanne and I portray Mr. & Mrs. Claus at Christmastime. We also do a comedic Ben and Debbie Franklin, where it's Mrs Franklin who actually gave Benjamin all his ideas, but never got credit for anything: 'It's time history was corrected!' We do other historical skits, too – my son, Earl, portrays Abraham Lincoln.

"I've always wanted to write a script – a dark comedy – on our very own Belle Gunness. She made sausage out of about 30 people here in LaPorte. But many of the actors in our community theater troupe are also members of the Historical Society; they were aghast at the thought of me altering any facts.

"Next year is going to be the 100th year anniversary of Gunness' alleged death caused by a mysterious fire. She lived about 8 blocks from here – attracted most of her victims through lonely heart letters."

Merle, this is such a cool place. You and Suzanne going to live out your days here?

"I don't know; they keep raising the taxes. By the time we pay the heat bill and the taxes, half of our Social Security check is gone.

"Let's have a seat at the kitchen table – it was an old drafting table. Suzanne said, 'I need a bigger table for Thanksgiving.' So I took it all apart and built the legs on Thanksgiving morning."

"What kind of dog is this?

"Brown," Merle said.

"Old," added Suzanne.

"Sasha is 14 1/2 years old now. A woman came up to me and said, 'Here's your puppy.' She put the dog in my hands, got in her car and left. Never saw her before or since."

So, how long have you two lovebirds been together, Merle?

"We have 23 years of happily married life – and 23 ain't a bad average for a 47-year marriage. After we got married, Suzanne and I moved to Vietnam. I went over there on a small aircraft carrier named the "Core." It got sunk two trips later in Saigon Bay.

"I felt my country needed me and I joined – Army Air Corps, back in 1962 and '63. I helped set up the first aircraft repair station in the middle of the jungle. We'd harvest aircraft that had crashed, then use the parts. Vietnam was the type of war we're not set up to fight. Same thing is going on now (in Iraq). You can't fight that with tanks."

Suzanne went to Vietnam, too?

"Yes, she had it pretty good. You could be living in town and everything was pleasant as can be, but two miles away in the jungle – all hell could be breaking loose."

Sounds pretty intense.

"They weren't that pretty."

Pardon me?

"The tents. We slept 'in tents.' I gotta a million of 'em!"

(The tinny sound of drumsticks meeting cymbals echoes in my head).

Let's back up a bit Dr. Quack – er, Merle. Your childhood?

"I graduated from Washington High in South Bend. When I attended there it went from kindergarten to 12th grade – all in one small building. Adams was the school where the rich kids went. Washington was the west end with all the poor kids.

"I'm a mechanical engineer. After my time in the service I went back to college and got a second degree. Suzanne gives me the third degree.

(Cymbals).

When did you move to LaPorte?

"In 1979; we moved to the school in '95. It was for sale for years and no one would touch it because it was too far gone. Being stupid, we bought it. Every pane of glass in this place was broken. We had a little help with the roof, but basically, these hands have done the whole thing. One thing at a time. Get up on the ladder. Get down from ladder. Up, down, up, down."

Children?

"Two boys and a girl; the two youngest grew up here. All the kids are in the show; all three became mechanical engineers."

How did "Dr. Quackenbush's Magic, Medicine and Music Show" come to be?

"Quackenbush just sort of developed. We went to libraries and did research on the old medicine wagons during the Gay '90s and early 1900s."

Some of those guys were kind of, well, rip-offs weren't they?

"They all were! Mountebanks and charlatans, the lot of them! The entertainment was pretty lame, too. Some of the stuff those guys peddled was 30 percent booze!"

How long has the 'medicine show' run at the Buckley Homestead Fall Festival?

"About 20 years; we don't advertise – all word of mouth. We've taken "Dr. Quackenbush's Magic, Medicine an Music Show" to Russia.

"My daughter Erin started performing in the show when she was 5 years old. She didn't understand why adults were laughing at some of her lines. As she got older she realized why the people were laughing.

"We've slacked off some since the kids have grown. Suzanne and I have staged a two-person show. She plays a 1920-made bass fiddle. I'm self-taught on the mandolin; I've written some of the music for it."

"Most of it," added Suzanne.

"I do rope tricks, magic and juggling. Suzanne does the ventriloquism; she has a dummy that looks like me.

"I also drive the train two days per week at the Potawatomi Zoo in South Bend. It's a lot of fun. I've written a spiel with a lot of jokes in it about the animals. The kids love it. There are adults who come back week after week to hear the same routine over again."

"He changes it all the time," said Suzanne.

* * *

Merle and Suzanne Miller. Latter-day vaudevillians who did comedy acts in war-torn Vietnam during the early 1960s, and continue to make the circuit with their traveling medicine show.

Together, they have performed a love story for 47 years.

Joe Mika *(Nov. 2008)*

Election Council President: "The chair recognizes it's old friend; that distinguished member of the Fourth Estate, founder, owner, publisher and editor of the Shinbone Express Star, Mr. Dutton Peabody, Esquire!"

Peabody (Edmond O'Brien): "No, no, no, you don't. No. I'm a newspaperman not a politician. Politicians are my meat. I build 'em up. I tear 'em down. But I, I wouldn't be one. I couldn't. It'd, it'd destroy me. Gimme a drink."

Bartender: The bar is closed, Mr. Editor, during voting.

Peabody: No exceptions for the working press? Why, that's carrying democracy too far!"

– From "The Man Who Shot Liberty Valance," 1962

It was Thursday, Oct. 16, when I pulled up to the Lake County Government Center in Crown Point. Folks were waiting in line to vote early, if not often. It was old-school politico Joe Mika that I'd come to chat with.

Mika lives in Crown Point now, but spent most of his adult life in Lowell. He was delivered by a midwife at 1007 Cherry Street in Hammond the year Babe Ruth swatted 60 homers – 1927.

Mika has served as South Lake County Democratic Chairman for 40 years; no chairperson has more tenure.

* * *

"Grab a seat, Jeff," Mika began. "Have any trouble finding me?"

No problem, Joe. I've visited every one of these buildings for one reason or another. You've resided in the north end as well as south county. Let's start from the beginning.

"I was a Depression baby; my folks had chickens and ducks right there in Hammond. We were a little north of 15th Street (169th) and Calumet Avenue. When beer first came back (1933), my dad had the first tavern in the neighborhood. We lived above it. It was called Helen's, named after one of my sisters.

"We served free fish back then. My mom and uncle would fry close to 100 pounds of lake perch every Friday night."

All that fish probably made those guys thirsty.

"Oh yeah, we also kept plenty of pretzels and popcorn on the bar, too. Free food was nothing to sneeze at in those days. On St Joseph's Day, my mom would dole out beef sandwiches; I was born on St. Joseph's Day.

"Both my parents were born in Czechoslovakia. All the time dad had the tavern, he also did plumbing and heating. This country is going through some tough economic times right now, but I've seen worse times, like when a meal was buttermilk and mashed potatoes. There were years when Christmas dinner consisted of mushroom soup and wafers from the church – Slovaks like mushrooms. But people helped each other back in those days.

"There was a guy named Steve who worked for Nagel Packing; he would stop at our tavern every night and have two shots and two beers, and then he would leave. My mom loaned him the money to start Marusczak's Polish Sausage.

"Ever heard of Kenny Gurley? He ran a little book at the Southtown Tap on Conkey Street. My mother loaned him money to get started, too. He bought the Yankee Inn over on Hoffman and Calumet Ave. Every place Kenny bought after that he made money because he was a good businessman."

Growing up above a saloon during the '30s must've provided for a flavorful childhood.

"It was back in '37 when the police got radios in there cars; when they stopped in the tavern, I'd sit in their squad cars and listen to calls for them. Closing time was 1 a.m.; the cops would say to my dad, 'Hey, Joe, that clock's no good, throw it out, it says one o'clock; it's only midnight.'

"I went to work for Junior Toy Corporation one summer when I was in high school, making bomb shells and bomb bases. They made bicycles and tricycles before the war. I worked the midnight shift. There was no air conditioning above the tavern; it was tough sleeping during the day – all you'd do is lay there and sweat."

Hammond High?

"Yeah, but as soon as I turned 17, I joined the Navy. When the war was over, I got my ruptured duck (discharge) and returned to the Region."

Always been a Democrat?

"Oh, yeah. I was raised around politics. My dad would have ham sandwiches and beer for the politicians in Hammond."

Joe, as far as Lake County goes, Hammond and Crown Point have been bastions of conservatism for years, have they not?

"If you look back through Hammond's history, since the Democrats took over in '33, there was only one mayoral election that the Republicans won easily. It was always like a 500-vote difference. I remember Dowling, a Democrat, beating Anderson, a Republican, by 500 votes."

Still, just the fact that it has been close shows the difference between Hammond, and say, East Chicago or Gary.

"You're right."

Lake County mayors you've admired in the past?

"Gary's Pete Mandich was a great mayor; so was George Chacharis. George had a big heart. He donated a lot of money to the churches. When Walter Jeorse was the mayor of East Chicago, he ran things with an iron fist.

"But it was (County Commissioner) J.J. Forszt who really controlled Lake County. He made a lot of guys. My mentor was Art Bush – one helluva guy.

"Years ago, they used to have what they called a 2 percent club. That's how they ran the campaigns. When you got a job with the county, you paid 2 percent. Everybody paid into it. That's how they funded the fall elections – with the 2 percent money. They don't have that no more. Now we have to have fund-raisers."

Let's talk a little about south county.

"I moved to Lowell in '48; I was 21. Most people probably don't know what all I've done for Lowell. I helped build the Lowell Volunteer Fire Department and had over 30 years as a volunteer fireman."

Joe, I was covering a Lowell High School football game the other night and I got to talking to a couple of guys who are about my age , Mark Sampson and Randy Lukasik. They claimed to have known you practically all their lives. When I asked them what you did for a living; neither of them knew.

"I'm retired from the Lake County Highway Department. I was the superintendent for years. The winters of '67 and '79 were rough, let me tell you.

"Randy Lukasik's dad and I are old friends. I could walk up to Stan right now and ask him for a couple of grand and he wouldn't blink an eye. He's that type of guy. If he likes you, he likes you. If he don't like you..."

Joe, being the liberal freethinking Democrat that you are, I'm sure you are in favor of the controversial subject of Lowell becoming a city.

"I'm against it."

Say it ain't so, Joe!

"Years ago, yeah. Why would you want to spend all that money? Just because you get federal funding, does that make up for the rest of it? Just changing all the logos on stationary, town trucks, etc. would cost a fortune. That's the way I look it."

Can Obama win Indiana?

"It's a distinct possibility. There's no doubt he's going to be the next president of the United States."

Joe, an enigma to me has always been the poor Republican.

"What really pisses me off is the farmer. Who saved their asses? Franklin Roosevelt. And now they're all Republicans? That's bullshit. I'm sorry. I've got one farmer there in Lowell that I might of converted. Old man Kalvaitis was a good Democrat.

"Jeff, I've had a good life. Violet and I just celebrated 57 years of marriage."

* * *

With our interview complete, Mika escorted me down the escalator and toward the door. At least a dozen people, some government employees, some John Q. Public, called him out by name: "Hi, Joe... How's it going, Joe... Good to see you, Joe..." Backs are slapped; hands are shaken. He's obviously a man who knows people.

And surely, a good Joe to know.

Gloria Lynn *(June 2007)*

"The only thing in the middle of the road is a yellow streak and dead armadillos."

– Jim Hightower

I traveled to the Tarrytown section of Gary to visit with Ms. Gloria Lynn. She'd given me apt directions. But, as usual, I was a block off. I believe it's a left-handed thing.

Three elderly fellas seated under a shade tree, eluding the hot sun while savoring cold suds, knew exactly where Gloria lived: "I done some work for Gloria once."

The trio seemed eager to get me to my destination. "You gonna interview Gloria, huh? Good luck." They smiled like Cheshire cats.

Good luck?

* * *

Nice aquarium.

"I used to have black angel fish and white angel fish, but they just couldn't get along," she said.

"I've set out all my scrap books for you. Some contain the resumes of guests who appeared on my radio program, 'Gloria Lynn With Her Common Sense.' WLNR FM, 106 on your dial."

How did you get started in radio?

"I had the Senior Citizens' Club, you see. I used to make crafts with flowers. I was a guest on Dorothy Ayres' herb show. She was very well known, lived out on Knickerbocker Avenue. She would tell people not to use sodium. Ironically, she got put in the hospital because she never ate salt."

We cannot survive without a little salt, Gloria.

"After my guest appearance, the manager of the station asked me to fill in for Libby Collins, who also had a radio show. She was going on vacation. Libby was Warren Freiberg's (the radio host) wife. I talked to my late husband Charles about it. Charles said, 'You talk all the time. You might as well get paid for it.'"

We'll get back to radio in a bit. Tarrytown?

"My mother told Charles and me about this development where black veterans could purchase a home with no money down. But your bills couldn't exceed $500 and your annual income had to be $13,000. Well, we didn't have any bills. We didn't even have a car. We qualified.

"People first came here from the other side of 21st Avenue in 1954. Some folks weren't all that gung-ho about buying these box houses because they were prefab. They also said the house wouldn't last more than 30 years. I planned to stay here for five years – I been here for 50."

Where were you born?

"Chicago. I graduated from Wendell Phillips High School on 39th and Pershing in 1945."

Tell me more about your mother.

"She was a Joshua from Louisiana. Her father was a doctor – Creole. He spoke French fluently. The reason we got all our history on paper is because his family was Catholic."

Are you Catholic?

"No. First African Methodist Episcopal. Mother used to take us to church every Sunday when we lived in the slums of Chicago. But I've since given all that up. I believe it's a God up there. But it's a God over all religions.

"The churches ain't too in love with Gloria because I talk about all of them. They should be in the streets doing more than they're doing.

"When Charles and I first moved from Chicago to Tarrytown, I used to shop at Jewel. I'd ask, 'Where are the colored people?' They'd say, 'This is Brunswick. We don't have any colored.' I'd say, 'Well, you should. I live in Tarrytown, we must have about 5,000 black people.'"

Gary?

"When Mayor Hatcher was in office, I didn't know there were poor people in Gary because everybody was working. Then the steel mills started slowing down. The people got sick of Hatcher. Said he wasn't doing anything. I always thought with Mayor Hatcher being the kingpin, that all these black people should have stuck together, like the Daleys did in Chicago. But no, they broke the chain. They splintered.

"Then we got Mayor Barnes in. He asked me to work with him. I said, 'No, I'm with Mayor Hatcher.' This was a model city. The United States, in my opinion, used us to watch and see if we could govern ourselves."

Martin Luther King? Scott King?

"I never was much for marching in the street and getting chewed up by the white man's police dogs so I could eat in the white man's restaurant. Build your own restaurant! With that said, you can't make a chocolate cake without a little white sugar. Mayor King's dream, with that baseball thing they got over there, he was for the new city that I been talking about on radio since 1974.

"Broadway would be condominiums to the lake and out there

would be your play land. I won't live to see it. The mill, it will be gone. The steelworker says, 'Well, I get a pension.' Yes, but everyday, they're trying to figure out how to take that pension away."

Radio, then came cable television.

"Yes. I had the radio program for 10 years. I've been on cable TV for 20. I've got over a 1,000 television programs stored away on tape. I've been a dishwasher and I've been a chef. Everything but a prostitute and a thief, I suppose. The best jobs I ever had was radio and televison."

What TV station are you on?

"Channel 21 in the old Sears building on Broadway. Million dollar studio. The city got the cable now; I'm waiting to see what they're going to do, whether or not they're going to try to hurt me, you understand?"

You mentioned Warren Freiberg, the radio host. Was your show as controversial?

"Probably so. A lot of people hated us both. We did it all. Warren was conservative."

Who have been some of your guests on radio or television?

"Fred 'The Hammer' Williamson, David Duke, Diane Burns, Wallace D Mohammed... I interviewed Linda Yu when she was very young.

"Congressman Pete Visclosky was on my show. When my mother was dying, Pete would come to see me. I had the guy on from Hammond with all the reptiles and snakes. I did a show from a plane that took off from the little airport in Hobart. I also picketed the Gary Police."

Reverend Jackson?

"I wouldn't have Jesse Jackson on my show; he's an opportunist. Now, John Buncich, he's my friend; I've had him on TV. When he lost, I had an asthma attack. Almost died. They sold us out. I worked hard for John.

"I also had the consul of South Africa come on my cable program; he wanted to take me back to Africa with him. My husband wouldn't let me go. The people who owned the botanical gardens, they were my friends, too. They send money to Africa to get their herbs."

How's your health?

"I had a stroke in 2004. Your brain is never the same. I used to get up at 6 a.m. and work in my garden. I had everything just perfect. I went out there a couple weeks ago with my hat and rubber shoes, and I knew I was gonna do this thing. I walked out into that backyard and it looked like it got bigger.

"The drug addicts help me with my yard. These people who use drugs, they do good work. But they're erratic, and that can be dangerous.

I'm like this, if you my friend, and you go to jail, you still my friend."

"People used to tell me I favored Eartha Kitt. But I was better looking than Eartha. They say if you have two first names you'll be rich. I'm still waiting."

* * *

Gloria Lynn. A woman who has ruffled some feathers, but doesn't see color when it comes to friends or enemies.

She's a piece of work. And she's a southpaw, too.

Walter Rich *(July 2010)*

"Do unto others as you would have them do unto you."
– Jesus of Nazareth

Walter Rich, 71, of Lake Village is a likeable cuss who often goes by W.W. He's a native Alabaman who has raised four children. And, he's a 32nd- degree Mason who portrays Kris Kringle at nursing homes, churches and schools.

But the delightful old scalawag's main claim to fame is the unique tourist attraction he's been creating on his 5-acre spread. "Wally's World" has been a work in progress since 1977.

* * *

How long have you lived in Indiana?

"I moved to Hammond in 1959," he said. "I worked on gondola cars at Standard Railway Corp. on Columbia Ave. for about 20 years, until it shut down, and then hired in at Thrall Car."

W.W., how about the dime tour of Wally's World?

"Yes, sir. Let's take a look at Scottsboro Depot first; it's inside this building."

Are you from that neck of the woods? That's where the notorious "Scottsboro Boys" scandel took place.

"My grandfather sat at the trial. I never did believe none of them was guilty. They was exonerated after several years. One of the women eventually admitted she wasn't raped... .

"Here we are: Welcome to Wally's World."

Oh my goodness. It's a microcosm of Newton, Jasper and southern Lake counties with a railroad running through it all.

"It's H.O. scale. I never had a train in my life until Carl Ferro gave me one. He runs Midtown Hardware in Lowell. Carl is like my brother; he ended up giving me all of his trains.

"Every scene tells a story: Here's a farmer slopping hogs. This is a young girl selling lemonade on the corner. Here's a lady putting flowers on a grave. And here's a young couple in the backseat of a convertible. This dog just jumped up on the grill and stole somebody's steak.

"Here's kids swimming and jumping off the railroad bridge. And these kids are playing basketball. See the one hanging on the rim after he dunked the ball?"

The detail is incredible.

"I have street lights that come on at dusk. The window of that machine shop lights up whenever the guy welding strikes an arc. I just put up these big windmills like you see near Fowler off of Interstate 65."

This is very educational.

"Jeff, I try to incorporate a little bit of everything; 50 years from now, kids might not know how we lived."

So much detail. You hand-paint all these Liliputian folks?

"Yes, sir. The inch-long fishin' poles those boys are using were made from individual hairs of a paint brush."

You use the names of real businesses on the storefronts. This area is obviously Lowell: Anco Appliance, the Cornerstone Mansion, Lowell Healthcare...

"I believe in goin' home with who I brought to the dance."

Huh?

"I trade with local merchants whenever possible. Lowell Healthcare was the nursing home that took care of my mama; she just passed. Over there is Norm's Pumpkin Patch in Creston. This here is Imperial Waste, they pick up my garbage – good people. This is Bruce Septic loading up Porta-Potties. And here's Sander's Cycle in Rensselaer.

"This is Hanford's Packing Co. in Thayer; Hans Kroll's body and paint shop in Lake Village; Studer's Corner Marathon station in Schneider... ."

What's that attached to the ceiling?

"The Enterprise from Star Trek; they're coming down to check on us. Since 1996, I've had people from all over the world sign my guest book."

Really? Let's see... . England, New Zealand, The Netherlands, South Korea, Costa Rica, Belgium... . Amazing.

"Brother, wait 'til I finish the park portion of Wally's World.

Everything will be G-gauge outdoors. Follow me."

...Wow! Where did you pick her up, Ellis Island?

"Not only will I showcase the Statue of Liberty, I plan on building the Eiffel Tower, Leaning Tower of Pisa, The Sphinx, Mount Rushmore, the Grand Canyon... . When the train meanders through all of it, the sign will say: 'See the Seven Wonders of Wally's World.'"

Do you have investors?

"Yes, sir. A lot of friends who have invested time, material and workmanship. Without friends, I'd have nothing.

"Let's have a seat in these wooden lawn chairs; they rock real nice. Jeff, I'm still in wonder of a good cloud, a soft rain, a sunset."

Before our interview began, you mentioned our mutual friend, the Rev. Stephen Snoich. Do you attend Mass regularly at St. Augusta Catholic Church?

No; I need to go. Father Steve is after me, but he don't pressure. I have a lamp in my bedroom that he made in seminary school. I love that man; he's good people. Want a beer?"

No, thanks; I'm working.

"Well, I do believe I will. Jeff, my mother's grandmother was full-blooded Cherokee. Some of my family wouldn't come to my great-grandfather's house after he married her. He was considered a 'squaw man.'

"But my immediate family told me my Cherokee great-grandmother was good people. I remember when her daughter, my grandmother, knocked a chicken hawk out of the sky with a rifle. My grandfather, who was of Irish stock, looked at me and winked, 'Don't ever mess with your grandma.'

"My grandma taught me, 'Always treat people like you want to be treated."

The golden rule.

"I had a man call me up and say, 'I need a favor.' I said, 'You got it.' He said, 'But you don't know what it is.' I said, 'I don't care; you're my friend.' He said, 'Lord, I've never had a friend.' I told him he probably had a lot of friends, but they didn't know what he needed."

W.W., I could listen to your delightful stories and southern drawl all day.

"Brother, there's probably some people who don't like me, but I ain't met too many of 'em yet. We all live on this little bitty planet, and it ain't getting no bigger. We gotta learn to get along with one another."

* * *

W.W. Rich is rich; he has a wealth of friends.
He's good people.

Fred Halpern *(Aug. 2011)*

"Have you ever walked through Sears and wondered what happened to Roebuck?"
– George Carlin

In 1905, Albert Rubinstein hung his shingle at the corner of Main Street and Broadway in East Chicago's Indiana Harbor neighborhood.

More than a century later, the business still is known as Albert's Jewelers, but a fellow named Fred has been running the show for 51 years.

Fred Halpern, 71, married Donna on Valentine's Day 44 years ago. They raised two children, Josh and Holly.

Josh, a gemologist, is vice president of Albert's Jewelers which was relocated from East Chicago to Schererville about eight years ago.

Fred and Donna live in Schererville, Briar Ridge to be exact. I don't interview many folks who live in gated communities, but Halpern is quite a character and has an incredible rags-to-riches story. He's also one of the most altruistic human beings I've ever met.

* * *

"I was born and raised in Chicago and went to South Shore High School," Halpern began. "My father was in the jewelry business in Chicago. A guy by the name of Bernie Davis managed one of Dad's stores.

"Davis was a great basketball player for Northwestern, but he loved the horses and loved the girls. He left my father and bought a store in Indiana Harbor called Albert's."

How did Davis fare?

"He got in some financial trouble... plus, in '59, the mills closed down because of the steel strike. Davis went bankrupt. At the time, I'm a 21-year old junior at the University of Alabama who was working summer help at Republic Steel. My dad tells me, 'We own that store in Indiana now; you got it.'"

Bad for Davis, but good for you.

"It was a bankrupt store with no inventory and no customers. My first year, we did $27,000 worth of business. I didn't get paid.

"I lived at home with my parents at 78th and Yates. The second year, I did $36,000. I still didn't get paid. The only stuff we sold was called memorandum."

Explain, please.

"A person would come around and say, 'Freddy, here's $100 worth of merchandise, if you sell it, you pay me at the end of the week.' There were times they shut off my water or electricity – no money."

What did you do?

"I said to hell with this shit; either I'm gonna to make it or I'm not. I started staying open until after every movie theater closed. All the other jewelry stores were closed; everything was closed but me. If a guy came out of the movies with his girlfriend he could buy her a pair of earrings for a buck."

Did things turn around for you?

"Slowly but surely, I still didn't get paid for five years. I basically lived off of my mom's home cooking. Eventually, I got married and we moved to Riverdale, (Ill.) and then to Glenwood, (Ill.).

"Jeff, I always was a gambler, not on the ponies or cards; I gambled in commodities. I borrowed $2,000 dollars and turned it into $100,000."

That was a lot of money in the 1960s. What did you do with it?

"I put a healthy down payment on my building and bought a house for my wife. I lost the rest. But I could've sold anything in those days. All you had to be was fair and honest with your customers..

"Not only were there about seven or eight theaters in town, you also had Inland (Steel Co.) and Youngstown. You had 50,000 people come to work in that town everyday. The population of East Chicago was maybe 35,000 to 40,000 back then. On Inland payday, they'd be lined up around the block cashing their checks right across from my store."

Were you ever robbed at Main Street and Broadway?

"Yeah, I had a guy come in and grab a purse or something. I go chasing after him into a pool hall. In the back room of this place, games were going on.

Games?

"Crap games, poker games, stuff like that. By that time, the cops are on the scene; we grabbed this guy and pulled him out of there, and nobody in the joint ever stops gambling.

"In that little half-mile area from where I was located, you had it all… . It was like the Roaring Twenties in the Sixties. It was fabulous."

Fred, it just hit me – your facial characteristics and mannerisms. Has anyone ever said that you bear a striking resemblance to the actor Roy Scheider?

"I get that a lot."

You're not a bad actor; I've watched your TV commercials for years. I liked the one where you dressed up like a swami. Let's switch gears. I used to see you at an occasional 5K road race. Do you still run?

"No, but I workout anaerobically every day for an hour. I had a brother, Kenneth, who was the city planner for New York City, one of the most prestigious jobs in the country. He designed this Frank Lloyd Wright-style home for me.

"One year, I ran the Chicago Marathon and he ran the New York Marathon when they were held on the same weekend."

You've also run in memory of that same brother while helping to raise money to find a cure for AIDS.

"I was the only person in the family he told. He broke the news to me at a restaurant. He figured he'd need to get me drunk first. Hell, I knew he was gay; the rest of my family was in denial."

Attitudes have changed somewhat since the '70s.

"I stayed with Ken at the hospital in NYC from morning until night for 11 days before he died. People from all over the world came to see him when they found out he was dying. It was very touching.

"Before he got real sick, Ken took in about five guys with AIDS, one by one, all of them died in his apartment. Their families had shunned them and they didn't have anyplace to go."

You've also helped raise money for multiple sclerosis research.

"More than $100,000 this year; we'll raise more next year. Donna has suffered from MS for decades."

The secret to your success?

"A positive mental attitude. You have to believe there is nothing you can't do. Also, be honest with your customers and find a way to out-hustle your competition. I wasn't smarter than my competition, but I stayed open until almost midnight."

* * *

Interesting man, Hapern. On one hand, he's a streetwise, pool shootin' son of a gun who has been known to take risks and out-hustle his competition. On the other hand, he's a kind soul who treats his customers right.

It would take far too much space to list all the groups Halpern supports by donating money or merchandise.

Suffice it to say that Fred Halpern is a diamond in the rough.

Mike Haviland *(July 2012)*

"... There'll be you, me, and old dog Trey, to doodle time away.
If we don't hook a perch or bass, we'll cool our toes in dewy grass,
Or else pull up a weed to chaw, and maybe set and jaw.
Hangin' around, takin' our ease, watchin' that hound, a scratchin' at his fleas."
– From the theme song of "The Andy Griffith Show."

Not everyone knows the lyrics to the above ditty, but most of us have whistled the tune a time or two. You best believe Mike Haviland knows all the words to "Fishin' Hole" by heart; he is the reigning 2011 Mayberry Trivia world champion.

Haviland, 63, was born and raised in Hammond but graduated from Lake Central High School. He lives in Lake Dalecarlia with Rhonda, his wife of 3 1/2 years. He has two adult daughters, Bonnie and Kelly, from a previous marriage.
Haviland is retired from the Dyer post office, but tends bar three days a week at Pop-O's Tap in Thayer.

Our interview recently took place in the Mayberry Room of his house overlooking Lake Dale. Several times during our conversation, Rhonda had to interrupt us: "Mike, that was Connie Niemeyer on the phone, sending her condolences."

It was the day Andy Griffith died.

* * *

Childhood memories of Hammond?

"It was a utopia; at age 6, I'd go down to the Civic Center by the park to fly kites and play ball without adult supervision," he said. "Nobody bothered anybody back then. I was into catching snakes and lizards over by Erie Hill."

Did you watch "The Andy Griffith Show" in those days?

"Oh, yeah. My parents used to use Opie as an example: 'Why don't you behave like Opie?'"

In your estimation, one of Opie's more precious lines?

"Pa, just what can you do with a grown woman?"

While we're on the subject, when you were Opie's age, who did you think was hotter, Helen Crump or Thelma Lou?

"Definitely, Thelma Lou (Betty Lynn). I've met Thelma Lou many times. Anita Corsaut (Helen Crump) died of cancer (in 1995) at the age of 62."

Mike, with a straight face, I'd tell some of the guys in the mill who from Hammond, East Chicago and Gary that I didn't realize "The Andy Griffith Show" was a comedy until I got out of high school. Coming from Lake Village, I thought it was a docudrama.

"That's funny."

We'll work our way up to you winning the world championship in North Carolina. When did you really start getting serious about Mayberry trivia?

"About 12 or 13 years ago. It's my kids' fault. Once you've bought dad everything, it becomes difficult to come up with something new. They knew I liked Andy Griffith, so they bought me that tin sign over there. Then, it was an 'Andy Griffith Show' calendar. As you can see, I'm a collector of 'Andy Griffith Show' memorabilia."

That's an understatement! Look at all this cool stuff. I really like the cookie jars, especially the one featuring Andy and Barney waving from their squad car.

"There were only 2,400 of those made. I have more than 500 items here in the Mayberry Room."

Mt. Airy, N.C.?

"That's Andy Griffith's hometown. Mayberry is patterned after Mt. Airy. I went down there and met a fella who owned a soda shop. He told me I had a great knowledge of the show and that I should come back and enter their trivia contest."

And?

"I took his advice and have attended the last three Mayberry Days in Mt Airy."

How did you fare?

"The first year, in 2009, I got blown away. The second year, I came in third. I was very disappointed because I knew the material, but just got nervous.

"I came home, took a month off, redid my room, and then I started studying every day."

Your persistence paid off.

"Yes, I won it by three questions."

When does Mayberry Days and the trivia contest take place?

"The last weekend in September. By the way, there are over 1,400 'Andy Griffith Show' fan clubs worldwide. Last year, people from 51 countries attended Mayberry Days. This will be the 22nd year of the festival."

Amazing. What is the population of Mt. Airy?

"Maybe a little bigger than Lowell. About 75,000 fans show up every year. In 2010, there were twice that many because it was the 50th anniversary of the show's premiere."

When was that?

"Oct. 3, 1960. The pilot episode actually aired in February of 1960; it was a spinoff of Danny Thomas' show 'Make Room for Daddy.' Mayberry is a fictitious place that was built at Desilu Studios."

Ernest T. Bass was one of my favorite characters.

"Howard Morris had four different roles in the 'Andy Griffith Show.' Not only was he Ernest T. Bass in five episodes; he also played George, a TV repairman. He was the voice of Barney's favorite radio personality, Leonard Blush, the masked singer out of Mt. Pilot, and he was one of the directors of the show."

Although he portrayed countrified simpleton Ernest T. Bass, the guy had a lot of talent.

"Howard Morris was a genius."

Thoughts on the spinoff "Mayberry RFD?" I never liked Howard Sprague.

"I never really watched it."

How many episodes of the original "Andy Griffith Show" are there?

"There are 249 of them; the show ran from 1960 to 1968."

One of your favorite episodes?

"Episode 145, when Otis rode the cow. He thought he'd won a horse: 'Put a clock on 'em, Andy!' Andy told him, 'Otis, you have a horse that gives milk.' Otis replied, 'I knew he was a good deal!'

"I also love episode 82 – 'The Class Reunion.' I'm a very sentimental kind of guy. When they're singing their high school class song, it's a real tear jerker for me."

Mike, one of my favorites centered around a bitter old man at Christmastime.

"Episode 11; that was the only time in eight seasons that they celebrated Christmas."

The geezer keeps peeking in the window while the Taylor family and friends are enjoying a Christmas get-together at the jailhouse. The old codger also keeps getting into mischief and is starting trouble all evening, but Andy won't arrest him because it's Christmas. Mike, I'm sentimental, too. Can you finish this story?

"Andy finally realizes the old man wants to be arrested so he can be near the festivities."

Thanks. Sniff.

"Some people don't realize that Briscoe Darling's boys, The Dillard Brothers; are in the Bluegrass Hall of Fame. They still perform at Mayberry Days."

I loved the one where Gomer is in awe of Goober's ridiculously twangy and terrible impersonations of Cary Grant and Edward G. Robinson.

"Episode 122, that's the only time you'll see Gomer and Goober in the same episode."

Floyd the barber was an odd bird.

"In an interview, Goober (George Lindsey), said they never should have paid Floyd (Howard McNair); he was not working or acting, that was his natural self. Goober went on to say there were many times when they had to stop production because Floyd had the entire cast cracking up."

OK, "Hotshot" Haviland, I'm no trivia slouch either. It's high time you and I slapped leather. Name two sets of cousins who appeared on the "Andy Griffith Show."

"Goober and Gomer Pyle and Andy Taylor and Barney Fife."

Not bad. Hit me!

"I'll ask you the easiest question they asked me at the world championship. What was checkout time at the Mayberry Hotel?"

Um, let me think – high noon.

"People in Mayberry don't get in a big hurry, checkout time was 4 p.m."

Alright, no more Mr. Nice Guy, wise guy. Who played the obscure character of town hypochondriac Emma Brand?

"That would be Cheerio Meredith."

You're getting on my nerves.

"Ernest T. Bass had a gold tooth painted on. How much did he pay for it?"

I'm taking my tape recorder and going home now. Nobody likes a showoff.

* * *

Mike Haviland is one of the friendliest guys you'd ever want to meet. I'm sure many readers would like to converse with him about their favorite Andy Griffith Show episodes like "Aunt Bee's Kerosene Cucumbers" or simply the comedic genius Don Knotts as deputy Barney Fife.

While working as a barkeep, Haviland often is quizzed by patrons. If they stump him, he'll buy that person a beer. Stop in for a cold one at Pop-O's on a Monday or Wednesday and say, "Hey."

Then, see about setting up an appointment to view Mike's Mayberry Room. The only stipulation is that you sign his guest book.

Cornelius House *(Feb. 2005)*

REGINA: (As she moves an armchair up to the table) Please now, do sit down, Pastor, and make yourself comfortable. (He sits; she slips a footstool under his feet.) That's it! Is that all right, Pastor?

MANDERS: Just perfect, thank you. (Regarding her.) You know, Miss Engstrand, I definitely think you've grown since I saw you last.

REGINA: Do you think so, Pastor? Mrs. Alving says that I've filled out, too.

MANDERS: Filled out – ? Well, yes, maybe a little – but acceptably (A short pause.)
– Henrik Ibsen

Through my picture window I watched him. He possessed the lively, quick step of a man in his mid-20s rather than someone 76. A long unbuttoned trench coat, reminiscent of Bogie, flapped in the brisk January breeze. A blue beret covered his balding bean.

I couldn't help but smile as Cornelius House side-stepped a mound of shoveled snow in front of my apartment. Mt. Kilimanjaro in comparison to the elfin professor.

A genius, the prof vaguely reminds me of the character Clarence in "It's a Wonderful Life"– after a few espressos.

Warily, I handed him a cup of Joe.

* * *

"I was born in 1929, in Kentucky," House began. "I have traveled a lot since then. I've enjoyed life. After graduating from the University of Kentucky in 1951 with a major in EduKAYSHUN, (the veteran lecturer has the whimsical -at times unsettling- wont of annunciating certain syllables or words in mid-sentence quite forcefully, part of his repertoire, no doubt) English, German and Sociology. I was sent to Heidelberg in Germany because our university had an exchange with them. In six weeks, I learned bushels and bushels of German.

"I taught for one year and was drafted. We were at war with

Korea, but because of my German, I ended up getting transferred to the 'Intelligence Corps' as it was known back then.

"I spent a year in Germany translating documents for the Army that were sensitive because the product that we produced was sent to the American State Department. It was espionage that was gathered by our people behind the Iron Curtain."

Interesting, but let's get back to education

"I would spend 3 or 4 years at various colleges and high schools throughout Indiana, Illinois, Ohio, and Missouri. That was my territory. The last place I taught high school was in Lake County, Ind. At Crown Point, I taught German; I also taught both German and World History at Andrean High School in 1980. It was quite the checkerboard career."

Continue, please.

"After that, I began teaching at Indiana University Northwest and then at Purdue University Calumet for a five-year term from 1997-2002. Today, I'm teaching at IUN again – English Composition. And I thought I'd try an experiment this particular semester, I'm also teaching German at Purdue Calumet."

Purdue Calumet, did you cross paths with Professor Tinkham perchance?

"Charlie Tinkham was a good friend of mine; I knew him very well. He taught English there – and poetry of course. He was sort of a poet laureate, not an official poet laureate, but he was a great poet and great teacher nonetheless."

Tell me about your memory, professor.

"This business of memory is a very, very unusual thing. I have never forgotten anything I have ever read in a book for over half a century. If it was anything I thought was important, I remembered it easily. So, I happen to have a rather extensive knowledge of ancient history, linguistics, archaeology, sociology, and the arts, and so on. I'll tell you an anecdote. When I was in the seventh-grade, I got into trouble for talking during study hall... ."

No!

"Yes. The teacher punished me by having me memorize the first verse of a poem. I memorized the entire poem. I could recite it right now, if I had the time. It's a long narrative that rhymes beautifully, 120 lines long. I've never looked at the poem since, on paper, but I've recited it many times at dinner parties and such. It runs past my mind like a movie film. I can see it.

"Two years ago, I memorized a 130-line poem, 'The Love Song of J. Alfred Prufrock' by T.S. Eliot. That one took me about 45 minutes to memorize. The Preamble of the Constitution, everybody should be able to recite the Preamble of the Constitution."

Yes they should Professor, you're darn tootin'.

"Do you know it?"

Well, nobutah...

"For shame."

Busted. (sotto voce)

"The Gettysburg Address – pure poetry. Why didn't Lincoln say 87 years ago? That's prosaic as all get out, four score and seven, now *that's* poetic."

Do you speak any other foreign languages besides German.

"No; I speak a little Spanish. French is a nice language. If I had time. OOOH, if I only had time, I would learn French perfectly. And I would learn Italian. I have this strange desire to learn French and Italian. Maybe Swedish. I'm not sure why Swedish attracts me."

You've been known to tread the boards a few times.

"I am passionately in love with the theater! I mean the legitimate stage. I've taken roles in many plays. I learn my part quickly and easily because I'm a quick study. In 1973, I was in a play by Ibsen, the great Norwegian playwright, it was 'Ghosts.'

One of my favorites.

"You've heard of it?"

Yes.

"No!"

Yes.

"What part do you think I portrayed?"

Professor. Who else? The parson.

"Yes, I was Pastor Manders."

Redemption. (sotto voce)

"I would love to direct a play. Nobody ever gave me the job."

Who are a few of your favorite poets?

"Longfellow is one of my favorites, although he's not taught much in high schools anymore, and that's a shame that he's been abandoned. The British poet Sir T.S. Eliot. I love T.S. Eliot."

Authors?

"My favorite author as a youngster was Thomas Wolfe. I love the book 'Raintree County' written at Indiana University in Bloomington by

Ross Lockridge Jr. He taught English at Bloomington."

Montgomery Clift and–

"Hated the movie. You can not film a book like 'Raintree County,' it contains an ethos of its own, a mystique. I have not read much fiction in the last 15 or 20 years, I'm sorry to say. But I'll tell you who I like, Dan Brown of 'The Da Vinci Code' and all those others he's written."

Prof, I'm about the only guy on the planet who hasn't read "The Da Vinci Code."

"You'd love it. They are all mystery driven, they're like Indiana Jones, except more exciting and full of scholarship and mediaeval lore, a very tasty treat, a very, very luscious kind of prose."

Actors?

"I'm dated when it comes to actors. I liked the actors of my generation. The movie actors like Cary Grant, Humphrey Bogart, Katherine Hepburn, Henry Fonda. I don't know the modern ones, I'm ashamed to say, but that's generational and impossible to prevent.

"As for theater, Shakespeare and Sir John Gielgud; those actors who did Shakespeare well. I thought Tennessee Williams was a wonderful playwright.

"Well, there you have it, my vitae. Do what you will with it, I must be off."

* * *

Professor Cornelius House. A brilliant chap who can recite the 23rd psalm in pidgin English or the Lord's Prayer in Olde English.

Nearly an octogenarian, House is blessed with near perfect health; which he attributes to having never damaged his body with tobacco, alcohol, or drugs.

A devout Catholic, he is a member of the Knights of Columbus and teaches an extremely popular. adult bible study class at St. Edwards.

With all of his university classes, the prof's plate is full; quite unfortunate for the area high school kids who simply adored him as a substitute teacher.

As we walked out to his car, Cornelius confided, "No one loves their work more than I do. I have always looked forward to Mondays. I just enjoy being at the place. With the high school students; with the college students."

Lil' Joe Gutierrez *(Apr. 2007)*

"We need to help students and parents cherish and preserve the ethnic and cultural diversity that nourishes this community and this nation."

– Cesar Chavez

"Joe's Place" is a poor man's Smithsonian. A librarian would blush at his collection of tomes and envy his cataloging techniques.

Oceans of books everywhere. Stacks of Huck Finns and Catch-22s on every stair lead to the top of his delightful two-story on Tod Avenue in East Chicago.

Gutierrez, 66, has shelves, but uses them to show off countless flea market knickknacks. I refrain from the use of mill vernacular when within these hallowed walls. Pictures of priests peek from nooks. Popes pop out from crannies. An upbeat Jesus welcomes me from a wall on high. A forlorn Jesus looks away.

* * *

Joe, those parakeets sure sing pretty – and loud. The interview...

"Spanish canaries, Jeff. There's something I wanted to show you, but it's like going on a mission finding something around here. I need a compass. I gotta write down what I'm lookin' for, too. I always find something else first, and forget what I was originally lookin' for."

You finished your novel.

"Yeah, after five years. I bunched short stories together based on growing up here in the neighborhood. Fictionalized actual events. I started on the corner here, because I grew up on Olcott.

"Used to be a grocery store there. I remember watching it burn down. I went right down the street with my stories. The pool room, the barber shop... There was a guy who shot his wife – caught her messin' around."

Did he work in the mill?

"They all worked in the mill. He went to jail. This is during World War II. They asked him, 'Do you want to stay in jail, or do you want to go and fight?'

"He went to Europe. He got a silver star. Died in France. Actual event, the names have been changed. I remember when Mr. Hooke died. I was like 8 years old. His dog was on the front porch, howling. Howling, sad. I never forgot that. It was all hillbillies down this street. We were the only Mexicans."

Joe, I realize you use that term affectionately. Where was your mother, Emma Champion, from?

Copper Hill, Tenn. The neighborhood has changed, but there's still good people here."

Your mom gave birth to 15 Gutierrez children. In what order did you come along?

"My memory isn't what used to be. All I know is about seven of us got in the same bed, and I got in the middle – I was guaranteed covers that way. I know Vince was born Dec 10 of '39 and I was born Dec 11 of '40. I was his birthday present. My brother Carl just passed away; he was a tremendous artist. My youngest brother, Mickey, fought in Vietnam. He was a medic with the 9th Cavalry."

Your father?

"Only one time did my father ever show me compassion. I was sick. He came into the bedroom and felt my forehead. He thought I was asleep. At first, he didn't speak English. Ma didn't speak Spanish. She was 14 when they got married."

School days?

"I went into the seminary when I was 15. Carmelites. I spent two years in Niagra Falls in Ontario – that's where the preparatory seminary was – and almost two in Massachusetts. After four years, I quit. I didn't become a priest, but I did become a father; I got married.

"Father Columba was my English teacher out East. I won the first-place award for short stories. I wrote about a bullfight. Jeff, I was raised in East Chicago. I never seen a bull in my life. Columba told me, 'If I ever find out that you plagiarized this story, I will break your back.' Me and the Father have remained in contact for the next 50 years – he's got Alzheimer's."

The mill?

"I hired in at Inland on June 16, 1959 – two days after I graduated high school. Monsignor Shea from St. Mary's got me in at No. 3 Cold Strip.

"At that time, Mexicans went to the yard department. Blacks were sent to the coke plants. We all went on strike for 116 days soon after. I ended up at Plant 1 Galvanizing Department. I was drafted in '63. We were on alert when (President John F.) Kennedy got shot."

The union?

"Jim Balanoff got me involved. He put me on the civil rights committee. When I first ran for griever, I wrote about waking up in the morning and hearing the whistle of the South Shore as I got ready for work. My opposition used that against me. 'Look at this guy, he wants to be griever and he's writing about train whistles!' I beat him, 9 to1.

"No griever was ever elected for a second consecutive term in the history of Plant 1 Galvanizing Department. I was elected to four straight terms. And then, I went full-time to the hall – base rate chairman."

Studs Terkel?

"I met Studs through Ed Sadlowski. Charlie Tinkham always wanted to meet Studs, so I took him to Studs' house – you think this place is cluttered."

Professor Tinkham?

"Charlie was my buddy. When he was hospitalized, I came to see him. I was writing a story called 'Friends.' We're arguing back and forth. The nurses rush in... Tinkham says: 'We're discussing Joe's beginning. Everything's fine.' I gave Charlie a cloth rosary. They buried it with him.

"Jeff, most of the people who have left the neighborhood are Republicans now. They bow their heads when they hear (President George W.) Bush's name. Here, take this with you. It's an 8-by-10 of St. Jude."

* * *

As the Patron Saint of Lost Causes and I head east toward Cline Avenue, I notice Beto's restaurant. Used to be Mehilo's watering hole.

Change.

Nearer the union hall, Pete and Mabel are but ghosts like Hot Dog

John or the no-legged man who sold pencils at the corner of Michigan and Guthrie. Busy Corner Drug Store – gone.

Joe stays.

Left the lights of my old Ford pick-up on while parked at 148th and Tod. Asked a couple fellas if they had cables.

They didn't ask me anything. Not in English, anyway. They simply produced the jumper cables. *Gracias, mis amigos.*

Still some good people in this neighborhood.

Lawrence Ginensky *(Mar. 2005)*

"My mechanic told me, 'I couldn't repair your brakes, so I made your horn louder.'"
– Steven Wright

Larry Ginensky is the moderator and founder of the Highland Writers' Group. I first met him at the Lowell Public Library about six years ago. Larry and his wife Sherry attended the Midwest Writers' Forum held there every Wednesday.

The Ginenskys live in Lansing, Ill. Larry, a retired licensed clinical psychologist, enjoys classical music and is a voracious reader. Born in 1930, he grew up on the streets of Brooklyn. Sherry, a native of the Kanawha Valley region of West Virginia, has come to be fluent in Brooklynese, serves as interpreter for Larry and The Kankakee Kid (me) when needed. She's a retired English teacher from Thornwood High School where she served as the English Department Chairperson.

* * *

Make yourself comfortable, Lawrence. Lie down upon the couch. Relax. Tell me about your childhood. Your father... .

"My faddah, he was bawn in Russia," Ginensky said. "He was a very – hey, what is this?"

I just wanted to see what it felt like being on the other end for once.

"My father was born in Russia. My mother was born in a part of Poland that is now Russia. They both spoke Russian, English and Yiddish. My brother was a philatelist. He died a very wealthy man."

FDR also collected stamps. Cool hobby, but what did your brother do for a living?

"I told you he was a philatelist. That's what he did!"

Calm down. Obviously, you are jealous of your sibling. Lawrence, do you feel your mother loved "Little Stamper" more?

"Knock it off."

You knew Alan Ginsberg.

"Yes, after I'd moved to Greenwich Village. I knew Carl Solomon, too. When Alan wrote 'Howl,' he made a name for himself. His father, Lewis, was a very famous poet. Alan died when he was about 60. Carl Solomon was a very brilliant and disturbed young man. I don't know what happened to Carl other than he was in and out of mental hospitals. That's part of what Alan was referring to when he began his mammoth poem, 'The Best Minds of My Generation.' It was a shame to see Carl go."

Interesting. Do you also believe that you knew Jack Kerouac, Saul Bellow, and Leo Tolstoy? Do you think you are Leo Tolstoy?

"Listen, you schmuck, if you..."

I'm done. You attended the City College of New York.

"Ahem. Yes. It took me nine years to complete a bachelor's degree and then a master's degree in psychology at CCNY because I had to support myself by driving a truck and a taxi.

"I eventually accepted an internship at Elgin State Hospital which brought me to the Midwest. I have resided in this part of the country ever since. I completed the course work for a Ph.D. in psychology, but ultimately chose not to write a thesis because it was not the type of writing I wanted to do. I also was a Good Humor man. I worked many jobs in the summah."

Summah?

"Yes."

"Summer."

Thanks, Sherry.

Added Sherry: "Larry maintained a private practice for 35 years. He was a consultant for Chicago's Alcoholic Treatment Center. He served as Clinical Director of the Illinois Visually Handicapped Institute, and then became Chief of Professional Staff at Tinley Park Mental Health Center where he received an award for his seminars and personal supervision with social workers, psychologists, and psychiatrists that enabled the institution to achieve accreditation after his first review. Isn't that right, dear? Larry? Larry!"

Let the old fella sleep.

"What?"

You also taught along the way.

"Yes. At many colleges and universities, including Roosevelt University in Chicago. That's where I met Sherry. She was one of my students."

"We dated *after* the course, of course," added Sherry, who is 18 years younger than her husband.

This is the second marriage for both of you.

"My first wife was Puerto Rican. She spoke only Spanish. My father was a kosher butcher, a very religious Jew. Just before we were married my brother calls me up and says, 'Dad wants me to tell you that he's lying in a gutter drinking on his back in the water. Unless you give up Tess, he's going to stay there until he dies.' I was mortified, 'Is that true?!' My brother answered, 'No, he's in the other room eating and enjoying himself. I'm just telling you, that he wants you to know that as long as you're with her, he's staying in the gutter, in the water getting wet, and dying.'"

Got any good taxi driver stories?

"I drove all night and would go to school during the daytime. The cab company had their regular drivers. I'd get whatever hack wasn't taken. On Sundays, I could have my pick, when most people wanted to be off. In other words, I got only the crappy cabs and unwanted hours.

"On one occasion, the only cab available didn't have a horn. I took it. I needed the money. This guy gets in. Traffic is horrendous. The car in front of me isn't going very fast. This is in Manhattan. My fare says, 'Give 'em your horn. Give 'em your horn!' No, I don't need to give 'em a horn. 'GIVE HIM YOUR HORN!!' Finally, I roll down my window, stick my head out, and shout: 'HONK! HONK! HONK!' I rolled my window back up. The guy told me, 'Calm down, everything is going to be okay. Don't be upset. We're not in a rush. I get off right here.'"

Probably a shrink. Larry, seriously now, I've always loved your short stories, many of which are filled with that wonderful Jewish sense of humor, like, "The Lies of White Men." But not all were comedic. Those recollections from your Brooklyn years are some of the most beautiful and touching stories I've ever read. Like "Minyan," or my personal favorite, "Izzy the Shiker."

"Izzy worked Belmont Avenue. He made good money along that 12 block stretch manning his own pushcart, hawking fresh vegetables. He was a hard worker. A good man."

Izzy was a moonlighter.

"Yes, I suppose he was. Every evening after Izzy sold the last of his wares, he would direct traffic in a very animated fashion – until someone helped him from the intersection."

A shiker is neither peddler nor policeman.

"No, Jeff. Shiker is the Yiddish term for a drunkard."

Anita Heath *(June 2006)*

"Every day I get in the queue
to get on the bus that takes me to you."
– "Magic Bus," by The Who

Anita Heath lives just east of Buckley Homestead on Belshaw Road in Lowell. She and her late husband, David, raised three children. It was summertime when I interviewed her.

Seated in lawn chairs, we were surrounded by a well-kept perennial border that wove in and around the backyard. Wind chimes and warblers made music while we chatted.

* * *

Were you raised here in Lowell?

"Yes, I was a farmer's daughter," she said. "Dad had 80 acres and no sons. I was the oldest; I did everything but put the crops in and take them out. My sister was eight years younger. While she was in the house, watching Howdy Dowdy, I was milking cows. Actually, I enjoyed the outside work more than cleaning and cooking."

You've driven a school bus forever. Anything else?

"I used to gut turkeys for Morrow's Turkey Farm – 21 years worth."

I've never interviewed a real-life turkey gutter. Tell me about it.

"We'd stand up at the old gut table, and oh, us women had a blast. The boys do all the killing. They decapitate 'em, dip 'em, and dunk 'em.

"I told a good friend of mine, who also is a bus driver, 'Come on, you have to give it a try, you make good money out at the turkey farm.' She was hesitant.

"'Well, what do the turkeys look like,'she asked?

"I said, 'Oh, they look just like when you buy them at the grocery store.'

"I didn't tell her she had to cut the behind out and reach in there to remove the guts. First day, her face was as green as a gourd! But she came back. Good money guttin' gobblers.

"You also had to separate the giblets from the intestines, rinse them, then replace them – 3,000 turkeys we'd gut. After about three or four days of it, you get kinda goofy. We'd end up draping the guts around our necks for necklaces."

School bus driving?

"I drove for 32 years, then retired. I thought it was the best thing to do when my husband's Parkinson's Disease worsened. Finally, I took him to Mayo's (Mayo Clinic). Mayo's took David off 26 of the 50-some pills he was on; my husband came back to life. I asked myself, 'What am I doing here? I miss driving Big Yella.'"

What year did you start driving a bus?

"In 1969. Stick shift. No power steering."

I could never park one of those things.

"Mirrors. If they'd put tape over a mirror, it would be nearly impossible."

Obviously, you love driving a bus. But it's a lot of responsibility, isn't it?

"I won't tolerate unruly behavior when I'm driving. I can't. From spring break until school's out is when they're the most rambunctious. They start thinking that they can talk at railroad tracks. Not on my route."

What was your first route like?

"When I first started out, I was approached by the school superintendent. He told me he had a route with special education kids. I told him, 'You won't believe this, but if I had gone to college, I would have wanted to become a special education teacher.'

"I got the route – 114 miles a day. There were 56 kids on the bus. No lift, nothing. It was a regular bus. There was no two-way radio if you broke down.

"I'd pick up children from old Oak Hill, Jane Ball, and Taft schools. Then, I'd truck them up north to eight different schools, come home for two-and-a-half hours, then, go back. I wasn't given an aide.

"Some of the children were blind, some deaf and some were emotionally disturbed. In order to get them to mind, I'd bribe them with Dairy Queen up in Highland on Fridays – it came out of my pocket.'"

That had to be difficult.

"Occasionally, I'd get permission from the parents to take some of the special needs kids home with me for a few hours. I probably got too attached to them."

Your middle child.

"Chuckie was born three months premature. His mother was 14 when she had him; no prenatal care. We adopted him when he was 2 months old. David was about 5 at the time. Two weeks after we found out that Chuckie had cerebral palsy, I found out I was pregnant with Amy.

"Chuckie had to have many surgeries at Shriner's Hospital. We didn't see a bill. My main goal was to keep him out of a wheel chair. He's always been very determined. I can still picture him, in the early days, with his braces and little walker with basket. It was heartbreaking. On the other hand, I also can picture those children who had much more severe issues.

"Chuckie wanted to be in the middle school band. They have to have their gait down just right – he was hurt by that. He is not a quitter. Chuckie got into choir instead. They'd set a chair out for him right in the front. He's loved music ever since.

"I used to have to bring Amy along every time he'd undergo surgery. She'd always hang around the therapy room. She'd watch the nurses.

Today, Amy's a surgical nurse at Methodist Hospital in Indianapolis. Our oldest son is going through the Masonic Lodge; he wants to be a Shriner. Chuckie has been a blessing."

* * *

She's a piece of work, Anita Heath.

When the afternoon bell rings on Halloween, soon-to-be trick-or-treaters are always delighted to see Mickey Mouse, Raggedy Ann, a nun or a whoopie cushion sitting behind the wheel of Big Yella waiting to take them home.

When the high school held its athletic banquet a few years back, the baseball team presented Mrs. Heath with a cap and jersey, calling her their good-luck charm. Nearly every time she drove the team bus, they won.

"Jeff, my stats were out of this world."

When a 7 year-old foster child stood waiting for the bus wearing a man's coat and a red face from the sting of cold and humiliation; it was Mrs. Heath who purchased a hat, mittens and proper coat.

"Jeff, her tiny hands only came to where the sleeves bent at the elbows."

When a teenage girl was the only young lady who didn't own a gown for a particular group performance out at the high school; it was Mrs. Heath who came through with a dress, slip, shoes, nylons and earrings.

"Jeff, I got paid that day."

Obviously, I was mistaken. It's not driving a bus that she loves.

Anita Heath loves children.

Caregivers & Do-gooders

Mark and Robyn Sepko *(Feb. 2007)*

"For I was an hungred, and ye gave me meat:
I was thirsty, and ye gave me drink:
I was a stranger, and ye took me in."
-Matthew 25:35

Upon entering the Sepko home, I noticed a smiling Bing Crosby propped atop a piano. Bing was wearing St. Nick's cap. On the kitchen wall hung a 1918 print depicting a bearded old-timer with hands folded and head bowed – a loaf of bread and a small bowl of gruel before him.

As I took a seat, a girl of 12 or 13 placed a copy of "Where the Red Fern Grows" upon the kitchen table.

Mark's sister-in-law played cupid by introducing Mark and Robyn in 1989. They were wed June 17 of the same year. The Sepkos both possess master's degrees. Mark is employed with Federal Signal, in the marketing division of their safety products branch. Robyn's degree is in special education.

The Lowellians live in a 3,800-square-foot house, and they need every inch of it. They now have 10 children living in their home. Jessica and Emily are their birth daughters. Dakota has been legally adopted. They also care for seven foster children. The 10 youths range from 14 months to 18 years.

* * *

How or when did you decide to become involved with foster care?

Mark: "Robyn has always had this dream. I'd tell her, 'That's really nice, honey.' In the back of my mind, I was hoping she'd change her mind (They both laugh.) One day I felt like God spoke to my heart, 'Mark, what do you have that is so important that you can't share it?'"

Robin: "Mark called me from work, 'Why don't you look into it for us?' I started looking into it that day! We knew a lady named Nancy Fisher who was involved with White's Agency."

Mark: "White's Family Services is the oldest private foster agency in the state of Indiana. White was a Quaker. He began an orphanage 150 years ago. Robyn and I are what is known as therapeutic foster parents. That's why we're given some of the more difficult children."

Robyn: "Dakota was our first foster child about four years ago. She was adoptive. We weren't really looking to adopt, but we were open to it. As soon as we opened up the door, Dakota ran toward me shouting, 'Mommy!' and put her arms around me. She was almost 5. She was still in diapers. She didn't use utensils. Dakota had been beaten since she was two days old..."

Mark: "The first six months was very difficult. She started out foster. We soon adopted her. She is the only one we've adopted. One of the girls will probably go home this summer. The boys may go home."

"We sign agreements that our goal is reunification. People ask us about that. 'How can you let them go?' It's tough. We are all family. But at least we had some influence in their lives," attests Mark. "We had to go through about six months of training to be therapeutic foster parents. You don't just walk through the door, say, 'OK, I want to be a foster parent.'"

Robyn: "When it is healthy and safe, they will return to their homes. I pray over these children everyday. Two of our children are sisters. They are African-American. They're both mentally handicapped. Here's a picture of them."

Bless their hearts – they're blind.

Mark: "Yes. So are their mother and grandmother. They have Peter's Anomaly. It gets worse each generation. One of the sisters has a heart condition. She wasn't supposed to live past the age of five. They sent her home from Riley's to die. She's 14 now."

"One of the boys was scared when he first saw the sisters. It can be a bit frightening. The younger sister has a prosthetic eye. When she first arrived they didn't provide her with one. We've learned to put it back in when it falls out."

"I'd like to say that I'm really impressed with the principal at Lowell Middle School, Mr. Alessia. The sisters used to go to the Indianapolis School of the Blind. We were petitioning to bring them here. There was reluctance at first, but now everybody absolutely loves them."

"Jessica had a hard time when we first started. She was a little older. She was an only child for five years. Emily had a hard time with Dakota. Usually, you don't adopt a child that is the same age as your birth child. You can run into problems. Emily has a half birthday. She is always 8 1/2 or whatever the case may be. That way they're never the same age."

Robyn: "When the sisters first came to live here, I blindfolded my three children so they could understand. I had them walk around the house for about an hour or so. They started getting really frustrated. I had them go in the store like that."

Mark: "We have our days when we ask ourselves, 'Why in the world are we even doing this?'"

Robyn: "I believe it is our faith that enables us to do it." .

Mark: "All this kind of pushes your comfort levels a little bit. It's rocked our world a little bit. Then, we realize, well that's not too bad. We did something for somebody else."

* * *

Robyn held the youngest in her arms. The tot reached out to me. I ruffled his hair and made my exit.

Mark and Robyn Sepko. Salt of the earth.

And for two sisters in particular, they are the light.

Tera Evans *(Jan. 2010)*

"You're happiest while you're making the greatest contribution."

– Robert F. Kennedy

I hadn't met Tera Evans before our interview, but she reads me and noted my obsessive if not hackneyed penchant for including famous quotes or lyrics from songs at the beginning of each column. She had RFK's above quote all picked out for me.

Evans, 37, is a graduate of Griffith High School. She lives in Valparaiso with husband Alex Evans. They've been married for two years. Both work for Opportunity Enterprises in Valparaiso.

* * *

Children?

"Nope," Evans began. "Three dogs."

What breeds?

"Yeah."

Yeah?

"They're mostly mixed, two from rescues."

College?

"I'm seven classes from graduating from (Indiana University Northwest) with a communications degree. Then, I'm going for an MBA in marketing."

How long have you worked at Opportunity Enterprises?

"Ten years, but I started working in this type of field 17 years ago."

Fill me in about OE and some of the work you do.

"We assist those who are developmentally disabled – anything to give meaning to their day. We want our participants to have a fulfilled life. My job description is employee development specialist."

Is there a member of your immediate family with a disability?

"No, but early on, my mother said I was going to be a nun or work in this population – I'm definitely not a nun. It's a reward working with these people, a privilege."

Not everybody could do what you do for a living.

"Jeff, when I was at another agency, there was a client with autism who didn't want to get out of bed in the morning. Nobody wanted to work with him because of his physically aggressive behavior. He'd also say some really horrible things."

Profanity?

"Oh, yeah. He had a mouth. But so do I at times, so I couldn't really criticize him for it. Besides, I liked that in him. It showed he had spirit.

"This was a guy in his 20s, whose parents never came to see him. He'd see all his house mates go home for the holidays. On Christmas, he never got to go anywhere.

"I knew he loved the movie 'Grease.' I decided I'd try to get him motivated. I informed him that 'Grease' was being re-released in the theaters.

"He said, 'I like that Tera. I like that movie a lot.'

"I told him I'd take him to see the movie if he would get up every morning during the work week.."

What did he say to that?

"'Grease is the word, Tera.' I brought the Grease soundtrack to work; drove the staff crazy, but I didn't care. I'd turn on the music, and he'd bolt out of his room, pointing his finger and shouting, 'Grease is the word, Tera. I'm getting up this morning!'

"He suffered from a severe seizure disorder and had to wear a protective helmet to the movie that evening. When the 'Grease' theme song was playing, he stood up in the theater and shouted, 'Grease is the word, Tera!' I've never seen a person so happy."

Please, don't tell me people in the audience gave him a hard time.

"He also had the most beautiful blue eyes. A row of high schools girls brought him popcorn, candy and pop. He told them, 'I love you all.' He had the entire theater singing, '...greased lightnin', go greased lightnin', go greased lightnin'... .' He totally came out of his shell."

There must be a wide range for the severity regarding your clients' disabilities.

"We try to stay away from the word 'client;' we like to refer to them as consumers or participants. But to answer your question – yes, some have a more curriculum-based kind of day. They can learn something as simple as tying their shoes or how to use a knife and fork.

"My husband works in the secure shred department with some of our higher functioning participants. Some have jobs at restaurants and supermarkets. Some do volunteer work at places like the Humane Society. We have a young woman who goes to the nursing home and paints the toenails and fingernails of the elderly ladies living there.

"We have another department that works with former participants who, because of their ages, have decided to retire from our daily workshops.

"I run the community book club. Twice a week, we go to different areas and read from a book so they can retain their reading skills."

You love your job, don't you?

"Yes, I'm really lucky. The people I work with save me every day, and they don't even know it. When I was 14, my mother died of cancer. My father died of the same disease by the time I was 21. You asked if I had children. My husband and I lost our baby – it was difficult taking down the nursery.

"Instead of thinking of the sad stuff that life can bring, I come here and see them. I came back to work about 10 days after the baby died and it was like they knew – they felt it. These amazing people rely on their emotional connection to people more than anything. I love them."

Tera, you told me some of the participants live with their parents and some receive 24-hour care in group homes. Who determines whether someone is eligible for these services? There must be some kind of process.

"The state ultimately decides who is needing and deserving of funding."

How many employees work for OE all together?

"More than 350. Jeff, it wasn't that long ago that facilities for challenged individuals were a disgrace. They were called horrible names like 'schools for social idiots' or 'lunatic asylums.' And now that funding is being cut, I worry we could revert back to those times.

"Not-for-profits are often the first to get cut by government. The people we serve are sometimes seen as socially undesirable because they don't vote. They don't have their own voice. We have to be their voice. There are those who don't believe our participants make a contribution. But they do. They changed my life; they saved me."

* * *

Human beings committing atrocious acts of violence against each other can be viewed on the six o'clock news or read in the newspaper everyday. It can bring you down.

It helps to think of a young volunteer with autism lovingly painting the fingernails of a former child in an old folks home.

Grease is the word, Tera!

And Bobby Kennedy's quote was a good choice.

Punchy Calloway *(May 2010)*

"Memories
Light the corners of my mind,
Misty watercolored memories,
Of the way we were.
Scattered pictures
Of the smiles we left behind... ."
– Alan and Marilyn Bergman

I once wrote a personal check that read: Pay to the order of: Punchy Calloway. No one I know calls him by his real name – Jim.

Calloway, 58, was born and raised in Lake Village, but has lived across the street from the VFW and Little League fields in Lowell since 1993. He designed and built his 3,200-square-foot house. Calloway was a union carpenter for 32 years.

* * *

Punchy, it's time. Since we were kids, you've avoided telling me how you got that nickname.

"My sister, Judy, loved the puppet show 'Punch and Judy.' Well, all of a sudden, I became Punchy."

I waited 50 years for that?

"I got my ass kicked the first 12 years of my life because of that name. It was sort of like being a boy named Sue. Roughnecks figured, 'Punchy, he must be tough; I'll have to try some of that.'"

Punchy, another thing. You're so dark-complected and brown-eyed with raven-black hair, I mean, you don't look Scottish or Irish.

"My dad was; my mother is part Iroquois Indian."

Tell me a little more about your parents.

"My folks moved to Lake Village about three or four years before I was born; they came from Whiting. My dad retired from Standard Oil. To give him something to do after he retired, he tended bar down in Schneider. He handed a guy change for a beer and fell over dead.

"Mom was originally from Missouri; she's 93 and living at George Ade Nursing Home in Kentland, the same place where my wife was."

Other childhood memories of Lake Village?

"Doug Rainford was my best friend."

He was my idol. I thought for sure he'd make the majors as a left-handed starting pitcher. Remember his parents' mushroom farm?

"Yeah, I worked there for one day. Chet (Rainford) caught me and Doug throwing mushrooms at each other and fired me. It broke my heart when Doug was killed in that automobile accident; he was like my brother.

"And Father Scholl was like my grandfather. He lived in that little house trailer across from St Augusta Catholic Church. Mom made all his meals and took them over to him every day when he became an invalid. He was one of the nicest people I ever met."

The old priest had a rich and famous relative.

"That's right – Dr. Scholl. I never met him."

You graduated from North Newton High School in 1970.

"As a freshman, I went to Morocco High School."

You were quite an athlete at North Newton.

"Yeah, the older I get, the better I was."

Remember guarding former NBA star Jack Sikma when he played for St. Anne (Ill.) High School?

"Yep, I 'held' him to 56 points. We were horrible."

You were a bunch of linebackers trying to play basketball. Hey, you got a full ride to play football and run track at New Mexico State.

"I hated New Mexico; I was so lonely out there. I called my dad a couple days after I got there and said, 'I want to come home.' Dad said, 'If you come home, I'll kick your ass the second you get off the plane.' He told me to stick it out one year and, if I still didn't like it, I could transfer."

And that's exactly what you did.

"Yeah, I ended up playing cornerback for Indiana State University."

Tell me about your lone collegiate track season at New Mexico State.

"I ran the 440 (yard) hurdles."

That's a grueling event.

"Oh, man. Those last two hurdles look like walls."

Personal best?

"I finished third at a meet in Texas in 56 seconds. The two guys who beat me both broke the world record in that race. They had a Coke and a hotdog by the time I crossed the line, but I got third."

You've had some ups and downs in 58 years.

"Yeah, Jeff, my life's been a roller coaster ride. I've had the highest highs and the lowest lows. It's like my golf game; I shank and slice, but, every once in a while, I hit one down the middle – just enough to keep me in the game."

Care to talk about your wife of 14 years?

"I don't mind."

Punchy, it's strange how some people get Alzheimer's disease and some don't.

"It's the luck of the draw; Laurie got ripped off. She came down with it when she was 49 and died at 56.

"The neurologist said he'd give her six years and she died almost six years to the day. The way they explained it to me, the younger you are when you get it, the faster you'll pass away. Your metabolism is faster when your younger. Older people suffer longer.

"Last June was her birthday; we took her to Dairy Queen. Kelly and Asa, my kids from previous marriages, were in the front seat. Laurie and I were in the back seat. She'd look at me, and ask, 'Are you married?' And I'd say, 'Yes.' And then she'd go, 'Oh, dammit.' She'd flirt with me. She was so cute. And it was so heart-wrenching.

"We went to the store one day, and I said, "Laurie, I forgot the hummingbird food; I'm getting worse than you.' She said: 'No, honey, the only thing wrong with you, is you have too much on your mind. Be like me, I have nothing on my mind.' She made jest of her disease. But I couldn't laugh.

"One day, she just sat down in the middle of the floor, and that was the last time she walked. She came down with pneumonia on a Sunday and died Saturday morning, Aug. 17 – three days after I retired."

* * *

Memories.

Rob Bailey *(Jan. 2011)*

"Past the seeker as he prayed came the crippled and the beggar and the beaten. And seeing them, he cried, 'Great God, how is it that a loving creator can see such things and yet do nothing about them?' God said, 'I did do something. I made you.'"
– Author unknown

I contacted Sister Peg Spindler of Sojourner Truth House in Gary asking for the names of a couple staff members for possible interviews. In the past, I've always written Sister Peg, but the thought of calling a nun on her cell phone delighted me.

Robert Bailey was one of the names Sister Peg gave me. He works as a maintenance assistant at STH.

Bailey, 27, lives in Hobart, is divorced and has two children, Falen, 9, and Asa, 8.

Brunch With Santa had concluded a few minutes before our interview took place. Rob had the starring role.

* * *

Rob, I didn't expect you to be a white guy.

"Well, I'm not the most common demographic in Gary."

Siblings?

"I had a younger brother, but he died about a year ago."

"I'm sorry to hear that. Parents?

"Dad died of complications from diabetes at age 50 in 2006. My mom is Lori Caldwell; she's a Gary crime reporter for the Post-Tribune."

Rob, I had no idea. I've read a thousand of her articles, but have never met her. Education?

"I graduated from Hobart High School and earned an associate's degree at Indiana University Northwest in '08 and a bachelor of science degree in radiologic technology in '09 – I'm an X-ray technician. Since I graduated college, I haven't been able to find work in my field. I became a permanent employee here a couple weeks ago."

Where else have you worked?

"I did hydroblasting and power vac in the mills for Kenny Manta out of Hammond."

Rob, a buddy of mine came around a corner of one of the batteries of No. 2 Coke Plant at Inland Steel and took a shot to his inner thigh from a guy using a water blaster. It cut him real deep. An inch or two higher and it would've desexed him.

"Yeah, 10,000 psi will cut you like a knife, and it's not clean water either. It was definitely dangerous, dirty work that motivated me to go to school. I was 17 when I started working for Manta; I did that for a couple of years. Then I bounced around working some stupid retail jobs; meanwhile, I had two kids to feed."

If a company like U.S. Steel called wanting you to work maintenance, would you take the job?

"In a heartbeat. There have been Baileys at U.S. Steel since they laid the foundation. My dad was still working there when he died."

How did you get hooked up with STH?

"I started volunteering here when I was a junior at IUN. In order to get my financial aid, I took what was called a seminar class. You could write a paper or do community service. I hate writing papers, so I did community service. I came here and did that for a couple of semesters. My mom couldn't afford to send me to college. I'm a blue-collar kid from NWI. I don't come from money.

"After I graduated from IUN, I continued to volunteer here. When a position opened up, they hired me, and here I am. I'm pretty good with my hands and have done mechanical stuff most of my life. I do all kinds of things here. My supervisor is Saul Barbosa; we drive around NWI in a box truck collecting donations – mostly furniture. We also drop off furniture."

Where to?

"STH helps woman get housing; we provide them with furniture. Most of them are moving in with nothing. Many of these women are homeless or have escaped from a very bad situation. We're able to provide a little bit of comfort for them."

Sister Peg?

"She's a wonderful woman; she really is. All the sisters here are bright and friendly and generous and wonderful to work with. Everyone who works here is great. I got no complaints about the place."

Aspirations?

"I'm hoping to get a full-time job in a hospital. I'm a fully qualified, accredited and licensed X-ray technologist."

Have you submitted applications?

"Let me show you this on my BlackBerry. Saul and I drive all over

NWI past all these doctor's offices and clinics. I've sent a resume to everyone of these places."

Wow, how many?

"At least 150."

Hobbies?

"I'm an apiarist."

Really? I used to keep bees, too.

"I've been having problems with swarm control. I just re-queened this fall. I went from a Hungarian breed called Carniolans to Italians."

Anything else?

"Photography; I think I took every photography course IUN offered. I like to take my camera to concerts; it's a good way to meet people and meet the band. I've made a lot of good friends that way. I was in a band for awhile. I've been playing bass for years. My brother was a drummer in the band. When he died, I just didn't want to do it anymore.

"In 2002, I started judging the NWI Science and Engineering Fair back when it was held at Purdue North Central; now, it's held at Valparaiso University. Last year, I started judging the Calumet Regional Science and Engineering Fair at IUN. I've always been a big science buff, and seeing the kids get excited about science and thinking is a blast for me."

Rob, I think you're a good-hearted soul who cares about people. Hey, like you said, you continued volunteering here at STH when you didn't have to.

"Jeff, do you remember a number of years ago when the Post-Tribune and The Newspaper Guild (the union for newsroom employees) used to have a program called Christmas Neediest? The Post-Trib did that for years and years. They would get things like Christmas presents and turkeys and make up big gift baskets. It was something the Post-Tribune and the Guild never advertised.

"People would often ask who sent us. We would never say we were from the Post-Tribune; we'd just say we were Santa's helpers. Mom and I would pick up the baskets at the Post-Tribune building at 11th Avenue and Broadway. The baskets were sent out all over NWI, but we always chose to deliver to the Gary addresses."

Why?

"My family has Gary roots. Gary has some of the nicest people I've ever met – absolute salt-of-the-earth, gracious people. This is my spiritual home. Some of the happiest moments of my life occurred while riding around Gary delivering food baskets with my mom ... I'm sorry."

Hey big fella, it's all right. You put a tear in my eye, too.

"I've always done charity stuff; it's a big part of who I am."

* * *

Bailey told me he never visualized himself being the type of person to get in a Santa costume and have kids crawl all over him. He said he's been known to be a tough guy.

I beg to differ; Rob Bailey is a good guy.

Rhonda Smith *(July 2007)*

"We make a living by what we do, but we make a life by what we give."
– Winston Churchill

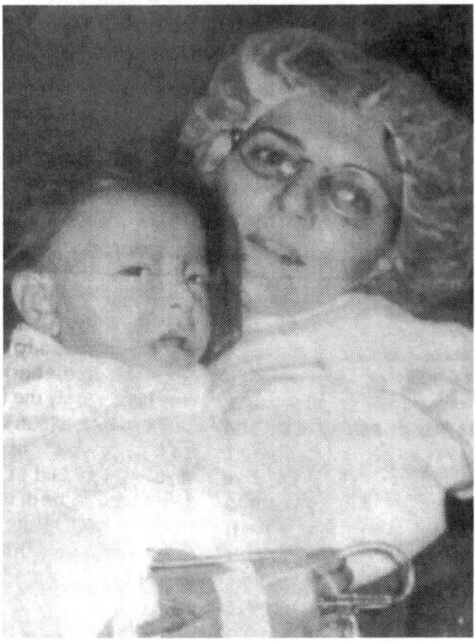

Rhonda Smith grew up on a farm in our original state capital, Corydon. She met Arden Smith of LaPorte at Indiana State University. Once she graduated they wed and moved to what is known as the Fairways near Lake Dalecarlia north of the Lowell town limits.

Arden took a job as a teacher at Hanover Central High School and Rhonda took a job as a registered nurse at St. Anthony Hospital. That was 1981. They've been at their respective jobs ever since.

The Smiths have three children. They are an athletic family. Arden, a crafty lefty, was the winning pitcher for LaPorte's state champion baseball team back in '76. Two of the Smith's children, Sarah and Steve, were excellent distance runners for Lowell High. Sarah ran for Carthage and Steve is currently running for Butler University. Scott, the youngest, is an avid bowler and basketball player; he has special needs. Rhonda waited 43 years to run a marathon but she fared well.

* * *

Did you run in high school?

"Girls cross country didn't exist at Corydon Central High School when I was there. I graduated in 1976. I feel like I missed out. My first road race was the Hub Run in Crown Point back in the early 90s."

Well, you made up for lost time, Rhonda. Running a 3:44 in your very first marathon back in 2000 at Chicago qualified you for Boston's prestigious affair – no small feat.

"I was so mad. I heard so many horror stories about Boston's notorious Heartbreak Hill. It was nothin'. I had way too much left. I hit my half a little bit fast. So I backed off. But I didn't feel bad at anytime. It's hard to get my miles in working these 12-hour days."

How long have you been working 12s?

"Since Steve started college two years ago."

Did you always want to be a nurse?

"Originally I wanted to be a teacher. Then one of the girls from high school decided to attend nursing school. I was impressed. I succumbed to peer pressure."

What department do you work in at St. Anthony's?

"I worked intensive care for a while. I'm in Pre-Op and Post-Op for surgery now."

You took a sabbatical in the spring.

"I went to Gracias, Honduras for seven days in late April and early May. It was a medical mission."

A medical mission?

"There's a national organization called The Smile Train. They perform plastic surgery on people with cleft palette or cleft lip. Have you ever known anybody who was born with – "

Yes, my mother.

"It's a genetic thing that runs rampant in the Asian and Central American countries. They really don't have the means to repair that kind of problem. A plastic surgeon by the name of Dr. Nicholas Retson started his own branch of The Smile Train called Healing, Health and Hope. He has an office in Merrillville and lives in Crown Point. A team member invited me to be part of the staff."

Were you paid to go?

"No. It actually cost me money. We take are own vacation time. We even buy items that the people can use down there. The staff believes in what they're doing. Some members have been on nearly a dozen such missions. This was my first one. They've been getting more donations from civic groups. In the past, some of the nurses and staff had to flip their own bill for airfare."

You and Arden are charter members of Cross of Christ Lutheran Church. You work for a Catholic hospital. Is it some kind of interfaith project?

"No. It's strictly a medical mission and has nothing to do with St Anthony's. There were 14 of us. Volunteers came from Porter Memorial, St. Anthony, St. Catherine, St. Mary... . A huge thing we needed was interpreters. Two of the nurses from St Catherine's could speak Spanish which was a tremendous help. Dr. Retson was the only surgeon. Dr. Janice is a geneticist who did a screening clinic to determine our case load while we did surgeries.

"Through word of mouth the villagers were informed that the Americans were coming with a plastic surgeon to help those born with cleft palette, lip or whatever. Posters were put up all over town just before we arrived informing them to be at the hospital at a specific date and time.

"Those of us who were working surgery set up our supplies while the anaesthesiologist, pediatrician and Dr Retson did all the screenings to see who our candidates for surgery would be; who they thought they could really help with a surgery intervention. It's like an evaluation of the patients who show up.

"There was a girl with a club foot. We couldn't help her. Dr. Retson is going back in August with a orthopaedic surgeon. Retson will do lips while the other doctor does feet.

"We did some burn victims, too. The man pictured here had been burned many years before. The scars on his neck were so thick he could barely move."

Those nurses from St. Cat's, near the mills, have seen this a time or two...

"Theoretically, he should not have survived with burns covering that percentage of his body."

How many of these poor people did you help?

"We did about 35 surgeries in seven days. Dr. Retson wanted to do more. If we wanted to take any kind of walk and sightsee, we had to get up by daybreak."

Why, because it gets so hot?

"Because we worked from early morning into the evening. Jeff, look at this little guy, he was a sweetheart. This girl was adorable; I loved her the most. One of our patients was a hospital administrator's child who had a lesion on the cheek. They brought her in so the Americans could work on her. That's how much they trusted us.

"The local youths performed a folk dance for us before we left. They have a Lion's Club down there that helped with our lodging. That whole country could be a gold mine. It's gorgeous. Mayan ruins, scuba diving, coffee, sugar cane... .

"I read a lot at night. I'm not used to somebody cooking for me. I'll work my brains out during the day if somebody can do that for me."

* * *

She's small but mighty. At nearly 49 years of age, I do believe she could run varsity for most high school boys cross country teams.

Rhonda said her parents worked relentlessly on that Corydon farm.

Father in the fields. Mother canning, freezing, and milking cows.

Rhonda can probably thank her parents for instilling a strong work ethic in her.

And there are some people living just north of Nicaragua and due west of Guatemala who are also thankful for volunteers like Rhonda. They're smiling proud now. And they're talking clear now. Can you hear them?

Children shoutin', "Thank you" from the humble village of Gracias.

Doc Forgey *(Dec. 2010)*

"...Blessed be ye poor: for yours is the kingdom of God."
– Luke 6:20

William Wallace "Doc" Forgey was named after the legendary Scotsman portrayed by Mel Gibson in the film "Braveheart." Like William Wallace, Doc Forgey also has been known to come to the aid of the poor and downtrodden. He will return from Haiti tomorrow and was interviewed before he left.

Forgey lives in Crown Point and practices medicine in Merrillville just south of the Methodist Hospitals Southlake Campus.

He's a lifetime bachelor who lives with his 13-year-old yellow Lab, Dawson.

* * *

What's up, Doc?

"I was born and raised in Gary," he said. "I went to Lew Wallace from first grade through the 12th grade. My mother graduated from the first class at Lew Wallace in 1932."

College?

"Indiana University; after four years, I earned a basic degree in chemistry."

Med school?

"Eventually, IU, but I enlisted in the Army first. It was 1964. I was out of money and yearning for adventure. 'Fun, travel and adventure' is the old motto of the Army. I bit hook, line and sinker. It taught me one good lesson."

What's that?

"To pay more attention to current events. I got sucked into the Vietnam War. I went through basic and advanced infantry (training) and then I got my commission in the infantry; I went through (Office Candidate School). I stayed in the Army in active duty about six years – 30 months in Vietnam."

What did you do for Uncle Sam?

"I was assigned to the Pentagon; I ended up with a very interesting job – propaganda, or psychological operations. But I realized maybe that wasn't the career path I wanted to take. Eventually, you figure you'll get killed if you keep that up."

Tell me more about psy-ops.

"In Vietnam, it was combat support with loud speakers, where you're yelling at the enemy to give up. Also dropping leaflets on them and radio broadcasting – stuff like that."

Tokyo Rose.

"Yes, we had our own version of Tokyo Rose blasting back in their direction. I was in logistics with that, so I was constantly all over Vietnam."

You're quite an outdoorsman.

"Yes, I was named the Outdoorsman of the Year in 1982 by the Post-Tribune's Jack Parry. I had been taking kids around here to expeditions in northern Canada. We'd either go for a long canoe trip or build a cabin. We also took winter trips 900 miles above the U.S. border. During the winter that's 30, 40, 50 degrees below zero, and we're not talking wind chill factor."

Sounds fun, but dangerous.

"We had full-arctic gear and would practice around here. So we had kids who were sleeping in their back-yards in weather like this, training for what would be three times worse."

Your first job as a doctor in this area?

"I was hired to work in the emergency room at the Ross Clinic in 1975, but I stipulated I wanted two months off per year – one month during the winter and one month during the summer to do expeditions. They agreed to that. For its time, the Ross Clinic was really quite sophisticated."

When did you leave Ross Clinic?

"In 1982; then I started my own family practice. I initially was in Twin Towers (Merrillville) until 1986, when I moved to my current location.

Retirement?

"I've flown 1 1/2 million miles on United Airlines and I fly mostly on American Airlines now. I've been everywhere, done a lot, and I've lectured all over the world – from Mt. Kilimanjaro to Mt. Blanc. I've dog sledded north of the Arctic Circle, and I've done all this while doing my job. There is no imperative for me to quit and say, 'Gee, I need to do something else.' I've done it, and I'm doin' it. Besides, if I retired, it would definitely decrease my ability to maintain this lifestyle; those expeditions are expensive."

Dawson?

"I got him from Central Indiana Lab Rescue. After Jack died, my previous yellow lab, I couldn't even face getting another dog for five years. Jack was a great camper; he canoed the Hudson Bay twice and rafted the Rio Grande."

Haiti?

"I teach a class in medical ethics at IUN. When the earthquake occurred, there was a concern in the class about what we could do. At first it was mostly fundraising, but then I said, 'What about a class project? Why don't we actually go down there as a medical team?'"

And?

"The students got real excited about that and formed a non-profit called Medical Student Missions. Our motto is 'Learning through Serving.' About 20 of us went down there in August.

"We networked with an outfit that had us set up a clinic in a orphanage in a remote area of northern Haiti. During a two-week period, we saw 1,600 patients."

How many doctors at the orphanage?

"Unfortunately, I was the only doctor. We had tables set up and we had interpreters. The medical students would assess each child and I'd go table to table. We could run seven stations simultaneously. We needed some of the students to do the triage as children were coming in – pick out the sickest ones."

Explain the triage.

"Well, it came down to this: Looks like shit, doesn't look like shit. And that was just for skin diseases and malaria before the cholera epidemic hit."

Have you been back since the cholera outbreak?

"Yes, in November. The medical students went to work in the cholera treatment facility. So, you have about 50 people on IVs; some serious cholera victims might need four bottles an hour. We were changing bottles like crazy."

What's next?

"About 17 of us are going back over Christmas break. Now is when they really need us because a lot of the volunteers go home for Christmas. We're leaving Dec. 18 and should get back on New Year's Eve. We're also putting together our February trip."

Haitians.

"What really impresses me is how kind and tender those people are to their children and how clean those children are; we're talking about people who have no running water. They are always dressed in their best clothes.

"Almost all of the clothing is American stuff that was sent down there since the earthquake. So, you're seeing this hodgepodge of screwball T-shirts. One little kid came in wearing a leather bomber jacket with fleece lining; it was 110 degrees. But that's what he owned, so that's what he wore."

Abject poverty?

"The wage for working from sunup until sundown is the equivalent of making $1.25, yet if you go downtown, a Coca Cola costs a dollar. Those guys will never drink a Coke in their lives."

* * *

I could have written a dozen columns on Dr. William W. Forgey. He has written 22 books. "Wilderness Medicine," first penned in 1979, is now in its sixth edition.

As for Haiti, I'm sure Doc could write a book on that, too.

Robin Perez *(June 2009)*

"And when the night is cloudy
There is still a light that shines on me
Shine until tomorrow
Let it be
I wake up to the sound of music
Mother Mary comes to me
Speaking words of wisdom
Let it be"
– Lennon/McCartney

Mother Mary Theresa was born Josephine Dudzik in Poland; she was raised on Chicago's impoverished Northwest side. In 1894, she founded the Franciscan Sisters of Chicago.

Robin Perez was raised in South Holland, Ill. In 1994, she became a nurse.

Since February, Perez has been the quality improvement and education coordinator for St. Anthony Hospice in Crown Point, sponsored by the Franciscan Sisters of Chicago.

Perez, 39, has two daughters ages 21 and 18; she has been married to Jose for 14 years. The four of them live in Lansing, Ill.

* * *

"I've always wanted to be a nurse," Perez began. "My Aunt Janet was a nurse. I had allergies; she gave me my shots every week. I idolized her. Whenever we went on vacations together, she would bring this little tackle box with all the first-aid stuff. I'd think, 'Oh, that's so neat!'"

You fulfilled your dream by getting your nursing degree from South Suburban College in South Holland.

"Yes; then I did a little over a year of med surg in Joliet, Ill."

Med surg?

"Medical-surgical. If patients had generic medical problems after surgery we'd tend to them – we took care of a lot of new hips and knees. I really liked it, but ... OK, I didn't really like it."

Why not?

"I just kept thinking, 'Why did I become a nurse, if this is what I'm going to do?' There were so many patients with so little time for them. So, I started interviewing at different health-care agencies. They all said, 'Oh, you belong in hospice.'"

And?

"They were right."

You have your own office now; do you still make house calls?

"Yes, and I also work in the in-patient unit."

Robin, some nurses help give birth. Then, there's your job.

"Some people say it's a calling. I never felt a special call or anything, but I do feel privileged. It's such a privilege when somebody allows you to be with them when they are dying. They trust us to take care of them and make sure they are comfortable. It's also a lot of responsibility; the nurses here are amazing."

How many nurses are there?

"We have 13 nurses and eight aides on staff. There also are approximately 30 volunteers, including a couple of volunteer nurses and aides. We have one volunteer who sings to our hospice patients in the nursing home; it's so nice."

Does a person have to be a Catholic from Lake County to be admitted to St. Anthony Hospice?

"Oh, no. We have chaplains for every patient: Methodist ministers, Catholic priests, rabbis ... . We're open to residents from Lake, Newton, Porter, Jasper and Starke Counties. There's also a St Anthony Hospice in Michigan City that covers LaPorte County.

"Part of our training is on the Franciscan values; it's a nice system to work for. My maiden name is Wilmington; I'm a Lutheran. My husband converted. His mother is aghast. First, he married a white woman. And now he's a Lutheran."

But there is one criterion each patient must meet.

"When they are admitted to hospice, the doctor has to feel that if the disease followed the normal course, they'd have six months or less."

Robin, you've been a hospice nurse since '96. I certainly don't want to give anyone false hope, but have you had any patients who were given six months to live and then had a miraculous recovery?

"I had a patient who had pancreatic cancer; usually, if you have that your prognosis isn't too good. But he lived for 18 months. He lived really well; he was golfing and going to the boat. His son took him places. Of course, he did die. There was a period of about three weeks that he was really sick and confined to bed.

"When I was working in Joliet, Ill., I had a lady who was 102; she had a really bad heart. The doctor signed her up for hospice; she stayed alive for two years. She was very active, volunteered to type things for us because she had been a secretary.

"Medicare actually said they weren't going to pay hospice because she didn't die within six months. We had what was like a hearing. The doctor took time from his practice, and said, 'Look at the scan of this lady's heart; she could drop over at any minute – of course she is appropriate.'"

What happened?

"Medicare ended up paying."

Do most insurance companies cover hospice care?

"Yes; we're anticipating that our patient load is going to increase."

The baby boomers are beginning to die.

"We're hiring more nurses and training them for that eventuality – we'll be prepared when our census goes up. Plus, more people are learning about hospice every year. We just started a new volunteer training."

What does that entail?

"The volunteers will be calling the families of patients who have died – asking them how they're doing, We send out four cards to the family in the year after the patient dies. We invite them to a support group for bereavement.

"We also try to attend the wake or funeral. And we have a memorial service every year for the patients that have died in that year. Some families memorialize their loved one by having the deceased's name etched on a brick in our secret garden. We just had the 'Blessing of the Bricks' last Sunday."

Your patients aren't always elderly.

"I had a patient who was 16. She'd had cancer almost her entire life. The other hospital I worked for told me: 'You know, we have helped her to live for 16 years. We can't do anything more to prolong her life. Now, we need you to help her die.'

"She had a lot of pain issues so we ended up keeping her on IV morphine. Her parents handled the morphine, the pump, the IV lines –

everything. They had done all that with her chemotherapy. They were amazing. I guess, in a way, they had prepared themselves for her death because she had been sick for so long. But it's hard.

"She was so active up until the very end. She made these little hemp bracelets and necklaces for all the nurses who took care of her. That was really heartbreaking.

"It was so nice that she got to stay at home. She didn't have to spend time in the hospital. She didn't have to go back and forth to the doctor. If one of us nurses went to the house and saw there was a problem, we were on the phone with the doctor and the doctor dealt with it just like that. We took care of it so she could spend time with her family and friends.

"That's usually when people come to hospice – when they've just had it: 'I've had it with the hospital; they wake me up every four hours to check my blood pressure. I don't want that anymore.'"

What about when problems occur after hours?

"The nurses are assigned a patient load, but are available for the patients around the clock every day. They take turns being on call.

"We have nine private rooms for in-patients who have symptoms that we can't control at home. We try to get them well enough so they can go back home because that's where everybody wants to be. That's the goal – get them back home.

"Jeff, people think hospice means death. It's about comfort. It's about maximizing the quality of life. Once you are able to get a patient to stop throwing up and having pain, they can spend time with their family. And it's more than just nursing – it's social services, volunteers. We're a good team and a good service. The earlier patients can enter into a hospice program the better their quality of life is going to be."

* * *

Not all hospice nurses last as long as Perez has; they tend to burn out. When Robin told me the story of the16-year-old girl with cancer who made the bracelets, her eyes were filled with tears. I wanted to ask her how long it had been since the girl passed away, but didn't.

I let it be.

Rosanne and George Kouris *(Feb. 2008)*

"She stretcheth out her hand to the poor;
yea, she reacheth out her hand to the needy."
-Proverbs 31: 20

Rosanne and George Kouris have lived in Lowell since 1984. They have been married 31 years and have five children. Rosanne home schools the two youngest.

They are members of St. Edward Catholic Church. He works at a factory in Shelby. She delivers the Post-Tribune.

The newspaper you are reading is dated February 3. It is an auspicious date for Rosanne and George; today they will board a plane for Sierra Leone, Africa where they help fund an orphanage.

It was five years ago that Rosanne heard Father John Gibson speak of the plight of the people of Freetown, Sierra Leone. Gibson had previously been a Missionary of Charity priest who worked with Mother Teresa in Albania. The Bishop requested that Father Gibson move on to Freetown soon after the end of Sierra Leone's civil war in 2002.

* * *

"Whatever money Father Gibson would get from friends back here he'd use to help the refugees of Freetown," Rosanne began. "A Muslim woman by the name of Louisa Aminata, who was 19 years old at the time, heard that a Catholic church nearby was handing out aid to people who needed it. She approached the father, telling him that her brother was dying, which he was, and that her family needed medicine which they couldn't afford.

"Father Gibson gave her the $500 she needed for the medication and then asked her when the last time her family had eaten. She said it had been three days. He gave her a bag of rice. Louisa was very grateful. Her brother survived.

"Louisa asked Father Gibson what she could do to repay him. He said come to mass every day. Gibson told her stories of Mother Teresa. She became inspired and also wanted to help people. Louisa became his assistant."

What happened then?

"When Father Gibson returned to the U.S., he'd speak at various parishes of the atrocities he saw," Rosanne said. "People were moved and would spontaneously give him $20 – or whatever. He'd send the money to trustworthy people like Louisa.

"George and I went on a pilgrimage with Father Gibson to Lourdes, France. He asked me to help him with the banking of the Sierra Leone donations because more and more people were donating. He couldn't do all the stuff he was trying to do and deal with the money.

"At first Louisa would go out in the neighborhood and get a list of people who needed help. She'd also ask the children living in the street if they had food or adequate clothing, most of whom had been orphaned during the civil war – a good number of them were amputees.

They'd lost limbs from roadside bombings?

"No, it was a terrorist tactic during the civil war," Rosanne said. "The Revolutionary United Front would round up people and asked the moms, 'Do you want long sleeves or short sleeves?' The moms thought maybe the RUF was going to give their children clothing. If they answered long sleeves, the RUF would cut off the child's hand. If the mothers said short sleeves, they would sever the child's arm near the shoulder."

"Jeff, people stand around in Freetown with no arms, begging," added George. "All you can do is put the money in their pocket."

"In the spring of 2004, Louisa asked Father Gibson if she could adopt the children," said Rosanne. "She felt that simply giving them food wasn't good enough. Louisa was 21 by then.

"We had raised enough money to rent a house for Louisa and the children for a year. We also had to be interviewed by the government officials of Sierra Leone. They wanted assurance that we weren't going to adopt the children out for child trafficking. There's a lot of that going on in Sierra Leone.

"Louisa adopted 20 children. She also took in mothers who had been raped. Louisa named her home Savior of the World."

What was the response?

"People were starting to become very generous," Rosanne said. "They also wanted tax receipts. We weren't a corporation, so we ended up incorporating and getting our nonprofit status as Savior of the World, Inc.

"I was named director because Father Gibson was sent to Rwanda. The whole thing ended up on me – I was in charge of the orphanage. The board consists of five people now, that includes my husband and my sister."

George, you and Rosanne were in Sierra Leone last February.

"Yes, when we showed up at the airport last year, I changed over $500. They handed me 1.75 million leones in a plastic bag.

"There are 30 children in the house right now. It's a 700 square foot flat – 16 boys in one room and 14 girls in the other room. They're doubled up in bunks."

Added Rosanne: "And they're happy. "They have a meal. They have clothes. They have someone who looks after them. They go to school now."

How many people live in Freetown, George?

"About 1.4 million. There is no running water in the entire country. If someone does have electricity, it comes from a generator."

Rosanne: "The whole country eats one meal per day – cassava leaves (greens) and rice," says Rosanne. 'The recipe also calls for peanuts, which are ground up with a mortar and pestle. Red pepper, onions and tin tomatoes (canned) are added to the cassava leaves and rice. Sometimes a fish is placed on top.

"There's 95 % unemployment. We would go down the streets of Freetown and see so many young men doing nothing. There are no jobs – just a bunch of young men with no future."

Ripe for another revolution?

"Now that the war is over, life expectancy is up to 45 years,"Rosanne said. "We were like the oldest people in the country. The sewer system runs along the streets in troughs. Malaria and typhoid are major problems.

"The buildings are all bombed out. There are little bamboo shops in the streets. There are cars, but no traffic lights or rules. You ask if they drive on the left or right side and they answer, 'Yes'.

Is English the national language?

"Yes. Sierra Leone was a British Territory until 1961," Rosanne said. "It was every man for himself once the British left. The RUF got to the point where they didn't even have military objectives anymore. They would just go into a village and start killing everybody except for the young boys who they would drug. These young boys would witness their families being murdered; the army would become their family.

"Eventually Louisa converted to Catholicism; she wants to become a nun. The building fund for the new orphanage is up to about $50,000. There will be a school."

Added George: "It's two levels of 2700 square feet. They're breaking ground as we speak."

* * *

Approximately 20,000 human beings lost a hand, an arm, an ear, or their lips thanks to axe or machete wielding members of the RUF in their quest to control Sierra Leone's blood diamonds. That's he equivalent of mutilating every man, woman and child in Crown Point.

Louisa Aminata cannot speak on behalf of her children here in the United States. Savior of the World, Inc. is about as grassroots as it gets. Rosanne and George Kouris welcome any help they can get – Catholic, Protestant, red and yellow, black or white.

John D. Wolf *(May 2008)*

"I hate war as only a soldier who has lived it can, only as one who has seen its brutality, its futility, its stupidity."
– Dwight D. Eisenhower

"...There is a certain level of blood lust, but we won't let it drive our reaction. We're steady, clear-eyed and patient, but pretty soon we'll have to start displaying scalps."
– George W. Bush

In 1942, John D. Wolf was exempt from the draft, but he volunteered anyway. He spent 23 months at sea and was part of six major combat engagements.

Wolf, an Iwo Jima survivor, was decorated for his service in World War II, but never fired a weapon.

John D. Wolf, chaplain, lieutenant commander, United States Navy Reserve, commands respect.

Wolf, 89, lives in Valparaiso with his wife, Carolyn. They have been married 67 years and have raised three sons. He is a retired Methodist pastor who has penned more than 800 local newspaper columns.

* * *

Mr. Wolf, are you a native Hoosier?

"No, I'm from Pocatello, Idaho, about five miles from a Shoshone-Bannock Indian reservation which is located at Fort Hall," he said.

Did you grow up on a farm?

"No, my father was a YMCA director; there were a good number of potato farmers in Pocatello.

"The Union Pacific Railroad has one of their major headquarters in Pocatello. Many of the workers were recruited by the railroad came straight from Italy and Greece. My best friend's name was Zaccardi; we played football together for Pocatello High.

"The Great Depression hit hard in Pocatello; the shops reduced themselves. During the Depression, my father led naturalization classes at the YMCA. The Greeks and Italians wanted to learn the language so they could become U.S. citizens. The second generation of them really produced once they got an education."

You eventually attended Union Theological Seminary in New York City.

"Yes, clergy and seminary students were exempt from the draft, but five of us enlisted and went to Norfolk, Va., for training in June of 1942. All of the chaplains in World War II were volunteers.

"They told me at the naval base in Norfolk that I was the youngest chaplain in the United States Navy; I was 23. There were 10,000 chaplains in World War II. There were 88 of us from Indiana who were United Methodists; I'm the only one left."

Talk about your deployment.

"I was ordered to the USS Frederick Funston; I was her first chaplain. We began our campaign in Sicily, then landed the 100th Battalion, 34th Division of Japanese-Americans at Salerno, Italy. Those young men from the 34th were the best troops we ever had.

"Returning from the Mediterranean, we dropped off the 82nd Airborne Division at Belfast, Ireland as they prepared for the Normandy landings. Europe took precedent; Hitler had to be stopped.

"Then, we had to be re-outfitted for the Pacific war. We were one of the first amphibious attack transports. All of the Pacific war was of that nature. You had to go from island to island. When we landed troops, we stayed around and took on casualties."

John, for Veteran's Day week a few years ago, I interviewed a man for this column by the name of Dorsey Ruley. He was aboard the Helena when she went down. Dorsey passed away about a year or so ago.

"That was the cruiser that got sunk in the battle of Guadalcanal; those guys really had it tough.

"Fifteen million Americans were in the service during World War II; our death rate is about 1,200 per day now. There are about a million-and-a-half of us remaining."

The duties of a chaplain?

"We serve all faiths by conducting services of worship. Often, we serve as librarian, recreation officer and counselor. During battle stations, we worked jointly with the medical staff in tending to the wounded. Immediately upon landing assault troops, we received casualties from the beaches – sometimes the same men we had a landed.

"All the chaplains in the Marine Corps are Navy. You are assigned to a ship or to the Marines. The men aboard the Funston played hard, fought hard and they prayed hard.

"I buried a lot guys off the fantail of a ship. I buried two on Iwo Jima. One was the son of my skipper, Capt. Charles Carter Anderson."

Do you mind talking about it?

"Charles Carter Anderson, Jr., USMC 4th Division and I had become acquainted back in Pearl Harbor. When the opportunity arose, he would visit his father aboard the Funston. The two of us played chess on occasion. We became friends. He was anxious to complete his education at Georgetown University.

"On Feb.19, 1945, Marines landed on the beaches of Iwo Jima. The Funston was carrying the 3rd Marine Division to be in reserve.

"On March 3, Capt. Anderson received a message from the flagship that a nearby ship was taking on casualties.

"While searching the stretchers waiting to be hoisted aboard, Capt. Anderson heard, 'Hey, Dad.' He hadn't recognized his son because of his extensive wounds.

"Shrapnel had cut off both his legs, the right one below the knee and the left above the knee. His right arm would eventually have to be amputated. He had serious head wounds over his right eye. Carter had enough consciousness to ask to be taken to his father's ship.

"Ships at Iwo got underway before it got dark because of the danger of kamikaze (suicide) planes. We would return and continue unloading and receiving casualties at dawn.

"Carter was rational throughout the night; Capt. Anderson came down frequently from the bridge to talk to his son.

"Although the Captain was a Protestant, his son was Roman Catholic. I contacted Chaplain James Finnigan, a Catholic Priest. Last rites were given.

"At times, Carter seemed to rally; he quipped about playing golf with one arm. He also pondered, 'I wonder how mother will take this?' He died at 9:45 a.m. on March 4.

"Chaplain Finnigan and I took the body ashore while the fighting was still raging on the north side of Iwo. The body was interred in grave No. 1,013, 13th grave in 21st row. Three years later, along with all those buried on Iwo Jima, Carter was interred at Arlington National Cemetery.

"I was so impressed by the heroic way that Carter faced death, coupled with the affection I felt for Capt. Anderson, I wrote a letter the day he died to my wife, Carolyn, 'If we are ever blessed with another son, with your permission, I would like to name him Carter Anderson Wolf.' Our second son was born March 9, 1946, and, on Mother's Day, Capt. Anderson and his wife, Viola, were sponsors to his baptism."

Mr. Wolf...

"Jeff, once you've experienced battle and have survived it, you have an obligation to work toward peace and not glorify war. War is not acceptable. That is why some of us are so opposed to the present war in Iraq. It's an unnecessary war; we were not attacked by Iraq.

"Our wounded in Iraq are not being treated right; every veteran should be paying attention to that. I worked with the wounded so much; I have the greatest empathy for them. When World War II was over, we had the GI Bill of Rights – they don't.

"I also believe that if the draft was on now, this war would be over. And it would be many of those proponents of this war who shouted, 'We're going to war,' who would suddenly change their way of thinking. Iwo Jima changed my way of thinking."

* * *

Before retiring, Pastor John D. Wolf ministered at six churches in Indiana – Evansville, Martinsville, South Bend, Hammond, Fort Wayne and Valparaiso.

Alongside his medals are six small stars: Sicily, Salerno, Saipan, Guam, Leyte-Lingayen Gulfs and Iwo Jima.

The Good Earth

Bryan McKay *(Sept. 2007)*

"I frequently tramped through eight or ten miles of the deepest snow to keep an appointment with a beech-tree or yellow birch..."
– Henry David Thoreau

South of Lowell, I turned off U.S. 41 and headed toward the state line. With maize to left of me and soy to the right, a ribbon of black pavement cut a swath through a sea of green leading to the home and seven acres of Bryan McKay.

McKay, 38, graduated from Purdue University, West Lafayette in 1992. He is a horticulturist for the Lake County Parks Department and is married to Ellen; they have one son, 4-year-old Jacob.

* * *

Where did you grow up?

"Merrillville. Ellen and I moved here 13 years ago."

Bryan, I'm dyin' to check out your arboretum. Is gardening a form of relaxation for you?

"Yes. I have a hectic job. Any time I can spend some time in my yard, it's way of relieving stress. My wife is more into vegetable gardening and canning and freezing; she lets me have carte blanche as far as the trees."

As a kid did you like gardening?

"Yes, my grandparents were big gardeners. My dad liked to garden a little bit. His garden was about the size of this kitchen table. Genetically, it must have skipped a generation. I was gardening soon after I was walking.

"I started making my dad's garden bigger. I'd landscape my parents' home; I'd cut neighbors' lawns. I guess I was born into the industry."

What did the place look like when you moved here?

"There was a total of four trees on the property. I cut down two of them. Everything else I've planted. I'm kind of a collector. I'm not that much of a flower person. I work with flowers a lot on the job. The heart of me is in woody ornamentals – trees and shrubs."

How many trees do you have back there?

"It's really hard telling. I don't have an exact number. If you asked me about a particular tree, I could tell you where I got it, how long it's been there, and its history. For the Lowell Garden Walk, I identified 125 trees. That was just scratching the surface."

Ballpark. You think you have 400 different species of trees?

"Easily."

The house was here already. You mentioned those four trees when you moved in. Which two stayed and which two got the axe?

"I kept a white birch and a sweet gum. They're about the biggest trees on the property and they're right in the center of the front yard. I cut down two crimson maples which a lot of people like, but I don't.

"I just felt like I wanted to personalize the place the way I wanted it. The white birch and sweet gum were fine. I could live with those."

Most people have a favorite flower. Do you have a favorite tree?

"I'd have to say a gingko. They are the oldest living tree on the face of the earth. I have several different cultivars of them."

What about a sequoia?

"Yes, I also have a hardy dawn redwood."

Bryan, let's take a walk. Oh, my. Shangri-la...

"I plant a lot of interesting and unusual stuff. I have a magnolia and a beech collection. Neither are known for their size, per se; it's more for their beauty.

"Now, this a Norway spruce which is a very common pine tree in this area, but it's the weeping form that crawls across the ground like a big serpent."

Bryan, I was told you were kind of shy and had to be coaxed into being a part of the garden walk.

"It's not that I'm really shy. It's more that they expected anywhere from 500 to 700 people to attend. That's 500 to 700 people parking on your lawn, trampling through your grass, pulling seed pods off of things. I love to share my garden or yard, but people don't always respect things."

Somebody carving their initials into your Gingko would probably be like drawing a moustache and sunglasses on Mickey Mantle's 1952 rookie card with a marker.

"Exactly!"

How deep is the pond?

"About 11 feet. As you can see I have lotuses, water poppies and several types of water lilies. The lilies close up by 3 p.m. It's filled with albino catfish, koi..."

Bullfrogs, too. What's this?

"Cypress. A tree that is known to grow down in the everglades."

I've seen this guy growing in the bayous of the Kankakee – river birch.

"Correct. They can tolerate flooded conditions."

And Staghorn Sumac. One of the first to turn red in the fall. I always liked their ferny leaves and velvety seed heads reminiscent of movie theater seats.

"I'm probably an extremist. I love growing things. People spend so much of their time doing things that I consider almost useless pleasures. Look at all the restaurants up in Crown Point or Merrillville – they're always packed.

"To me, that's just a passing satisfaction. Whereas you plant a tree or do some landscaping in your yard, it's going to pay dividends to you and your property. A tree is there for the long run. And hopefully, after you're gone the trees will still be there.

"A lot of them will live for hundreds of years. So many people have to have the fanciest car and the huge house. Materialism isn't important to me. I like having a nice home, but I don't need the Taj Mahal.

"People say, 'Oh, you must run yourself ragged out here.' Not really. No doubt I work at it. But if I didn't, and just sat inside behind a computer or in front of a television set, I'd probably weigh about 400 pounds. This keeps me in shape – it's a healthy habit.

"Half-jokingly, I tell people that I've done my part to help fight global warming. All these trees give off a lot of oxygen. This is a big leaf magnolia. The flowers are about 18 inches wide. They bloom around Memorial Day."

What's that nice shaped tree?

"Cimarron Ash. That tree will probably eventually die because of the emerald ash borer. I would like it to not die. It's a beautiful tree.

"Here's the sequoia. See how massive the trunk is? If you look up higher, you can see it dwindles quite a bit."

Is this a mountain ash?

"European ash. In the winter the bark is yellow like a yellow twig dogwood."

Hey, you've got Hoosier bananas! Do you eat 'em?

"Oh, yes. Pawpaws are delicious. They'll ripen in October. The Pawpaw is the northern most growing tropical tree there is."

Are you organic?

"As close to being organic as I can get. I use integrated pest management. I don't want to lock myself into an entire summer of spraying. On weekends, I average about 15 hours per day watering. I water seven days per week – we have a separate well for watering.

"I usually buy a semitrailer load of mulch per year for all my trees. My neighbors say, 'You're constantly ripping something out and putting something else back in.' I tell them, 'I'm a horticulturist; that's what people like us do.'"

Well, you have an above ground swimming pool. I guess you do kick back once in a while.

"I wanted to make a water garden out of it. Ellen said no."

* * *

Bryan worries as to who will take care of his tall woody perennials after he's been planted beneath this earth. And there will be those who read a paragraph of this column, call McKay a tree hugger, and turn the page.

As for a fool like me, I store away what I've just witnessed: birch, beech, bullfrogs, bluebirds and a tiger swallowtail resting on the weed Native American Joe Pye used medicinally.

And I'm glad to have met Bryan McKay.

He keeps good company.

Alan Resetar *(Dec. 2011)*

"Never try to catch two frogs with one hand."
– Chinese proverb

Alan Resetar is acting divisional manager & collection manager, division of amphibians and reptiles, at The Field Museum in Chicago.

Resetar lives in Valparaiso with his wife, Donna. Other members of the household include a cat, an African plated lizard, a beagle, and a rottweiler-Lab mix named Gary who was a junkyard dog found in Gary.

Resetar also is the owner of a turtle he purchased from Ernie's Pet Shop in Gary almost 45 years ago.

Resetar, 57, has degrees in zoology from Purdue University Calumet and information sciences from the University of Wisconsin, Milwaukee.

* * *

Lived in Valparaiso all your life?

"No, I grew up in Hammond and graduated from Gavit High School."

What ethnicity is Resetar?

"Slovak; my dad is from Whiting. Some of my first amphibian and reptile expeditions took place in Whiting with my cousin, Joe Stahura, who is now the mayor of Whiting."

Childhood memories of Hammond?

"The turtle races they used to have downtown. My sister Elizabeth and I went once and I gave her a large Blandings turtle that I had found and she actually won the race. The Blandings turtle is now a state-endangered species in Indiana."

Sounds like your interest in amphibians and reptiles started at an early age.

"I first got interested in creatures watching 'Garfield Goose' (on WGN, Ch.9) when they'd show these five-minute segments called 'Journey to the Beginning of Time.'"

I used to love "Journey to the Beginning of Time;" every segment had a different title, like: "Part XVII: The Mastodon's Tusk."

"Once I discovered modern amphibians and reptiles, I completely forgot about dinosaurs."

You've studied or surveyed the habitats of the Grand Calumet and Little Calumet rivers.

"The water of the Grand Calumet River is fairly clean; it's the sediments where you have issues. There are 14 (beneficial use impairments); the Grand Cal is the only body of water that has all 14. But there are places where there are actual presettlement natural habitat going right up to the Grand Cal."

Mother Nature can be a resilient old dame, if she's given a fighting chance.

"Believe it or not, there are frogs, turtles and water snakes in the Grand Cal, and some interesting fish species, too."

I bet.

"The Grand Cal does have a distinct odor that's not natural."

I bet.

"We were doing some surveys in the Grand Cal using dip nets and I went a little too deep into the sediment with the net and when I brought up the net, it smelled like fuel oil, yet, there was a beaver swimming about 30 feet from me."

Tell me about The Field Museum.

"The museum has 22 million objects within it; less than 1 percent of those are on exhibit. Even if you go there and spend all day looking at things, you're only scratching the surface."

A typical day at work?

"My job is taking care of and providing access to 290,000 specimens of preserved amphibians and reptiles."

In what are specimens contained?

"Anything up to 5-gallon jars to stainless-steel tanks filled with everything from tiny cricket frogs that were collected at Wolf Lake during the early 1900s to Komodo dragons."

Fieldwork?

"Locally, I do. I haven't done any foreign fieldwork since I went to Libya in 1981. A lot of my day is spent corresponding with people from all over the world through email. People can actually borrow our specimens just like checking out a book at a library."

Are the specimens kept in formaldehyde?

"They are preserved with formaldehyde, but stored in ethanol. We use a technique that was developed in the mid-17th century when people realized they could take a freshly killed animal, slit it open, put it in strong wine and arrest the decay."

A favorite amphibian or reptile?

"Oh, gosh, I like them all, from the biggest snake to the tiniest tadpole. We have 50 different species of amphibians and reptiles in Northwest Indiana, which is a tremendous amount for a small area.

"This is an area where the eastern deciduous forests meet the western prairies, so there are different amphibians and reptiles found from each major habitat."

Alan, when I was a kid growing up on the Kankakee Sands of northern Newton County, I remember catching 5-foot-long blue racers and trying to catch these little green lizards with blue tails, but they were too fast.

"You're probably referring to the six-lined racerunner. You wouldn't find that lizard or a snake like the blue racer in, say, East Chicago."

Serpent trivia?

"As an embryo, the snake's eyelids actually fuse together clear. So, in a sense, a snake's eyes are always closed, but always open. Snakes do not have internal ear openings; lizards do."

Do you ever come across a species that hadn't previously existed in Lake County or Porter County?

"Yes, we're still finding new county records even though herpetologists have been studying this area for at least120 years."

As a whole, how are amphibians and reptiles faring in the 21st century?

"Amphibian and reptile decline is happening all over the world.

Take the cricket frog for example, it has declined in the Great Lakes area, but there are still sites in Lake County where that frog can be found. It's actually an inch-long tree frog, but it lives like a bull frog in that it likes areas along the margin of open water."

You mentioned the bull frog, that's a tenacious creature.

"Oh, gosh, I've seen photos of a bull frog that had choked to death trying to swallow a bullhead. They're quite the predator."

I always was fascinated by the mud puppy.

"The mud puppy would be one of my favorites among the salamanders; they get to be about 18 inches long and are active all year long; ice fishermen catch them. They have external gills and they never become terrestrial."

Explain the latter, please.

"Mud puppies remain as giant larvae in adulthood; the mud puppy retains its aquatic habits and external gills."

Whereas other species of salamanders eventually live on land.

"Exactly."

"Grand Cal Al," its been a pleasure.

"Same here, 'Kankakee Kid.'"

* * *

Concerning his pet turtle, Resetar is grandfathered because he can prove George was acquired before 2005. Box turtles are a protected species in Indiana and cannot be collected in the wild.

Resetar informed me that George will be bequeathed to someone; box turtles can live more than a century. I'm sure it will be a sad day for George when Alan's time comes.

Those two have been friends a long time.

Stephanie Frischie *(Oct. 2011)*

"Everywhere we beheld the works of God in nature... I have been in France and Germany; I was raised in England, but I have never seen anything in those countries that equaled the beauty of this western prairie."

– Thomas Rogers Barker

Tom Barker was describing the Beaver Lake area in what became the northern portion of Newton County when he spoke those words at the Iroquois Old Settlers' Reunion in 1879.

Stephanie Frischie, 38, is a single vegetarian who grew up in Kentland and now lives in an unincorporated area between Mount Ayr, Morocco and Rensselaer. She graduated from South Newton High School and Purdue University West Lafayette.

Frischie works at The Nature Conservancy's 8,000-acre Kankakee Sands project in northern Newton County. She is plant materials and conservation programs coordinator.

And you can bet your sweet-smellin' Matricaria matricarioides Steph knows the scientific name of every form of flora growing on the property.

* * *

Are you a farmer's daughter?

"My dad was a vocational agriculture teacher at South Newton High School; he also did some farming."

What was your degree in at Purdue?

"I began as a botany major and graduated with a degree in international agronomy."

Was this your first job after college?

"No, right after college I was an intern with Pioneer Hybrid at a soybean breeding facility in Napoleon, Ohio. We picked through a lot of beans."

Then what?

"I joined the Peace Corps and was sent to southeastern Bolivia."

Your workmate, Alyssa Nyberg, also was in the Peace Corp.

"Yes, Alyssa was in Nepal while I was in Bolivia; we didn't know each other at the time. Alyssa oversees the nursery and greenhouse and I harvest the ripe pods and seeds."

Steph, tell me a little more about Bolivia.

"I was there for almost three years. Bolivia is a very diverse country; it has the Andes Mountains, but half of the country is actually Amazon rain forest. Other portions are valleys and scrub forests.

"Packing for the Peace Corps, you're only allowed two suitcases and you don't know where you're going to end up. I was sent where it was hot and humid."

What were your duties?

"The indigenous people that I worked with were already very good gardeners, but we helped them to diversify their crops; they grew mostly corn. Not only is it unhealthy to eat nothing but corn everyday, it also isn't healthy economically if corn prices are bad.

"Yucca is a starchy root that is native to that area so we grew more of that and also planted a lot more peanuts and sweet potatoes."

Have you ever been back?

"Many times."

What did you do when you returned to the United States?

"I worked at a wheat research lab and a sorghum lab. Then, I went back to Bolivia on my own and did some watermelon and potato farming. Then, I came back to Indiana in the summer of 2001 and started volunteering here. Eventually, I became a fulltime employee."

When did TNC purchase this land?

"TNC bought the land in Newton County in 1996 and started its first restoration planting in '97."

Steph, are there old-timers who believe this ground should be planted in corn and beans rather than wet prairie or black oak savanna?

"There are as many opinions as there are people. In general, people are polite and respectful and we can agree to disagree. There are reasons for farming and there are reasons for not farming."

Explain, please.

"This is an area with really sandy soil and a high water table which is not ideal for corn and soybean production. It is a wonderful habitat for many plants and animals."

You get to work outside a lot, which I know you enjoy, but inside the seed barn is really cool, too. It sure smells good in there with all the different seed heads and pods. Tell me about the machinery you have in there.

"We have a hammer mill, a stationary thresher and two fanning mills which are still made by the A.T. Farrell Company."

What are your major tasks?

"I determine the plants that are native to this area and get them to grow here. That involves a lot of research and visiting other local remnants or preserves. I also collect the seeds and get them ready. We're primarily here for conservation purposes, but the property is open to the public for hiking and nature."

How many threatened or endangered species of flora and fauna are thriving at Kankakee Sands?

"More than 130 species."

That's remarkable. How long can a seed remain in the soil and still germinate if given the chance?

"Some seeds don't live very long at all; they need to germinate and become a plant. But there are some seeds that can last in the soil for decades."

What are a few of the state-endangered or threatened species of animal-life found at Kankakee Sands? Common names, please.

"The Henslow's sparrow, the plains pocket gopher, and we have something that's really neat called a slender glass lizard. It's a legless lizard that looks like a snake; it thrives in sandy soils and black oak savannas. We also have many, many types of insects. Certainly, one of the most spectacular is the regal fritillary."

My friend Patty Wisniewski got one on film a couple months ago; it was flitting among the wild flowers on TNC property near the seed barn – beautiful butterfly.

"The caterpillars of the regal frittilary will only eat the leaves of violet plants. We've planted a lot of violets here."

Rare plants?

"We have the Carolina woolly white or old plainsman on the property. Some of our St. John's wort species are really rare. It's always fun to find a rare plant that you've read about or heard about. It's probably like a bird watcher spotting a bald eagle for the first time."

* * *

One-tenth of 1 percent of the world's black oak savanna remain today.

Thomas Rogers Barker is considered the father of Newton County; he died in 1899. Some say he wasn't meant for the 20th Century.

But I like to think Barker is smiling down on the Kankakee Sands from that big blue stem and blazing star-filled prairie in the sky.

And in my reverie, I envision him nodding his head in approval regarding the restoration work being done by the likes of Stephanie Frischie in the 21st Century.

Lester Klein *(July 2007)*

"The harder you work, the harder it is to surrender."
– Vincent Lombardi

When I was a boy, my father told me, "Son, I have found two topics upon which men of reasonable integrity and honesty have a tendency to lie about: the gas mileage of their pickup trucks and the length of their blue gills' (Dad's a fly fisherman)." I can't even remember my old man using exaggeration for emphasis – let alone telling a bald-faced lie.

When he was a boy, his family moved from Chicago's 87th and Cottage Grove neighborhood to a formidable grove of oaks in Lake Village. It was the Great Depression. Hardwood was hewed during hard times.

When my father says he was performing a man's labor by the age of 6, I believe him. He also told me if any children growing up in that neck of the woods worked any harder than the Manes kids, it was the brothers Klein.

Les Klein has resided with his wife, Trudy, in Portage since 1970. Klein is 70, but has the physique of a 30-year-old. Les and Trudy have raised two adult daughters.

* * *

"Both mom and dad were from the Cook-Cedar Lake area," Klein began. "My father decided to move to Lake Village. He bought a 110-acre farm for $2,500 back in the 1930s. He also worked at Keen Foundry in Griffith for 40-some years.

"There were six of us kids. I was raised on that Lake Village farm. It was exactly one mile from your Grandpa Vito's place – as the crow flies.

"Our house was very old. It stood on what we called 'Hungry Hill.' We raised a lot of cane. Literally. Sugar cane. We made sorghum molasses from it and sold it in gallon jugs.

"We always raised at least three acres of pickles and sold them at the pickle factory in town. Pickles put my brother, Ken, through college. We'd pick pickles from mid-July until it was time to go to school.

"Actually, my older brothers didn't even attend school until about the third week because that's when we were making molasses. Dad would say, 'We need you here in the fields.'Blueberries, asparagus, if you could pick it, we picked it. If you could sell it, we sold it.

"As hard as we worked, we never missed Mass. Father Woods would come from Shelby and say a Mass for us in the Lake Village gymnasium. By the mid-1940s, we started going to St. Pat's in Momence, Ill., which became our parish until St. Augusta was built at Ind.10 and U.S. 41."

You played for the Beavers back in high school.

"Yep; football, basketball, and ran track. I graduated from Morocco High School in 1956."

What position on the gridiron?

"Running back; in those days, the halfback would throw a lot of passes, too. It was like a tailback in a single wing. We lost three games in four years at Morocco. We played both 11 and six-man football. When we played 11-man, most of the schools like Lowell, Rensselaer and Monticello had more kids in their senior class than we had in our entire school."

Track?

"I held the school records in both the 100-yard dash and the shot put. I was fortunate enough to garner a college education at St. Joseph's College in Rensselaer because of an athletic scholarship.

"I graduated from St. Joe in 1960. That fall, I went to Wendell Willkie High School in Elwood for two years, where I was an assistant coach for three sports. In the fall of '62, I went to North Judson for four years as head coach. I became head football and track coach at Lowell in '66. I stayed there for four years."

Tell me about your stint at Lowell High.

"We came into the program as a whole new staff. They had not won a ballgame in three years – and we didn't help the situation. Well, we did get a forfeit that first year. The next year, we were 5-4. By '68, we were 8-1. We were undefeated going into the playoff game versus Chesterton. That's back when you had the North and South Calumet Conference."

Portage?

"I went to Portage in the fall of '70. Little did I know I would retire from the Portage school system 30 years later. Nineteen of those years, I was head football coach. I was also the athletic director for 20-plus years."

When I worked at Inland Steel's Coke Plant, I lockered next to a guy named Randy Leggett. He punted for your 1977 Class 3A state championship team.

"Do you ever see Randy?"

Not for several years.

"The reason I ask you, in the championship against Evansville Reitz, the turnaround of the game came when they called roughing the punter. I swear the ball was deflected.

"Well, you know you can't rough the punter if you get a piece of the ball. To this day, when I ask Randy if the guy from Evansville got a piece of ball or just him, he won't tell me. He just smiles, 'Can't say, Coach.'"

Les, Leggett confided in me after a midnight turn regarding that fateful play.

"What did he say?"

Can't say, Coach. Are you a Bears fan?

"I'm a die-hard White Sox fan. That made me a Chicago Cardinal fan (now the Phoenix Cardinals). They both played at Comiskey Park. I despised the two teams (Cubs and Bears) that played at Wrigley Field. While at St. Joseph's, we had to follow the Bears through the chow line. We got all the leftovers – wasn't much."

The kids today?

"It seems a kid can no longer play if he isn't attending an organized practice. I don't see kids throwing a ball up on a roof, practicing catching it when it comes down. I don't see kids bouncing a ball off a wall.

"Right here in Indiana, where every barn or driveway had a basketball rim, you don't see many kids playing. You have to provide an open gym for them. They have Game-Boys today. With that said, I was never that thrilled about Pop Warner Football – starting kids at such a young age – from the contact aspect of it."

A couple of the best you ever coached?

"There's been a lot of good ones. From Portage, Mike Wishnevski and Eric Jones. From Lowell, Terry Padgett was a great three-sport athlete. Padgett ranked right up there with any of them."

Final thoughts?

"You have to separate the chaff from the grain. And, if you're not the sharpest knife in the cutlery, you better be working harder than the rest of them." Down through the years, I've realized that without good teammates or assistant coaches, you don't go anywhere."

* * *

Les Klein is a member of both the St. Joseph's College and Indiana High School Football Halls of Fame. He has many fond football memories.

He reminisced about another fellow hall-of-famer who just happened to be my mother's first cousin, Ken "Zip" Sypult. They named a football field after him at Highland High School.

"We had some good battles, then joked about it afterward," Klein said. "I loved that man. Zip had the kind of sense of humor that I enjoyed in a coach."

Although raised in Hammond, Zip Sypult also was born in Lake Village.

Lester Klein has no regrets regarding his hardscrabble roots. That's where his strong work ethic was first cultivated...

Atop a plot of land they called "Hungry Hill."

Patricia Riley-Churilla *(July 2010)*

"I hear the voices of the grandmothers calling me...
May the rivers all run clear
May the mountains be unspoiled
May the trees grow tall
May the air be pure
May the earth be shared by all
May the earth be shared by all"
– author unknown

On those rare occasions when I receive disparaging e-mails from disgruntled readers, they usually come from Porter County residents of the conservative persuasion. In an effort to make amends and new friends, I decided to interview someone from Chesterton.

Patricia Riley-Churilla, 47, has been married to Patrick Churilla for six years. They don't have any children, but they do have two cats, a dog, and an aquarium full of fish.

Patricia is an animal lover who feeds the neighborhood birds. She enjoys camping, reading and going to the movies. She crochets a bit, likes to do Sudoku and just finished her first semester at Purdue University North Central where she is studying sign language.

Riley-Churilla's is of Irish, Cherokee, Welsh, Scottish and German ancestry. In other words, the redhead born Patricia Riley is as American as apple pie. I don't know whether or not Riley-Churilla is a right-wing Republican, but I do know she's a Porter County Pagan.

* * *

Are you a secular humanist?

"No, and by the way, don't be afraid to ask me anything," she said. "There really are no stupid questions."

It's really good to hear you say that. What's a Pagan?

"If you'd ask 10 Pagans, you'd probably get about 20 definitions. My definition of Paganism would be that it's an earth-centered or nature-based religion. Some Pagans are secular humanists; a Pagan might or might not be a polytheist. That's where I'd place myself, in the polytheism area of Paganism."

Is your husband a Pagan?

"Yes; we met in church."

What church was that?

"The First Unitarian Church of Hobart; I became a member in '91. We did a survey years back and determined that our church broke down to about 20 percent each: Christian, Pagan, Humanist, Buddhist and other. We don't agree theologically, but we get along."

Wasn't Thomas Jefferson a Unitarian?

"We claim him. Jefferson was actually a Deist; he believed God created the world, sent it spinning and walked away. And whatever it's doing now, it's doing on its own. Jefferson didn't believe in divine intervention."

Patricia, there have been some extremely intelligent people who didn't believe in God: Isaac Asimov, Carl Sagan, Jonas Salk, Kurt Vonnegut and Charles M. Schultz, just to name a few. They were all secular humanists.

"Most of our Founding Fathers weren't religious men. I think it was President John Adams who said this country is no more a Christian nation than it is a Mohammedan nation; that was the word they used to describe Muslims. We fled from religious persecution; that's why we came here."

Wicca?

"I'd say Wicca is a Pagan denomination like Catholic is a Christian denomination. Not all Pagans are Wiccans and not all witches are Wiccan – not all witches are even Pagan."

Are you a Wiccan?

"No; Wicca is a religion that people spend a lot of time learning by degree. There are 1st, 2nd and 3rd degree Wiccans."

Sort of like the martial arts or the Masons for that matter.

"I didn't take that training and I don't like diminishing the people who have, by calling myself a Wiccan. What I learned was from my grandmother; she did things."

Did things?

"She called it 'the work.' Other people call it 'the craft.' And that's what witchcraft is – a craft."

Tell me more about Grandma.

"My grandmother was born in 1906. She wouldn't have called herself a Pagan; she used the Bible, but only the Old Testament."

Similar to those of Jewish faith.

"My grandmother's mother was a German Jew."

So your grandmother got the cauldron boiling. I would've guessed the Paganism evolved from your ancient Celtic or American Indian side of the family.

"Actually, I'm seventh generation. My maternal grandmother learned 'the work' from her mother who learned from her father who learned from his mother who learned from her mother who learned from her father."

You're telling me that your great-times-five-granddaddy was a warlock?

"My family is just like other families who hand down their religious beliefs from one generation to the next."

Back to Grandma's "work."

"She would light different-colored candles; for example, if somebody needed money, she'd burn a green candle and go into meditation. Then, she'd get out her Bible and go to an Old Testament passage.

"She did a lot of things with herbs. We use poultices as folk remedies a lot. Grandma would soak bread or mash down a potato, which would hold the herbs in a mass onto things like bee stings, hang nails or stubbed toes. The difference between grandmother's practice and my practice is I do more rituals."

An example, please?

"I cast a circle and ask the four directions to be present and bless my work. Sometimes, I use implements and ornaments. The candles or symbols that you might put at the four corners are just helpers. It's more a visual thing, more a right-brain thing. You need to tap into that right brain and leave the left brain outside of it."

Ouija boards?

"Grandmother thought Ouija boards were doorways best not opened. I consider them something made by Parker Brothers. I have no interest in using them."

Tarot cards?

"I use them. Grandmother used one special deck of playing cards. They were her reading cards and used solely for that purpose.

"Jeff, this is the book that changed my life: 'Drawing Down the Moon: Witches, Druids, Goddess-worshipers and Other Pagans in America Today,' by Margot Adler. I didn't get very far into it when I started seeing things my family did."

I'm not familiar with that particular tome. Animal sacrifices?

"That's an ancient device that was used in most cultures. I have not seen or heard of animal sacrifices like the kind you see on television. I liken animal sacrifice to Thanksgiving."

Really?

"You have this big bird on the table and you thank God that all the family is there and you're enjoying this great meal that was provided by God – somebody had to slaughter that turkey for you."

Beelzebub, Lord of the Flies?

"We believe the devil is a Christian concept. The devil is not part of the Pagan pantheon."

Heaven and hell?

"I think most Pagans agree that heaven and hell aren't the only two possibilities. Many Pagans believe that you go to a place called the summerland where you review what you did in your life. And, you get a chance to learn from those mistakes. You come back until you get it right."

Edgar Cayce, "The Sleeping Prophet," was a devout Christian who believed in reincarnation.

"My grandmother read everything ever written about Cayce."

Patricia, thanks. I learned a lot from you. Some readers, however, strongly disagree with your beliefs.

"I have no problem with that. We want to be open with the public and also want to give people who are curious access to find out what this is all about.

"By and large, we're a diverse lot; we don't make distinctions as far as race, class, sexual orientation, ethnicity or gender."

* * *

It's just a hunch, but I don't think she's a right-wing Republican.

Jim Sweeney *(Jan. 2008)*

"When the earth is sick, the animals will begin to disappear. Continue to contaminate your bed, and you will one night suffocate in your own waste."
– Chief Seattle, 1855

"We were in a nest of pollution. What got me active about it all was the Calumet River. People were complaining that by 2 a.m., they would wake up choking as if they were drowning in sewage."
– Betty Balanoff, 2007

The first time I met Jim Sweeney he was chairing a Friends of the Kankakee River meeting held at the Grand Kankakee Marsh about seven years ago.

His eclectic entourage ranged from a young man who was a member of Greenpeace to an elderly woman who was a member of the Audubon Society.

Sweeney is a lifelong bachelor who has resided in Schererville since 1984. He grew up in Lansing, Ill., and graduated from Thornton Fractional South High School in 1973.

A wall within Sweeney's home is covered with various plaques bestowed upon him for his efforts regarding environmentalism and conservation.

He's the kind of guy who speaks with concern regarding ivory-billed woodpeckers. He's the kind of guy who speaks with passion when referring to a nocturnal chorus of coyotes or the sweet serenade of the brown thrush. He finds blizzards and thunderstorms magnificent.

* * *

Jim, you were named Environmentalist of the Year by the Izaak Walton League, and you are one of the IWLA's 13-member National Executive Board. You also work for Enbridge Inc., a major pipeline supplier of oil and natural gas. Is it possible for man to have an industrial and a natural environment?

"I believe so. People like Lee Botts (Lake Michigan Federation) and Herb and Charlotte Read (Save the Dunes) would probably say the same thing. The dunes area was an absolute paradise 150 years ago when Lake County was half swamp – dunes and swales.

"Now that we've ruined a whole bunch of it, there is plenty of room to protect and restore natural areas and still have an industrial economy. Still, if George Bush had his way, we wouldn't have half the regulations we do have."

Exxon Valdez.

"Because of that disaster, the regulations were tightened quite a bit – but it's still not clean. The fisheries still haven't come back.

"Big changes only come after disasters. Personally, I try to get as much preventive information out ahead of time to people as possible."

When did you get interested in bird watching?

"One of the jobs I had with Enbridge was called line walker. Every other week, my partner and I would hopscotch from Elgin (Ill.) to Merrillville, taking turns walking in five-mile increments and picking up each other with the truck. Those two years of walking the line got me interested in birds. I gravitated toward wetlands because wherever you have a wet spot, you're going to have wildlife."

How did you get involved with the Izaak Walton League?

"It met a man by the name of Howard Anderson who talked me into becoming an 'Ike' back in 1988. Howard worked for Inland Steel (now ArcelorMittal); he was stationed at their waste-water treatment facility. He also was a founding member of Local 1010's Environmental Committee.

"Because of Howard, I learned about what had been one of the largest marshes in the world along the Kankakee River – and what it had become. I had no idea. Since then, I decided that I would work for the rest of life to promote large-scale restoration along the Kankakee River.

"The Kankakee is a really high-quality river and it is being threatened in Illinois by the way it's managed in Indiana. All that sand is rolling down our artificial ditch into Illinois.

"Before the dredging, the river meandered for 250 miles from South Bend to the state line. Today, it's 90 miles long. It will never be a million-acre marsh again, but I feel that 50,000 acres would be better served to hold the water coming off of the rest."

Continue, please.

"The 1996 National Wildlife Refuge Proposal was for 30,000 acres – 20,000 would be along the river in Indiana, 10,000 would be in Iroquois County, including prairie and savannah. The proposal is on hold. We've had (Hurricane) Katrina. We have a war going on. We have to wait until the political climate changes.

"One of the big reasons I'm promoting Kankakee Restoration is because it's so wide open. There's a chance to do the restoration in a way that could be effective, economical and also could be done in a way where it becomes a tourist destination.

"Eventually, this juggernaut of development is going to get down there. So, if we protect a lot of it now, or soon, it's something we could all utilize down the road.

"My biggest fear is that if I live another100 years, I'm going to see a flood- control project on the Kankakee River that looks just like the one on the Little Calumet River. It will cost billions of dollars and it's going to do the same thing; it's going to give you a flood control project that has minimal wildlife benefit, minimal water quality benefit, and minimal recreational benefit – all because there's development and an expressway running right through the middle of it.

"If we generate enough support, we can get a flood-plain restoration project down there before the development gets there. We can do it in a way that is really good for wildlife, water quality and recreational values. We can give people a place to see wildlife, to hike, bike, camp, hunt, fish – and then go home at night. Maybe a few bed and breakfasts will pop up. Why not have a big trail right along both sides of the river from South Bend to Momence?

"Jeff, I don't care about being famous. But when I'm gone, maybe someone will write that I made a difference; maybe it will be you."

* * *

Jim Sweeney already has made a difference. And he will continue to fight the good fight.

Liz and Corey Aquino *(June 2008)*

"To own a bit of ground, to scratch it with a hoe, to plant seeds, and watch the renewal of life – this is the commonest delight, the most satisfactory thing a person can do."

-- Charles Dudley Warner, 1870

Liz and Corey Aquino are too young to be old hippies but they are one of the grooviest couples I know.

They are organic farmers. Their home sits on 20 acres northeast of Lowell; it was a former pole barn. They have raised two children; Erin will be a senior at Butler University and Rand just graduated from Lowell High School.

We conversed in a screened-in porch. Liz was sipping from a cup of her homemade applemint tea. Corey, who also is a member of the IBEW was sipping from a can of Miller High Life.

* * *

Corey, were those hops and grains organically raised?

"Hey, it's union-made – gotta keep 'em workin'."

On the way here I saw some mighty fancy shacks – mansions.

"Liz and I were talking about that today; a guy down the street is building a $10 million house. Why would anybody build a $10 million house?"

You both graduated from Lowell High?

"Yes, I graduated in '79; Corey was class of '80," Liz said. "We were middle school sweethearts."

Corey, you took an electrical apprenticeship right out of high school. Which do you prefer, bending wires or busting sod?

"I tried walking away from the trade when work was really good back in the late '90s. I'd take a 7-12 gig (seven days a week, 12 hours per day) for about two weeks, then I'd take four or five weeks off to work on the farm.

"Originally, we had a little house in Crown Point. Liz and Erin came home and said we have to buy this place. I didn't want to live in a pole barn. I was going to build a new house over on the Nine-mile Stretch on a one-acre lot – we kind of chucked all that.

"Liz wanted a garden – we started gardening. I started reading about organics. I had never planted a thing in my life, but once you're in there and you get the bug – that's it."

Added Liz: "My maternal grandfather, Melvin Rosenthal was a corn and bean farmer. "When we started growing organically he understood because that's how he started out; there were no chemicals. He gave us a lot of advice."

Corey said, "That old man was a conservative Republican, but we could sit down and talk all day."

The three of you shared a mutual love for Mother Nature.

"Right," Liz said. "Grandpa never questioned what we did."

Added Corey: "When I was a kid growing up right here in this neighborhood, there were five dairy farmers – they're all gone. Those guys raised their families farming 400 acres or less. Now you can't make it unless you're farming 2,000 – and they're having a rough time."

Let's talk about chemical-free farming.

"We don't even use organic sprays," Liz said. "The organic sprays are still broad spectrum and will also kill the beneficial insects. When you're killing the beneficials, you're messing up the environment. We hand pick bugs. We use mulch and compost."

Added Corey: "What's interesting is, there was a movement to go organic on the coasts and, eventually, in the Midwest. We had a hard time selling at first. People would say, 'I'm not buying organic, you people use shit to grow your produce – that's nasty'.

"Eventually the idea of consuming organically grown vegetables became mainstream. Well, it has become so mainstream that the word organic has become completely diluted. The federal government has their own set of organic standards. You have to be certified in order to adhere to those standards. We can't even call ourselves organic because we're not certified – I don't want to be certified.

"Year after year the market share for organics was growing. The Monsantos of the world started thinking, 'We've got to get these larger growers in on this marketplace.' So now organic produce shipped from

California, Argentina or Chile is not organic by definition because you just shipped the damn stuff thousands of miles expending fossil fuels to get it here. How many hands have touched it? How many gases have gassed it? They're not adhering to the basic principals of why we started organic – why little growers do what we do."

Added Liz: "It's not just the non-use of chemicals – it's the whole thing.. It's working with the environment instead of against it."

Heavy equipment?

"A 1972 John Deere 10-20 – it came with the place," Corey said. "This was a 60-acre apple orchard; we bought 20 acres of it. We farm seven."

How did the apple grower fare?

"He started out doing pretty well," Corey said. "Apples were selling for $12 a bushel. When he got out, apples were down to five bucks a bushel. He couldn't make it. His name was Chapman."

Corey, there was another guy with the surname of Chapman who also planted quite a few apple trees years ago. He was an eccentric old cuss folks nicknamed Johnny Appleseed.

"You just about have to spray apples," Corey said. "We don't mess with the orchard; it's too time-consuming mowing around the trees. I just let it grow wild. The way I look it at, it's a safe haven for wildlife to hang out."

Is garlic still one of your best sellers?

"Yes," Corey said. "We always take one-third of our crop and set it aside for the next year's planting. What happens is we're kind of genetically modifying by using natural evolution. Those plants just keep getting stronger."

Added Liz: "It has become our own stock; it's Lane's End Farm garlic. It's no longer the wild strain of garlic we originally started with."

Corey said: "And with that you're getting into stuff like GATT," says Corey. "The big seed companies say no farmer around here is supposed to save their seed because they own rights to those living organisms. Because the giants modify and hybridize them, now they declare the seeds theirs."

Liz explained: "That's why we grow heirloom tomatoes; we can save those seeds. Nobody can say, 'I'm going to take the Black Prince and make it mine'.

Black Prince – gotta love the names of those heirloom varieties.

"Heirloom tomatoes are unbelievable – their depth of flavor and color," Corey said. "People fight over the tomatoes. Liz, tell Jeff some market stories."

Liz: "Customers would ask us to hold back tomatoes at the markets. It got to the point where I was holding so many back that there were none displayed on the stand."

At how many markets do you sell?

"We do two every week in Chicago," Liz said. "On Saturdays, is Division Street; on Tuesdays we set up on the plaza in front of the Museum of Contemporary Art. This is our 10th year of going to Chicago. We have very loyal customers, but I never cut a deal. I'd rather bring it home and compost it.

"Learning marketing and setting up a stand is just as important and difficult as growing the vegetables. You don't just throw the stuff on a table.

"We also have the CSA (Community Supported Agriculture). There are 80 members hailing from Miller, Lowell, Valpo, Wheatfield, Crown Point... There are four different pick up sites on Wednesdays. People also stop by here on harvest day (Mondays and Fridays) and buy whatever we have."

Added Corey: "It's not about competition; it's about cooperation. If you have an acre-and-a-half of land, you can have a decent part-time job. I'd like to think that we've paved a little road. We can't grow everything; we don't want to grow everything."

Liz said: "This really was a good way to raise our kids; they know how to work."

Added Corey: "I think that's how it all started. We wanted to spend more time with the kids. We haven't been able to go on family vacations because of the farm; this is where we play."

"One of the most fun times here is the week we harvest garlic. It's an event – a national holiday on the farm."

* * *

Lane's End Farm... Folks who don't even like tomatoes become afficionados of the fruit once they've sampled a Green Zebra, Cherokee Purple, Striped German, Anna Russian or Black Prince raised by Liz and Corey Aquino.

Bob Engel *(Oct. 2008)*

"...Goodnight ladies
Sorry if I stayed too long
So long it's been good to know you
I love the way I sing that song."
–Randy Newman, "Old Man On The Farm"

Crimson leaves of staghorn sumac match the throat of the hummingbird flitting about Bob Engel's back yard in Hebron.

Time to head south, little fella. It's October; the frost is on the pumpkin; the hay is in the barn, and apiarists like Engel,76, have put their girls to bed until spring.

* * *

How long have you been keeping bees, Bob?

"Since I was 14," he said. "I grew up around 47th (Avenue) and Roosevelt (Street) in Gary. I worked for three different beekeepers."

How long have you and the wife been hitched?

"Elizabeth and I have been married for 56 years – five good ones."

I know you're an avid member of the Northwest Indiana Beekeepers Association but what did you do for a living?

"I was a heavy equipment operator for 39 years. We didn't have mufflers, cabs or heaters when I started out. There was no oscillation on a D8 dozer – no nothin'. All you could do was raise the blade up with a cable and let it drop. The weight of the blade is what made it cut into the ground.

"Back around '46 the D6 came along; that was the first hydraulic blade we had ever seen. It was fantastic.

"Just off Indiana 55 in Crown Point there's a big machine sittin' out front of Local 150; that's an old D8 cable bulldozer. I stare at it every time I drive by."

How long have you lived in Hebron?

Eighteen years; I lived in Merrillville for 38 years before that. Had a neighbor move in next to me; he didn't like my bees so I moved to Hebron. Honeybees get a bad rap."

You're also an instructor.

"Yep, I've taught over 500 beekeepers. I had a class of 71 this spring. When the state gives lessons it's a one-shot, four-hour class and that's it – you're a beekeeper. I teach five, three- to four-hour lessons.

"I also teach people how to make a basswood container to store their cut comb honey in. It's an art that we like to keep going."

What are some good sources of nectar for the honeybee?

"What the bees really need in the early spring is what everybody hates – dandelions and creeping Charlie. Those are two of the first nectar sources available. And people poison them.

"If I see that a customer has paid some company to spray their yard, I will never sell them another jar of honey. If they're going to kill my girls' food sources, they do not deserve the honey. If you're gonna to steal the dog food, why pet the dog? Two of the worst places for spraying are golf courses and cemeteries."

Bob, I kept bees for a couple years back in the late '80s. They complimented the three acres of organic produce I raised. Mites infested my hives; that put me in a predicament. There were chemicals I could have used to kill the mite, but I chose not to. My bees died.

"You should have tried powdered sugar. When you're not collecting honey, you can sprinkle it all over the bees. When the bees clean themselves off, they remove the mites in the process. Mineral oil is good, too."

It was Bill McKinney from Lowell who got me started.

"Bill was a good friend of mine, too. He kept a hive of bees on his front porch to deter peddlers from pestering him."

Bob, McKinney told me he needed to get stung every once in a while. Said he needed the venom – it was good for his arthritis. Tell me about Colony Collapse Disorder.

"The EPA has been reluctant to admit to the public that CCD is caused by pesticides such as clothianidin. When the bee took the pollen from a plant that had been treated, it lost its memory for home. Some of the same pesticides are used on corn. If it affects a bee like that, what will it do to a five-year old kid eating corn?"

Pretty scary stuff, Bob. I've read where beekeepers have lost as much as 90 percent of their bees because of CCD. And not only does the honeybee pollinate $15 billion worth of crops annually in America, there are many who believe when the honeybee goes extinct, so do we.

"Jeff, I'd like to get a couple schoolteachers who want to learn about beekeeping so they can teach kids the truth about honeybees in their classrooms. On televison the other day, I watched, oh, I forget her name.. The one who went to prison.."

Martha Stewart?

"Yeah, her. She did a segment on beekeeping and got it all wrong."

I noticed your beehives when I pulled up to the house. Is that the extent of it?

"No, I have eight other yards within a 50-mile radius. I only run about 25 hives now; I used to run 500. I started harvesting honey Oct. 1; I'm usually done within two weeks."

How much does a hive produce per season?

"In its third year, a hive should produce its full amount – five gallons. The fourth year, it usually produces another five gallons, but that's when bees swarm and divide. You should leave the bees with a fourth of the honey to survive the winter."

How many bees reside in a healthy hive during the summer?

"About 70,000. Come spring, maybe three or four thousand survive."

You mentioned spring nectar sources; what about later in the season?

"I get my biggest good crop of honey in August off of goldenrod. Once you eat my goldenrod honey, you won't want any other honey. Spring honey is the lightest; the fall honey is darker – it has more minerals in it."

Which do you prefer?

"I like it almost black."

Bob, sometimes I get up close and personal in this column; let's talk sex.

"What?"

I know the queen gets fed royal jelly; that's why she has reproductive organs. Explain the differences between bees of the common herd – the workers and the drones.

“The workers are all females. The first thing a worker bee does when she emerges from her cell is eat. The second thing – she goes to work. They do every job there is to do within the hive.

“After 42 days, she will fly for 21 days or until her wings get damaged; if the latter occurs, she is killed upon returning to the hive. Nothing is allowed in that hive but perfection. The drones service the queen.”

Bob, all things considered, I’d want to be a drone.

“It’s no fun to be a drone when the temps start to drop like they did last night. A drone cannot eat entirely by himself; he has to be fed by the workers.

Well, after a while, they quit feeding him. They are not going to cater to him all winter long for no reason. When he gets weak, a couple of the ladies will carry him out to the front porch and boot him out.”

Ahem. Sounds vaguely familiar.

“Jeff, let’s take a walk out to the hives. I’d like to mention that I don’t charge for my lessons. I want to share the enjoyment I’ve received from beekeeping in my lifetime.

“Everything in life is there. You’re touching life with your fingers. You’re seeing life born in front of you. Beekeeping helps you to live your own life a little better.

“You’ll never make a fortune at beekeeping, but it’s a hobby that pays for itself. All this honey you see here wasn’t my doing; the bees did it.

“Go ahead, walk right up to them; they won’t sting you. My bees are a cross. They’re half Italian and half German blacks.

No problem, Bob. So am I.

Don Randolph *(Mar. 2012)*

"The farmer is the only man in our economy who buys everything at retail, sells everything at wholesale, and pays the freight both ways."

– President John F. Kennedy

Don Randolph is the fourth generation to farm the land in Center Township on which he lives. He's 82, so that's going back a ways. One of Randolph's father's aunts was the wife of Crown Point founder Solon Robinson.

Randolph also is a Korean War veteran who was married for 57 1/2 years. His wife passed away three years ago. They raised three children.

While being interviewed, Randolph sat in the same recliner that his maternal great-grandfather, Conrad Jergens, recuperated in after being released from Camp Sumter Civil War prison in Andersonville, Ga..Jergens was part of Union Gen. William Sherman's March to the Sea. His name is listed on a statue honoring Civil War veterans in Lowell.

* * *

"I was born in the bedroom I sleep in today," Randolph began. "When I was growing up, Crown Point was South Street, North Street, East Street and West Street, and that was it. There were no subdivisions. I was born in '29 and remember all the (John) Dillinger stories. I was 5 when he broke out of the (Lake County) jail."

Tell me more.

"Dillinger was a jerk. My mother knew Lou Baker real well; he was the turnkey when Dillinger escaped. Later, Lou Baker opened a nice jewelry shop and everybody said Dillinger paid him off."

Small-town gossip. Your mother?

"My mother was the only girl in her high school class; that's how tiny it was. She put half of her classmates through school; she was real smart."

Did your father come to America from England?

"Oh, no. We're going to become members of the Mayflower Society; my great-great-great-great grandfather built the 13th house in

Plymouth Colony."

Wow, pilgrim. My Grandpa Vito came here in 1910. When did Randolphs move to this farm?

"This land was bought from the government by Josiah Randolph in 1851 for $1.25 per acre."

Probably part of the Swampland Act.

"Just a little east of us is Niles Marsh. My dad could ice skate from the Gary Railroad to Leroy. Did you know the Kankakee Marsh was the second largest wetland in the world?"

Well, I know it was one of the largest inland wetlands in the North America.

"Dignitaries from all over the world came to the Grand Kankakee Marsh to hunt and fish. Think what Indiana had, and they horsed it up."

Don, I'm helping make a documentary film on the subject; it's scheduled to air this spring.

"That's great. Old Man Niles used a floating dredge to drain Niles Marsh. He owned most of the land back there; he made the Niles Ditch. I remember the (Civilian Conservation Corps) boys in the 1930s cleaning out the ditch. This house is all oak; it came from the Kankakee Marsh."

Timber from the Kankakee River helped rebuild Chicago after the Great Fire in October of 1871. Don, I know you were a dairy farmer, did you also grow corn and soy beans?

"Yes. Alfalfa, too. Dad said corn was selling for a dime a bushel in the early 1900s. He raised wheat; I never did. Back in the days when I was young, everybody raised wheat; that's how you fed your chickens. Dad also raised the first soybeans in Lake County."

Soybeans were introduced to this area in the 1930s.

"Yes, '35, '36."

Back in the mid-1800s, many of the farmers were actually against draining the marsh along the Kankakee River because they were marsh hay farmers.

"Oh, yeah. Marsh hay was a big deal. I remember when the Brown Ranch down by Shelby had hoof-and-mouth disease; it wiped out their cattle."

A good friend of mine, Sig Boezeman, has a farm a little south of there. He showed me a spot on his property where a herd of cattle had to be destroyed because of hoof-and-mouth.

"My son didn't want to farm, which was all right with me; a person should do what they want to do. He works at U.S. Steel.

"Farming has changed so much; I'm actually glad he didn't get into it. But I will say this: People should thank the Lord every day for the farmers."

Don, I'll say that in our film. As much as I would've loved seeing the Grand Kankakee Marsh in all its splendor, before it was drained for agricultural purposes, the farmers of the Midwest fed us; hell, they fed much of the world.

"My dad farmed with horses, of course. He had five workhorses; one was a Clydesdale. I loved that horse; Jumbo was a huge horse and was so gentle.

"My grandfather wasn't a very good farmer; he was a professional horse trader. My dad was the one who built up this farm. We'd husk corn by hand in those days."

When did your family purchase its first tractor?

"In 1941, just before the war. It was an Allis Chalmers WC."

Being a dairy farmer is one heck of a job.

"Yeah, it's a lot of work; 12 hours a day and 365 days a year."

To whom did you sell the milk?

"My dad was the first shipper to Cloverleaf Dairy. We also shipped to Dixie and Borden's at one time. When I was a kid, there were five dairies in Crown Point."

How many acres was the entire farm?

"We had 120 acres; we've kept the original homestead, which is two acres. We're going to keep it in the family."

Your time in the service?

"The day I got discharged, I hitchhiked 1,000 miles to get home."

Where did you begin this trek?

"Fort Stewart, in Georgia. It was called Camp Stewart back then. I didn't have any money. My dad got hurt in a corn picker, so I got out of the service on an emergency leave for a while.

"Well, they kept my mustering out pay; I had to pay 'em back. I could have asked my folks or my wife for money, but I was too proud to ask for money.

"I had 10 bucks and a good thumb. I made it to Atlanta that night. I was wearing my uniform and I'd get out of one car and right into another."

What an experience.

"There were no interstates back then. I slept in a bus station; it was pouring rain. A taxi driver told me to get on in and he'd take me where I could get a ride; he didn't charge me.

"I rode in a fruit truck through the Smokey Mountains. I made it to Indianapolis; a couple dropped me off at a hotel. I asked the guy if he had a room for five bucks. He said, 'No.' So I turned around and started to walk out."

And?

"He hollered out, 'I'll give you a room for five bucks.' I got up the next morning and jumped into a semi that was headed for Chicago with a load of hogs. The trucker dropped me off at Route 8. A real estate salesman by the name of Ed Bennett from Crown Point took me home. My journey from Camp Stewart to Crown Point took 48 hours."

* * *

Salt of the earth, Don Randolph.

Rufus Reyes *(June 2006)*

"In this world it is possible to achieve great material wealth, to live an opulent life. But a life built upon those things alone leaves a shallow legacy, in the end, we will be judged by other standards."
– Cesar Chavez

I'm one year older than Rufus Reyes; we grew up one mile apart – just west of Indiana 10 and U.S. 41. We sat together on Stanley Madison's school bus the year Rufus entered first grade. Rufus didn't say much. When he did speak, it was in a language I was not familiar with. Still, we connected.

By the time second grade rolled around, third for me, Rufus could speak English as well as any of us ragamuffins raised south of the Kankakee River – not that a great a compliment, I suppose.

Father's Day nears. Rufus and his lovely wife have brought five children into this world. Frank, Rick, Julia, Andy, and Ashley range between 27 and 11 years of age, respectively.

As for the prodigal son, I have come back home to Lake Village for a day to see my old friend. It's been at least 20 years.

With rows of zinnias behind us to the south, and an ancient airport on the horizon to the north, we took a seat in his garage. There was a constant rumble of rigs whirring westward toward the State Line Tap and Illinois 114 while we talked.

* * *

¿Qué pasa, flaco?

"Jeff? Jeff Manes!"

Good to see you, Rufus. You've lost weight.

"Diabetes, man. Can't eat none of the good stuff no more."

How's the flower business treating you?

"I quit wholesale because they were screwing with me left and right; I'm strictly retail now – the farmer's markets in Chicago."

Flowers only?

"Yeah, no more vegetables. Flowers were always the gig here on this place anyway – way before I was ever born. Last year was tough. My sales were down 50 percent. Had to borrow money. I was gonna get a job in the mill, but no one wanted to hire me, 'Man, we don't want you –

you're too freakin' old, man.'"

Rufus, you've been working with fresh-cut flowers all your life. How long have you been running the business on your own?

"Twenty years. Ten, 15 years ago, I was makin' a lot of money, man. Payin' all my bills. You know, makin' a comfortable living. Right after 9-11, everything went to hell. I was in Chicago yesterday, the Daley Plaza, downtown. We were having a tough time. Finally, I had to drop my prices. It's rough out there."

What do you sell, bouquets?

"Yeah, lilac bouquets, rose bouquets... ."

Do you grow the roses?

"No, not the roses, I buy them out of South America – through brokers in Chicago."

You know, Rufus, when I was laid off from the mill, I worked the Gary Farmer's Market. I had a tough time growing sweet potatoes in the Lowell clay. I'd go to the water market near Chinatown at 2 a.m. and buy cases of them to resell. Hey, when in Rome. The good folks of Gary like their yams. Had an elderly customer bring me a sweet potato pie one Saturday; I was more accustomed to pumpkin, but it was pretty tasty.

"Jeff, sometimes it's cheaper to buy it and resell it than grow it yourself."

What are some of your heavy hitters?

"Cockscomb in the fall, lilacs in the spring; I grow a lot of sunflowers – city people eat them up. Sunflowers bring life to the city. We do a lot of zinnias in the summer. Pussy willows are good sellers. I buy eucalyptus out of California. I had customers asking me for eucalyptus yesterday, people really dig the smell, but eucalyptus won't come in for a couple of weeks. We do a lot of winterberry, too – right after Thanksgiving.

"We don't get into as much variety as we used to. It's better to stay small. I know a guy in Huntington who just went broke. Big-time pumpkin grower. Grew pumpkins all the way from Huntington to South Bend. They're gonna have a sale next month. He's out of business – big-time. Too much waste."

How many people work for you?

"Just two, right now. During the summer about five. My dad still helps. My kids... When things were really going good I had about 25 Mexican people helping me. Business is just not there.

"Last year, in Chicago, there were 220 retail flower growers that went out of business. Sam's Club, Costco, Kmart – they're killin' us. Two dozen roses for $9.89? They're puttin' the squeeze on us, man. They're buyin' direct from the farms, these guys. They're still makin' money because they sell huge quantities. You know what I mean, man?

"They're cutting everybody's throat. And it's not just my line of work. Look at all the pig farmers, the small dairy farms, all the mom-and-pop shops all over the country. I know someone who works at one of those huge dairy farms, he said, 'I'll never drink milk again. The stuff they feed the cows is so hot (chemicals) it puts holes in their stomachs.'"

Rufus, you've probably had to spray too, haven't you?

"With the flowers, very seldom. With the vegetables, yes. It was terrible. Pure poison, man. I sprayed sweet corn with this stuff called Pytron. Had the skull and cross bones right on the container. Here I am wearing all this protective gear from head to toe to spray the corn. I get to thinking, 'I'm going to sell this so somebody can eat it? I stopped growing corn. I couldn't do that. I just couldn't do that. The big timers? They don't care. They just care about the money comin' in.

"I was way up in Palatine doing a craft show. People are walking by my pussy willow bouquets – buying soaps, jewelry.... They'd say things like, 'We can buy stuff like that off the Internet.'"

I remember when we were kids; your father was kind of the go-between for former owner, Angeles Kocoshis, and his Hispanic field hands.

"My dad was never really a boss, but yes, he would translate the orders from Angeles, which were usually spoken in a mixture of English, Greek, and Spanish, to the rest of the Mexican workers."

Rufus, it's not my intention to solve the nation's immigration problems, but... .

"There are a lot of educated people across the border, but the Mexican government has their thumb on them. You can't just become, say, a doctor. And if you were so fortunate, the pay would suck. Most people are oppressed. Jeff, as a kid, you worked for the Greeks in the fields. You've weeded and worked your own couple of acres. It's a hard, hot way to go. If you were making $5 a day in the fields of Mexico, but could make $75 a day here, doing the same thing, wouldn't you be tempted to cross over?

"All those people want to do is take care of their families. And yes, like any other nationality, there's riff raff. Hey, I say if they're not here in this country to work – kick 'em out! The Mexicans who want to work – let 'em stay. My father worked for Angeles for 28 years. Angeles fixed my parents up with an apartment behind Christenson Chevrolet. Once he saw my dad would bust his ass for him, he had a guy by the name of Oliver build this house for my father."

Rufus, where were you born?

"Cleveland; my family moved to Gary when I was six months old, soon after, they moved to Lake Village. My parents and my wife were born in Mexico. My wife learned English from our children. I don't like it that the kids can't speak Spanish. They can understand it, but they can't speak it.

"I've never had any problems in Lake Village. I've been all over, but Lake Village is my home. I get along with people. I like people. I thank God that I'm liked in this town, that my sons are liked, and my family is respected. It doesn't make any difference how much money you make. If you're not respected, you're not going to get anywhere.

"Jeff, when I go down to Mexico, the first thing that hits me is the poverty. I've been in the little huts with the dirt floors; their wooden tables are old, but their tablecloths are clean. When those people offer you a bowl of beans, they offer it with their heart. A good vibe you get from those people, man. They ain't got shit, but the love is there, man.

"Sometimes, I fear we're losing that in this country. And yet, on my way back, coming into Texas, I see that American flag flying, and I feel it, man. It's a great country we live in, but the government is fucking it up. Why? Greed! That, *mi amigo,* you can plaster on the front page of your newspaper."

* * *

I can still remember when Rufus called our house late in the afternoon so many winters ago. It was probably not an easy call for him to make. It was a few hours before the annual father/son basketball game for boys in the sixth-grade and their dads. Being a year older, I was attending junior high school in Morocco. My mother answered the phone, she said, 'It's the Reyes boy, it's for you.' She wasn't talking to me, she was addressing my father.

Rufus' father, Frank, was and is a good and hardworking man, but maybe wasn't so familiar with the game of basketball – not 40 years ago.

The Manes *famiglia* was one generation ahead of the Reyes *familia*. Although of Italian ancestry, my father, like Rufus, is first-generation. Maybe that's why Rufus chose to call my dad, hoping that he'd be his 'father' for a day.

I didn't go to the basketball game that night. Thought it best to stay home. Later that evening, upon my father's return, I remember my little brother asking him if he made any baskets.

Let it be known, my old man scored that night; he scored a few points indeed. The second he stepped out on the floor of Lake Village gymnasium with my friend, Rufus Reyes, he scored points with me.

Kindred Spirits

Ronnie Robinson *(Feb. 2005)*

"...I've seen fire and I've seen rain,
I've seen sunny days that I
thought would never end,
I've seen lonely times when I
could not find a friend,
But I always thought that I'd
see you again."
– James Taylor

I'm heading south along U.S. 41. Crossing the Kankakee River and entering Newton County.

At Indiana 10, I drive west for a half-mile. Getting out of my old F150, I plant my feet upon sandy loam. I'm greeted by acid-loving oaks, prickly pear and the pods of last season's wild yucca plants. Lake Village.

It's been a while since I've chatted with my old friend, Ron Robinson. Always more talkative, I begin the conversation.

* * *

Finally getting some rest, huh, Ronnie? Well, good for you; after all, you worked all your life.

While just a boy, you were shelling pink-eye purple hull crowders for your mother, plus slopping hogs and baling hay.

Remember the summer before seventh grade, when they removed that tumor from your lung? Silly question. Of course, you do. Heck, they removed 90 percent of your lung. You didn't let it stop you though – back to that hayloft, shooting baskets. You worked at it. Hey, it paid off – a three-year starter for North Newton High School before graduating in 1974, a year ahead of me. I can still picture you knockin' down 25-footers from the corner before the advent of the 3-point shot.

Yeah, the glory days came and went. Fresh out of high school, you found employment at Youngstown as it was known back then. But they kept laying you off, so you tried your luck across the canal, taking a job at Inland Steel in East Chicago.

You always had to stay busy. You lived to work. Management

handed you a set of flame-retardant greens and sent you to the armpit of the mill – the coke plant. Eventually, they gave you a respirator.

I remember how you shunned those wooden clogs they tried to get us to strap to our steel-toed boots so our feet wouldn't burn up. I didn't like them, either; they were too clumsy and unsafe.

I remember one afternoon when a sales rep hung a thermometer from one of the standpipes while we were working – 208 degrees. Our long underwear stayed drenched in those days, didn't it, kiddo? But you stayed out there longer than most, because you were steeled and tempered early.

You knew work, Ronnie.

How about when we used to clad those huge gas mains on the battery top? Our eyebrows and eyelashes were burned almost completely off a few times when she spiked. Nothin' smells like singed hair...

Hey, there were guys hurt worse than us – much worse. You always respected the dangers and watched out for me like a hawk.

Remember when you wired that bathroom fan for me? I can still see you wriggling that lanky frame of yours inside my cramped attic, fighting insulation, spider webs and mouse shit the entire way.

While you were working, I told you about the time your Grandpa Harvey mounted a security light for my widowed grandmother. Old Harvey had never mentioned it to you; he just did the work for free. Bought the light, too.

Yep, my Grandpa Vito (Local 597) and your Grandpa Harvey (IBEW Local 697) worked on the same job sites many times down through the years, right, Ron?

I learned a lot about you, car pooling all those years to and from the mill. Without a doubt, two people who left a lasting impression on you were your Grandpa Harvey and your mother. Although they had passed away, you often reminisced about them while you drove. I know, your ma left this world too young; it happens sometimes.

You were always a moonlighter, hauling our native black sandy loam north so the city folk wouldn't have to plant their petunias in clay. Heck, you held positions for the town of Schneider like head of the Water Department and Street Department. You were a jack-of-all-trades for Ashland Products. You knew work.

In May of '92, we ran into the fire while 300 coke-plant employees were evacuated to the Big Lake. Only about six or eight of us stayed back. Didn't do much good; two good men had already perished. Then Fred took his life a week later – 10 feet from where his buddies died.

Being a union rep, I had to go through his belongings with his loved ones. Did I ever tell you that?

Ronnie, I came home that evening, after being in that hell for four hours, just knowing every second we were going to get burned alive or blown up, and I looked at my little twins and told myself: "You didn't hire in that place to be a fireman. No, sir, if something like that happens again, get out."

March 16, 2001. Sixth floor of No. 4 BOF. Moon dust. Graphite City. Live, 10-inch oxygen line. Wessie, Tom, Ponziano, and I, we ran one way. You and Norm ran another.

That steel mill is Hades hot, Ron; you know that, but the powers that be can be truly cold. They'll use you and abuse you.

Ronald Lee Robinson, keep watching out for me.

* * *

As I pull out of Lake Village Cemetery, I think of the reassuring words the pastor spoke at Sheets Funeral Home as family and steelworkers mourned. They were simple words, really.

Jesus wept.

Jimmie Kunis *(Oct. 2012)*

"Whenever I take up a newspaper and read it, I fancy I see ghosts creeping between the lines. There must be ghosts all over the world."

– Henrik Ibsen

Do not read this interview if you are afraid of things that go bump in the night.

Jimmie Kunis might not live on Elm Street, but hers is the last house on the left of a dead-end country road which is a tombstone's toss from Gypsy Graveyard in extreme northeast Lowell.

Fitting. Kunis has been known to see, hear and talk to dead people. She's a ghost tracker.

Kunis, 50, has been married to William for 11 years. They have five children between them from previous marriages. Jimmie is the mother of former Lowell Red Devil star defensive end Jeff Barker.

* * *

"The first 13 years of my life were spent growing up in Whiting," Kunis began. "But I graduated from Griffith High School."

When did you start believing in ghosts?

"When we lived on Schrage Avenue in Whiting, my room was really small, I remember waking up in the middle of the night and seeing this black-hooded figure walking toward my bed. It had its head down.

"I was thinking, what if its somebody that had broken into the house. It sat down at the side of the bed not looking at me with its head down and that hood over it."

Can we turn on a few more lights while you tell me the rest of this story?

"I remember laying there and saying to myself, 'Jimmie, you're dreaming, wake up.' I also remember having the covers pulled up just below my eyeballs, not wanting this thing to know I was awake. Then, all of a sudden it just vanished. They say if the Grim Reaper looks at you, it's your time. But it never looked at me."

That's comforting.

"I know what I saw. They do say that kids see more than adults. I'm pretty much a skeptic; I try to prove false positives.

"I may be a ghost tracker, but when I walk into a place that's supposedly haunted, I'll keep in mind that it could be a vent that's making a strange noise or a car headlight that's coming through a window – things like that. I've debunked quite a few ghostly occurrences, but I've also had quite a few that were real."

Did you eventually join some sort of ghost tracker club?

"Yes, in 2000, I started with Indiana Ghost Trackers. It was just kind of a hobby thing where I'd go to their meetings and then we'd go ghost hunting afterwards.

"I'm part of a very small group now. It's called Aftershock RSI – research science investigators."

Tell me more ghost stories.

"When I was in Indiana Ghost Trackers, I would have people contact me because they had things happening in their houses."

Details; we need details?

"I don't want to mention any names, but I had a woman whose grandchildren – they were 3 and 4 years old – woke up in the middle of the night and were pointing at the door. They kept repeating, 'The man! The man!' But the mother and grandmother saw nothing but the door. It continued night after night, the kids would wake up screaming, scared to death of this man."

Was this in Lowell?

"No, in Hammond. I brought a woman named Vera with me; I don't know if I'd call her psychic or a medium. She believes in Mother Earth and she does cleansings of houses.

"While sitting at these people's kitchen table, I felt a burning at my back. I immediately lifted up my shirt and saw that I'd been scratched. The scratches were in the shape of a half moon that had a line through it."

Yikes!

"That kind of stuff really upsets me; I mean that's demonic. I can see a ghost, but don't touch me. You're not allowed to hurt me. My girlfriend was there also; she gave me a rosary and I walked out the door."

What happened next?

"When I came back into the house, the woman who owns the place took me into the bedroom. In crayon, the little girl had drawn the half moon with a line through it on the sheet where she slept. I guess 'the man' didn't like the fact I'd brought a cleanser to the house, so he decided to scratch me."

Did Vera get rid of the poltergeist or whatever it was?

"Yes, she basically builds a staircase and tells the ghost: 'There is a bright light at the top of the staircase; you need to follow it and move on. You don't need to stay in this home.' She did this, and miracles happened."

Tell me one more, please?

"I don't consider myself to be a psychic or a medium, but I do believe if a spirit wants to work with me, they can. And I've had them do it with me."

Continue.

"My husband had a job in Wilmington, Ill., so I decided to take a ride with him. While in Wilmington, we decided to have lunch. I spotted a sign that read: Marina Restaurant & Bar.

"We sat down to have lunch and the bartender said: 'If ashtrays start flying off the bar don't worry about it, it's just our ghost.' This guy doesn't know me from Adam."

Yeah?

"I got up to use the restroom, and when I returned, my husband had this concerned look on his face. He asked me why I was in the restroom so long.

"I told him: 'I know who their ghost is. She's a lady who has reddish-brown hair down to her shoulders and she's about 5-feet, six-inches tall. She was driving a little yellow car out of here and she hit that tree at the end of the dirt road. That's how she died."

Mercy.

"Astonished, the bartender said: 'You're talking about Rose, and how do you know Rose? She was the former owner here, and that was years ago.'

"I said, 'I don't know Rose and I don't know how I know this."

You're giving me goose bumps.

"It gets better. The bartender takes me into Rose's former office and it's ice cold. You could see your breath. Nothing happened.

"We returned to the bar and the phone rang. The bartender answered it and there was a lot of static, but over the static, a voice asked, 'Is Rose there?' Then (the caller) hung up. The bartender, pale as a ghost, turned to me and asked what the hell was going on?'

"I told him to dial star-67. The call had come from the boathouse on the Kankakee River. There was two feet of snow on the ground when my husband and I walked over to the boathouse. There were no footprints anywhere; it had been closed down all winter."

Eerie.

"When we re-entered the bar, I shouted out loud and clear: 'Everybody in here needs to know that Rose got a phone call the night she died. The message was that her husband was cheating on her. She hung up the phone, ran out of here, got in her car, peeled out, hit the tree, and that's how she died!'

"Excuse me, I get tears in my eyes when I tell this story. You see, that's what Rose wanted; she wanted to use me. Why was I drawn to that little marina-restaurant-bar located on the Kankakee River?"

* * *

Jimmie Kunis lives about 15 minutes from my apartment. When I returned home, I received a phone call from her. Jimmie wanted to tell me that soon after I left her house, she entered her basement and while down there, the lights flickered three times although it was windless evening without lightning.

Jimmie figures it was the tormented soul from Wilmington, wanting to thank her for letting us, the living, know what really happened on that tragic night.

May you finally rest in peace, Rose.

Gordon Johanson *(June 2011)*

"This day and age we're living in
Gives cause for apprehension.
With speed and new invention
And things like fourth dimension.
...You must remember this
A kiss is just a kiss, a sigh is just a sigh.
The fundamental things apply
As time goes by."
– Herman Hupefeld

The above lyrics ring as true today as they did back in 1942, when Dooley Wilson reluctantly sang those words for Bogie in the classic film "Casablanca."

Gordon Johanson not only owns an antique store named As Time Goes By in LaPorte, he's been known to dabble in things like fourth dimension – he's a medium.

Among many other jobs, Johanson has bagged groceries, dug ditches, was an apprentice butcher in Rantoul, Ill., worked at a pizza joint in Columbus, Miss., and operated a brass-rubbing business in England.

Johanson, 65, also was a 20-year man in the Air Force. Two of those years – 1971 and '72 – were spent in Saigon. He has been a competitive volleyball player since 1965 and will be participating in the Senior Olympics this month in Houston.

Johanson attends LaPorte New Church, which draws its faith from the Bible as illuminated by the teachings of Emanuel Swedenborg (1688-1772).

Johanson has been married to Jodell for 45 years; they raised two children.

* * *

Born and raised in LaPorte?

"I'm actually from Hudson Lake; we moved out there from Chicago in 1946. Jodell and I moved to LaPorte in '96."

Where is Hudson Lake?

"About 12 miles east of here, near New Carlisle. I graduated from New Carlisle High School in 1963."

Are you Swedish?

"Yes, Mom's mom and Dad's dad were born in Sweden."

How long have you been dealing in antiques in this area?

"Since '96; we've been at this particular store for three years."

Which of these clocks is the oldest?

"That grandfather's clock standing right over there; it was made in England in 1810."

Wow, 201 years old. How much you asking?

"I've got $3,500 on it."

These clocks aren't as tall.

"Those are grandmother's clocks."

I realize part of your business is repairing clocks; did you serve some sort of apprenticeship?

"I took a clock apart and my wife said, 'You *will* put that back together.' So, I put it back together and it worked – that was the start of it back in 1974."

You've got a little bit of everything here, where do you get these antiques?

"Auctions, estates, people come in and sell things... ."

Gordon, let's switch gears – ghosts and the like?

"We started out in that building across the street. There was a little place next to it we were going to rent out; Jodell and I put an ad in the newspaper.

"Four ladies showed up saying they were interested. I asked them, 'What are you going to put in there?' They told me a metaphysical store. Then, they told me they were witches."

Interesting.

"I showed them around the place, and all of a sudden, they start saying, 'Hello.'

So?

"They weren't talking to me. I saw absolutely nothing. The witches proceeded to introduce me to a fella named Albert, an elderly woman who would go around and straighten doilies at night, and a couple of kids. I asked the four witches how they were able to see ghosts."

Excellent question.

"They told me they were going to hold classes every Thursday night. So for years, I was the only guy out of about 14 people who attended the classes.

"After awhile, I asked, 'How come you ladies get to see all these ghosts and spirits and I get nothin'?' And all of a sudden a chill went through me like you wouldn't believe."

Gordon, I believe you.

"I asked them what had just happened to me. They laughed and said, 'Never ask for anything you don't want.' The witch who was second in command told me her mother had just walked right through me. I told her, 'Well, don't mess with me because *my* mother is right behind me protecting me.' She said: 'No, she isn't. Put your hand out as if you were going to hold hands with someone at your side. I did what she said and my hand became really, really cold. Then the witch said, '*That,* is your mother.' And that is what started me on my life-quest for ghosts."

Gordon, look, the hair is standing up on my arms.

"They come back and check on us. They loved us in life; why wouldn't they love us in death?

"My gift is past lives. Anytime someone comes back to Earth, they learn a lesson. It could be humility, happiness... . When you learn that lesson, then you pass on and when you want to learn another lesson, you come back again.

"I can see different lives that you've lived. Some of the traits you had then, you have now."

Really? And how would you know that? We've never met.

"Because I've done a reading on you."

You Googled me?

"You were about 35 in 1826. You had two good friends, enjoyed sitting in front of a fireplace and you liked to wear hats, both formal and informal."

Hmm. I'm not wearing one today, but usually do. Of course, I mentioned to you when I first walked in that I really liked that grey, felt fedora you have displayed.

"Here, I wrote this out for you a few days ago. As you can see, the part about the hats is included in the list. You're favorite colors were or are black and white. You're favorite movie or book is or was, 'A Christmas Carol.' You've lived in a small house in the woods with a small library in it."

How do you know?

"You're a good listener, but also like to tell stories. You're good at what you do. You've liked dogs and tall ships."

Have you ever read my column?

"Never."

Shame on you. But seriously, who have you been talking to?

"My guardian angel."

Explain, please.

"My guardian angel can talk to your guardian angel. When I wanted to know about you, I asked my guardian angel to ask your guardian angel about you and my spirit guide gave me impressions of what you were like then and now."

* * *

I get this vague feeling that I've met the multifaceted Johanson somewhere before, but can't put my finger on it.

Maybe it will come to me as time goes by.

Leona *(May 2005)*

"You are beautiful...
Like an old opera tune
played upon a harpsichord."
-Amy Lowell

It was comforting to hear your guttural chuckle when amused.

You were born the 16th of 18 children, including two sets of twins – you were a twin.

All 18 born at home. All 18 given at least a half-dozen names. Leona Rosina Carolina Anna Helena Wilhelmina... .

You worked so hard all your life, yet lived in poverty. I can't imagine what you might have accomplished with a college education, but you never complained – about anything.

"God is good to us," you would say.

And you read to me.

Was it true that your father was friends with William F. Cody? And that "Buffalo Bill" always made sure, "the man with all the children" and his family were allowed to view the "Wild West Show" free of charge?

I remember an old country cuckoo clock and the smell of your lotion. Was it Jergen's or Noxzema?

I think of pomegranates; what did you call them? Christmas apples?

And bacon, lettuce and tomato sandwiches with Miracle Whip.

I also recall half-and-half, chocolate chip pie, and lemon meringue pie so tart only you and I could eat it. That lemon squeezer got quite a workout, didn't it?

I think you were the first person on Earth to try the Rice Krispies Squares recipe on the back of the cereal box.

There was piping-hot Jell-O water, good for the fingernails, you said, and ice water, good for everything.

You nourished me; you read to me.

I remember Crayola crayons and coloring books, "Yahtzee," crossword puzzles, endless hours of "Youth Scrabble" and eventually,

“Scrabble.”

And stacks of clipped newspaper articles that you found interesting or humorous cached away – old-fashioned cut-and-paste.

I wonder what you would have thought about the Internet?

There was a wondrous garden in the backyard of your modest Lake Village home that included vine-ripened tomatoes, hummingbirds, mammoth sunflowers, lightning bugs, horseradish, green beans and rhubarb.

Your modest home – a former chicken coop, I was told. You had no indoor plumbing until the late 1950s. A more immaculate place or person I’ve yet to meet. In fact, you were so good at scrubbing and scouring that others hired you, so their fancy houses also could sparkle.

In my eyes, you were next to godliness.

I think back to when you would hold me up in your arms; we waltzed to Lawrence Welk.

And you read to me.

The things you taught me. The way you taught me. In the beginning, the Bible, “The Velveteen Rabbit,” “The Little Match Girl,” “Grimm’s Fairy Tales,” books on dinosaurs, all of these and so many more you read to me.

Although widowed young in life, you were of the hardiest stock. I believe you might have lived a century.

Too many miles, too little sleep. Eighteen wheels crumpled your tiny Chevy, compressing your chest against the steering wheel.

“Better to kill ‘em then cripple ‘em,” some callous fellas have been known to say.

Well, you survived, but soon after, a spot. Then a mastectomy, then a wig. Pallbearers – I was the youngest and smallest of the six.

The weight of it.

Many years have passed; it is still difficult to gaze at your name etched in stone. I find it somewhat easier poring over the written words of this shaking piece of paper.

See, Grandma? My turn now.

I read to you.

The Behrens family. Twins Leonard and Leona are sitting on their father's lap

- Jeff Manes